HOW ENGLISH WORKS

A Grammar Handbook with Readings

HOW ENGLISH WORKS

*A Grammar Handbook
with Readings*

ANN RAIMES

Hunter College, City University of New York

CAMBRIDGE
UNIVERSITY PRESS

PUBLISHED BY THE PRESS SYNDICATE OF THE UNIVERSITY OF CAMBRIDGE
The Pitt Building, Trumpington Street, Cambridge CB2 1RP, United Kingdom

CAMBRIDGE UNIVERSITY PRESS
The Edinburgh Building, Cambridge CB2 2RU, UK   http://www.cup.cam.ac.uk
40 West 20th Street, New York, NY 10011-4211, USA   http://www.cup.org
10 Stamford Road, Oakleigh, Melbourne 3166, Australia

First published by St. Martin's Press, Inc. 1990
Reprinted 1998

Printed in the United States of America

Library of Congress Cataloging-in-Publication Data Available

ISBN 0 521 65758 X Student's Book
ISBN 0 521 657571 Instructor's Manual

Acknowledgments are given on page(s) 379–380

This book is dedicated to my daughters
Emily Raimes and Lucy Raimes,
whose adventures with language constantly divert
and inspire me

Preface:
To the Instructor

How English Works: A Grammar Handbook with Readings is designed for classroom use with intermediate and advanced students of English. Such a range of abilities can easily be addressed in a book of this kind: as we teachers know only too well, even advanced students who speak and understand English with apparent ease can still make many errors when they write and can still have surprising gaps in understanding.

THE DESIGN OF THE BOOK

How English Works is unique in that it offers grammatical instruction and exercises based on published readings. Part II contains sixteen glossed readings; Part I contains grammar chapters that use the readings for examples and exercises.

In Part I, each grammar chapter (1 through 27) contains the following:

- An excerpt from one of the sixteen readings in Part II
- A series of tasks for inductive analysis of the form and function of a grammar point in the reading
- Explanations of grammar points, with charts, tables, and examples
- Exercises, both oral and written
- Authentic student writing for editing
- A focused writing task that elicits the structure
- Editing advice

Chapters 28 and 29 address concerns of style and punctuation. These chapters also provide examples and exercises from the readings. In addition, the appendices provide students with easy access to irregular verb forms and spelling conventions.

The book, with its inductive approach to grammar, has four distinctive teaching features: readings, clear presentation of the basic principles of grammar, a wide variety of exercises, and tasks for writing and editing.

hand-me-downs.
= Used Clothes

Readings

The grammar points are introduced and illustrated in the real-life context of authentic, unadapted readings. The sixteen glossed readings cover a variety of topics and levels of difficulty. These readings, from nonfiction, journalism, and textbooks, have been carefully chosen as representative of the sorts of writing students are likely to come across at this stage of their studies (in both assigned reading for courses and pleasure reading). Each reading provides the introductory focus for one or more grammar chapters as well as the basis for exercises in other chapters.

Why readings? Why not just isolated sentences written to illustrate a grammatical structure? Well, quite apart from the fact that they are, I believe, far more interesting in themselves than any passages concocted with the sole purpose of illustrating grammatical points in a textbook, these readings show students the real thing. This is indeed "how English works." Students see grammar in action, grammar as it is used in real life and real language.

Clear Presentation of the Basic Principles of Grammar

The book presents the basic principles of how English works for general academic purposes. It describes the common, frequently used structures of English for intermediate students and for more advanced students who have gaps in their knowledge or need review. It explains common exceptions to general principles, helping students to make sense of the patterns they see when they read. However, it does not attempt to cover every nuance of the language, every exception to every rule, every facet of specialized disciplines. Students need to know patterns that they can rely on, that will work for them *most* of the time. This book, then, offers broad strokes, not minute detail. Wherever possible, boxes, charts, and tables are used to clarify and highlight grammatical structures.

A Wide Variety of Exercises

To suit as many different learning (and teaching) styles as possible, the exercises include

- Group tasks
- Individual writing tasks
- Communicative oral exercises
- Error identification exercises
- "Right answer" selection exercises
- Open-ended exercises

- Exercises related to the readings
- Exercises using short, illustrative sentences

Some of the exercises allow students to focus on a grammatical feature by presenting it in a short, illustrative pattern sentence of a type familiar to them from other language-learning activities. Many other exercises, however, use the readings to provide subject matter and context. Exercises designated as "oral" can be used in class. Others, primarily written, can be done in class or as a homework assignment. Linguistically challenging exercises, more suitable for advanced students, are marked with a five-point star (☆).

Tasks for Writing and Editing

How English Works is based on the premise that students can't really work on improving their grammar while they are speaking. The nature of spoken communication simply does not leave room for extensive monitoring or for review of the language produced. While the book provides frequent opportunity for oral practice, many of its exercises are designed to focus on reading and writing, when students have time to analyze, recall, discuss, and apply principles of grammar. In addition, each chapter ends with a writing task designed to elicit the principles of the chapter. Students produce a text they can examine and revise, thus seeing how *their* English works.

The book links writing and grammar with editing techniques. At the end of each chapter, editing guidelines that focus on the grammar principle of the chapter are presented. Students are encouraged to use what they have learned about the workings of English to correct errors and make improvements—and they do this both with their own writing and with the samples of authentic student writing included in each chapter.

So in each chapter, reading leads to analysis, which leads to study of principles followed by practice, which then leads to writing and editing—that is, to the application of principles of grammar.

HOW TO USE THE BOOK

How English Works provides you with flexibility. You can begin with the grammar chapters, referring to the complete readings only when necessary. Or, if your focus is more on accuracy in writing than on a systematic, overall review of grammar, you can begin with the readings and their associated writing topics; then you can let the students' needs (as revealed in their written assignments) determine which grammar chapters you address.

If you want to spend more time with the complete readings before turning to grammar analysis, additional activities (under the headings "Preview Questions," "Response Questions," and "Analysis") appear in the Instructor's Manual. The Instructor's Manual also provides guidelines for organizing a course, teaching the chapters, dealing with errors, and preparing students for essay examinations, as well as an answer key for the exercises.

With *How English Works,* my students say that they start to see grammar as an interesting, vital part of a living language, not just as something to get right or wrong in textbook sentences. I hope the book works as well for you and your students as it has for us.

ACKNOWLEDGMENTS

Warm thanks go to the students in my ESL writing classes at Hunter College, many of whose names appear in this book. They helped me by working and commenting on exercises developed here and generously allowed me to include samples of their own writing. Their enthusiasm and willingness to learn were a constant source of inspiration.

Thanks, too, to the readers of the manuscript at its various stages, who all took time from their busy schedules to read with great care and sensitivity: Margaret Lindstrom, Colorado State University; Patrick Aquilina, American Language Program, Columbia University; Robert Kantor, Ohio State University; Stephen Thewlis, San Francisco State University; Cheryl Ruggiero, Virginia Polytechnic; and Amy Sales, Boston University. I am grateful to all of them for their valuable advice.

All the staff members at St. Martin's Press continue to impress me with their creativity and efficiency. It was especially rewarding to work with Joyce Hinnefeld, project editor, who kept track of cuts, changes, and last-minute revising without getting flustered. Susan Anker, editor-in-chief, helped guide the development of this book; thanks go to her again for giving me the benefit of her knowledge, common sense, and warm encouragement.

A colleague once told me that he'd noticed how acknowledgments in my books always mentioned my family and seemed to escalate in praise of their contribution. No wonder. By the sixth or seventh book, they must be tired of seeing me sitting at my processor while they make dinner and do all those nasty household chores. So at the risk of repetition and even more escalation, I'll end again by acknowledging my huge debt to James, Emily, and Lucy Raimes. So much of this is really their book.

ANN RAIMES

Contents

Verbals   207

Connecting Sentences 242

22 · Coordinating Conjunctions 243

SELECTED READING PASSAGES

23 · Transitions 252

SELECTED READING PASSAGES

Combining Sentences 260

24 · Adjectival Clauses 261

SELECTED READING PASSAGES

Principles of Written Discourse 310

PART II READINGS

PART I

GRAMMAR

BASIC SENTENCE STRUCTURE

NOUN PHRASES

VERB PHRASES

MODIFIERS

AGREEMENT

VERBALS

CONNECTING SENTENCES

COMBINING SENTENCES

PRINCIPLES OF WRITTEN DISCOURSE

Basic Sentence Structure

1. **SUBJECT AND PREDICATE**
   a. The independent clause: subject + verb
   b. The verb phrase
   c. The position of the subject
   d. What not to do with the subject of the sentence
   e. Filler subjects *it* and *there*
   f. The six basic requirements of a written sentence

2. **PHRASES AND CLAUSES**
   a. Packing a sentence with information
   b. Adding information at the beginning
   c. Including information to modify and identify the subject
   d. Inserting additional information after the subject
   e. Adding a verb
   f. Expanding the object: direct and indirect object
   g. Adding information about the sentence at the end

3. **QUESTIONS AND NEGATIVES**
   a. The form of questions
   b. *Why?* and *What for?*
   c. Negatives
   d. Alternative forms of negation
   e. Tag questions
   f. Tag questions: summary

Subject and Predicate

1

READ

Read the following excerpt from "Room with View—and No People." The complete selection, with vocabulary glosses, appears on p. 334.

> We talk a lot about the fact that no one ever sits in the living room. It makes us all sad. The living room is the prettiest room in the apartment. It has a fireplace and moldings. It has a slice of a view of the river. It is a cheerful room furnished in light colors. The couches in it were
>
> 5   recently cleaned by men with small machines. It always looks neat and tidy.

ANALYZE

1. Underline the words *talk* and *sits* (the verbs) in the first sentence. Now follow this lead, and continue underlining all the verbs throughout the passage. (One of them consists of more than one word.)

2. Now circle *we* and *no one* in the first sentence. These are the subjects of the verbs. They tell us who or what is *talking* and *sitting*. Again, follow this lead and continue circling all the subjects throughout the rest of the passage. (Some of the subjects consist of more than one word.)

3. In each sentence, use a slash to separate the subject you have circled from the rest of the sentence, like this:

    (We) / <u>talk</u> a lot . . .

What you are doing here is separating the subject from the predicate. The predicate in a simple sentence consists of the verb and what comes after it.

4. The reading passage at the beginning of this chapter consists of eight sentences. Look at them closely and, with other students, make a list of the features that are common to all these sentences and also to all sentences in general (for example, one feature is that each sentence begins with a capital letter).

STUDY

1a. The independent clause: subject + verb

A complete sentence in standard written English must have its own subject and verb. That is enough to make a sentence. The box shows that a verb is a necessary part of the predicate.

Subject	Predicate	
	VERB	REST OF PREDICATE
Babies	cry.	
Children	like	ice cream.
The children in the park	are eating	some delicious ice cream.

This basic unit of meaning—the subject and the predicate—along with its attachments, is called an *independent clause*. So every sentence you write must have at least one independent clause with a subject and a verb. It can have more than one independent clause, provided that the clauses are connected with words like *and* or *but* (see Chapter 22). Only commands regularly omit the subject:

Go away!
[You] go away.

You can always check that you have written complete sentences by identifying the independent clause and then underlining the verb and circling the subject. Remember that the core of any sentence is this structure:

S	+	V

subject + verb

EXERCISE 1

In the following passages from students' descriptions of a room, indicate which passages contain well-constructed, correctly punctuated sentences (OK) and which ones have problems (X).

_____ 1. There were not too many things in the room. Everything nice and clean.

_____ 2. The person who lives in the apartment needed something from his drawer, and I have never seen such an organized drawer in my life. He had made small wooden boxes for everything.

_____ 3. From the first look, I realized that the person who lived there was very neat and clean and also interested in art and antiques. The colorful furniture, the marble table with antique look.

_____ 4. In the living room, there are portraits hanging everywhere. A tea set with lion decoration that looks so gorgeous.

_____ 5. Although the walls and the ceiling are plain white and the furniture is white too and very simple, the floor is covered with a rug, which has an exotic blue and red pattern on it.

_____ 6. The table is covered with books and papers. A big desk in front of the window.

_____ 7. The main thing about the room is that it has a lot of chairs. Very big and comfortable chairs.

_____ 8. She wanted only bright colors. To make her room a more exciting place to be.

EXERCISE 2

Look at the painter van Gogh's painting of his own room in Arles, France, on p. 6. Write a description of it. Imagine that someone will have to draw the room according to your description, so make your description as full and accurate as you can. When you have done that, exchange papers with another student; tell each other about any details you have left out. On your partner's paper, draw a slash to separate the subject from the predicate in each independent clause.

1b. The verb phrase

An independent clause in standard written English needs a verb or, more accurately (since verbs can consist of more than one word), a complete verb phrase.

VERB PHRASES IN INDEPENDENT CLAUSES	
Subject	**Verb Phrase**
	Verb in present (one word)
It	makes
We	talk
	Verb in past (one word)
It	made
We	talked
	auxiliaries (one or more) + main verb
The couches	were cleaned
The couches	might have been cleaned

The Artist's Room in Arles, VINCENT VAN GOGH (1889)

A complete verb phrase can be a one-word phrase, with the main verb indicating past or present time:

She *waited* for an hour.
He *works* for a big company.

The verbs here are *wait* and *work*. The form of the verb shows past tense *(-ed)* and present tense *(-s)*, respectively.

A complete verb phrase can also be composed of one or more auxiliary verbs + the corresponding form of the main verb following them (see Chapter 13 for a summary of verb forms). In the following examples, the main verbs used are *waiting, worked,* and *decorated,* but note that they are accompanied by auxiliaries to add more—and necessary—information:

She *was waiting* for two hours.
He *has worked* for that company for two years.
They *should have decorated* their living room.

In some languages, it is possible to mention a topic and then to make a comment about it without using a verb phrase. A speaker of Mandarin, for example, could write

他很高

which translates literally as *"He very tall."[†] In English, such topic-comment constructions are not acceptable in expository writing. When you read, though, you might sometimes find such structures used consciously by the writer as a stylistic device:

My sister became a doctor. My brother, a lawyer.

Some more examples of topic-comment structures used in specific circumstances occur in Exercise 3.

☆*EXERCISE 3*[‡]

The artist Vincent van Gogh wrote to his brother, Theo, to explain his intentions in the painting of his room. Read what he wrote.

I had a new idea in my head and here is the sketch to it. . . . This time it's just simply my bedroom, only here color must do everything, and, as it gives a grander style to things when it is simple, it will be suggestive here of rest or of sleep in general. In a word, to look at the picture ought to rest the brain or rather the imagination.

The walls are pale violet. The ground is of red tiles. The wood of the bed and chairs is the yellow of fresh butter, the sheets and pillows

---

[†]An asterisk (*) indicates incorrect usage.

[‡]A star (☆) indicates a linguistically challenging exercise.

very light greenish lemon. The coverlet scarlet. The window green. The toilet-table orange, the basin blue. The doors lilac.

And that is all—there is nothing in this room with closed shutters. The broad lines of the furniture, again, must express absolute rest.

Adapted from a translation quoted in E. H. Gombrich, The Story of Art
(Oxford: Phaidon Press, 1978), p. 438.

Because Vincent van Gogh was writing to his brother, he could write in his own personal and stylized way. He did not keep on repeating a form of the verb *be*, but he left out the verb phrase in some of the basic sentence structures. Where did he do that? How would those structures be written in an academic description of the painting?

EXERCISE 4

For Exercise 2, you wrote a description of van Gogh's room and a partner indicated the division between the subject and predicate in each sentence. Underline the verb phrase you used in each independent clause, and then underline the main verb (not the auxiliaries) twice.

Note that a form of *be, do,* or *have* can serve as either a main verb or an auxiliary.

1c. The position of the subject

The subject of a sentence is frequently a noun phrase: either a noun + determiners (words like *a, an, the, this,* etc.) or a pronoun (*he, they,* etc.). The usual and common sentence order in English is this:

S-V-O: subject-verb-object ("The boy ate the cake.")

Or

S-V-C: subject-linking verb-complement ("The boy was hungry.")

Linking verbs are verbs like *be, seem, appear, look,* and *feel.*

A speaker of English tends to watch out for the subject when reading in order to determine what the sentence will be about. Very often, the subject appears in first position in the sentence. But when a phrase or clause precedes the subject, a comma is usually—though not always—used to signal this (as in this very sentence!) and to prepare the reader for the appearance of the subject:

 , S + V

EXERCISE 5

In the following sentences from the passage by Nora Ephron, the author includes information in the sentence before the subject. Underline the part of the sentence that precedes the subject.

1. Last year, I came to believe that the main reason was the lamps.
2. Also, they make the room much brighter.
3. Years ago, when I lived in a two-room apartment, I never used the living room either.
4. Sometimes I think about moving the bed into the living room.
5. Every time I walk from the bedroom or the study to the kitchen I pass the living room and take a long, fond look at it.
6. When I was growing up, I had a friend named Lillian.

1d. What not to do with the subject of the sentence

There are three important things to remember about the subject.

- The subject should not be omitted. ("My town is pretty; *is big, too.")
- The subject should not be repeated. (*"My town Kafarselwan it is marvelous and exciting.")
- The subject should not be buried inside a prepositional phrase. (*"In my town Kafarselwan is marvelous and exciting." What is the subject of *is?* The student can rewrite this as "My town Kafarselwan is marvelous and exciting" or "In my town Kafarselwan, everything is marvelous and exciting.")

In some languages—Spanish or Japanese, for example—the subject of the sentence does not have to be stated when it is a pronoun like *I, we, he,* or *they:*

SPANISH
Tengo muchos libros. (I have a lot of books.)
tengo = I have

JAPANESE
Hon wo kaimashita. (*X* bought a book—the pronoun is inferred from the context.)
kaimashita = I bought, you bought, he/she bought, etc.

In English, however, both in speech and writing, a pronoun subject may never be omitted.

EXERCISE 6 (oral)

The following students' sentences contain errors. Can you identify the errors and fix them?

1. The big chair it is very comfortable.
2. The bedroom is extremely pretty; has a lot of antique furniture.
3. The pictures that are on the walls around the room, they are mostly landscapes.
4. By buying expensive furniture has made the room look like a museum.
5. My mother wanted a new carpet. Then wanted a new table, too.
6. The lamp on the table next to the window it belonged to my grandmother.

1e. Filler subjects *it* and *there*

Both *it* and *there* can be used to fill the subject position in an English sentence. Some languages can omit the subject. Since the subject is obligatory in an English sentence, *it* and *there* are often used to fill that position. They occur in different contexts, however, and should not be confused:

- *It* is used with time, distance, weather, temperature, and the environment:

  It is 8 o'clock.
  It's 200 miles away.
  It's raining and soon *it* will be snowing.
  It was hot yesterday.
  It got too crowded at the party, so I left.

The filler subject *it* is always singular, followed by a third-person singular verb form (see Chapter 17).

Note that the uses of *it* as a subject in the reading passage introducing this chapter do not represent a filler subject. These uses are referential: each *it* refers to something previously mentioned in the text.

- *There* postpones the logical subject and indicates position or existence:

  There are 20 people in the room.
  There was once a school on that corner.
  There is a reason for my absence.
  There is a God.

The filler subject *there* merely postpones the logical subject, so the noun phrase that follows the verb (the logical subject) determines whether the verb form is singular or plural:

There is a reason.
There are some reasons.

See also Chapter 17, "Subject-Verb Agreement."

EXERCISE 7

Look at the picture of van Gogh's room on p. 00. Produce as many sentences of description as you can that begin with the word *there*.

EXAMPLE

There are some pictures on the walls.

EXERCISE 8 (oral)

In pairs, produce questions and answers about your present environment (date, day, time, year, weather, temperature, distances in the room and larger environment). Use *it* as a filler subject in the response.

EXAMPLES

What is the date today? It's . . .
What time is it? It's . . .
How far is it from here to . . . ? It's . . .

1f. The six basic requirements of a written sentence

REQUIREMENTS OF A WRITTEN SENTENCE

- A capital letter at the beginning
- Punctuation at the end (a period, a question mark, or an exclamation point)
- A subject
- A predicate containing a complete verb phrase
- Standard word order (commonly subject-verb-object or complement)
- An independent clause, that is, a core idea that can stand alone with its own subject and verb

---

EXERCISE 9 (oral)

This is to be done with a partner. Follow the pattern and examples below:

STUDENT 1	STUDENT 2
"Tell me something about . . ."	Says a sentence in response. Then adds another sentence.

EXAMPLES

Tell me something about your sister.	My sister is 22 years old. She is in Bangkok now.
Tell me something about your room.	My room is very dark. It has only one small window.

Listen carefully to each other to make sure that each sentence contains a subject and a complete verb phrase.

EXERCISE 10

In each sentence, four words or phrases are underlined. One of them should be corrected or rewritten. Which one, and what is the correct form?

_____ 1. Big rooms with a lot of windows they help to make us feel
            _a_   _b_ _c_   _d_
cheerful. _____

_____ 2. Mr. Johnson, a friend of mine, he always chooses antique
                              _a_   _b_   _c_
furniture. _____
  _d_

_____ 3. Architects studying how different people live and work and
                    _a_   _b_   _c_
what they need. _____
      _d_

_____ 4. By fixing up the room cost us more money than we could
         _a_   _b_   _c_
afford. _____
  _d_

_____ 5. The pictures hanging on the wall near the window they were
                                                        _a_   _b_
given to me as graduation gifts by my grandparents.
  _c_   _d_

EDIT

Read the following piece of student writing on the topic "My Ideal Room." Underline the three places where there are problems with basic sentence structure. Why do you think these problems occurred? What changes should the student make to edit this passage?

Isn't it lovely to live in New York, where an inch of space costs a lot of money? I live in a studio apartment, and I dream of having an extra room. This is the best subject I was ever asked to write about.

In terms of size this room should be at least as big as my actual studio apartment. One big window would be enough, but I would want it to face south to get the afternoon sunlight as well as to watch my favorite time of the day. The winter sunsets and the lights coming on in the city. The room should have high ceilings. The walls, painted in matte white, and a big, dark, polished wooden desk. A few shelves for books they should occupy one corner, and the rest of the space should be covered with pillows with red roses designed on a white background.

I don't like rooms to look cluttered. In addition, don't like them to be dark. So I would want one more thing in it that is necessary: a red and white rounded Spanish marble lamp.

Carlos Gomariz, Argentina

WRITE

Write two paragraphs to describe a room that you think of as your ideal room, one that you would like to spend time in. Make sure that your readers will be able to understand what makes this room special for you. Describe the room in detail in the first paragraph, so that readers will feel they are looking at a photograph. In the second paragraph, tell your reader why you like that kind of room so much. If you want to, add an introductory paragraph that captures your readers' attention and introduces them to the idea of an ideal room. When you have written your description, examine the structure of each sentence.

**EDITING
ADVICE**

1. Go through your piece of writing and examine carefully all the groups of words that end with a period (.) or a semicolon (;). Then identify all the verbs that occur in the independent clauses of those sentences. Make sure they are complete verb phrases (an *-ing* form by itself with no auxiliary is not complete). Underline the verbs.

2. Circle the subjects of those verbs.

3. If you have difficulty finding an independent clause or identifying the verb or its subject, take that as a warning sign. There may be something wrong with the structure of the sentence.

4. Once you have checked that your sentences have all the six requirements of a sentence, make sure that the end punctuation of each one is clear and that the first letter of the first word is clearly written as a capital letter.

Phrases and Clauses

2

READ

Read some of the simple sentences (subject + predicate) that students wrote about the picture.

Outside a Bistro in France, Henri Cartier-Bresson (1968–1969)

They are living in Paris.
They are outside a bistro.
They are kissing.
He loves her.
She loves him.
There is a dog under the table.
The dog is watching them.
No people are watching.
The man is smoking.

Add some simple sentences of your own about the picture.

Now read one of the longer, extended sentences that a group of students wrote.

> **Outside a bistro in Paris last spring, when there were no people watching, a man who was smoking a cigarette tenderly and lovingly kissed the woman sitting opposite him, while his dog watched approvingly.**

ANALYZE

1. In the extended sentence just given, underline the verb of the independent clause and circle its subject. Remember that an independent clause has a subject and a complete verb phrase, can stand alone grammatically, and is not introduced with subordinating conjunctions like *although, if, because,* or *when.*

2. Identify the S + V of the independent clause. Then copy down in a list the parts of the sentence that exist outside of the S + V (subject + verb), for example, "outside a bistro," "who was smoking a cigarette."

3. Discuss with other students how you might name the sentence parts you have listed in order to identify and classify them (according to their position in the sentence, according to the type of expression, according to the type of first word, etc.).

STUDY

2a. Packing a sentence with information

The subject-predicate structure is preserved even when the sentence is packed with additional information. The S + V core remains and does not change.

Look again at the picture by Henri Cartier-Bresson. A basic subject + predicate sentence (S + V + C/O) about this picture could be

> **The man kissed the woman.**

or, indeed,

> **The woman kissed the man.**

or

> **They kissed each other.**

These are all independent clauses.

Let's look at the first one in detail. It has a verb phrase, *kissed,* a subject, *The man,* and an object, *the woman.* We can add a lot more information to this basic sentence, yet the sentence may still have only one independent clause. The information can take the form of many different grammatical structures.

16

EXERCISE 1

Freewrite (write as much as you can and as quickly as you can) for five minutes to tell a reader about your own reactions to the photograph at the beginning of this chapter. For example, would such a scene be possible in your country? Do you think people should kiss in public? How do you feel when you see incidents like this?

Exchange papers with another student and discuss the ideas you expressed. Read each other's freewriting carefully, and underline all verbs that occur as the complete verb of a S + V structure in an independent clause. Note where you have packed in more information.

2b. Adding information at the beginning

We can add information at the beginning of the sentence that will tell us more about the sentence as a whole or simply about the subject of the sentence. Usually, when this information is longer than one word, it will be separated from the subject with a comma. That comma is a signal to the reader that the introductory material has ended. The reader expects the subject to come next. The accompanying box gives some examples of structures that can introduce a sentence. Read them aloud; both reader and listener will wait for the subject of the sentence to appear.

FRONT STRUCTURES		
Front Structure	**Example**	**Independent Clause**
Time phrase	Yesterday	
Place phrase	On a busy street,	
Descriptive phrase	Happy to be on vacation,	
Adverb (See also Chapter 15.)	Enthusiastically,	
Prepositional phrase	With only the dog watching,	
-ing phrase (See also Chapter 20.)	Sitting outside a restaurant,	the man kissed the woman.
Participle phrase (See also Chapter 21.)	Watched only by the dog,	
Infinitive phrase (See also Chapter 19.)	To show his love,	
Dependent clause (adverbial) (See also Chapter 26.)	Because he felt romantic,	

A phrase does not contain a *subject + verb* structure; a clause does.

EXERCISE 2

Choose a photograph that you own, or choose one from a magazine. Write a simple sentence that expresses the idea of the picture. Then write sentences about the picture, adding phrases or clauses before the subject of the simple sentence you chose.

2c. Including information to modify and identify the subject

Here are some examples of the types of informational structures you can use to modify or identify a noun phrase (a noun with its modifiers: *the tall man, one lonely man, her former husband,* etc.). In the examples, the noun phrase that is modified or identified is *The man,* the subject of the sentence *The man kissed the woman.*

STRUCTURES TO MODIFY THE SUBJECT	
Modifying Structure	*Example*
Adjective(s)	The happy, smiling man kissed the woman.
Noun as adjective	The family man kissed the woman.
Prepositional phrase	The man in the dark shirt kissed the woman.
-ing phrase (See also Chapter 20.)	The man sitting outside the restaurant kissed the woman.
Participle phrase (See also Chapter 21.)	The man selected as the best chef of the year kissed the woman.
Dependent clause (adjectival) (See also Chapter 24.)	The man who brought the brown-and-white dog with him kissed the woman. The man [whom/that] you saw in the restaurant kissed the woman.

EXERCISE 3 (oral)

Complete the following sentences, using *kissed the woman* as the predicate.

EXAMPLE

The man [what did he have with him?]
The man with a dog at his feet kissed the woman.

1. The man [what was he wearing?]
2. The man [where had you seen him previously?]
3. The man [were the police looking for him?]
4. The man [what did he do?]
5. The man [what was he eating?]
6. The man [where was he?]

2d. Inserting additional information after the subject

We can use certain structures to insert additional information after the subject of a sentence.

STRUCTURES INSERTED AFTER THE SUBJECT	
Inserted Structure	*Example*
Noun phrase (appositive)	The man, a young movie star, kissed the woman.
-ing phrase (See also Chapter 20.)	The man, feeling in a romantic mood, kissed the woman.
Participle phrase (See also Chapter 21.)	The man, inspired by the beautiful spring weather, kissed the woman.
Dependent clause (adjectival) (See also Chapter 24.)	Pierre Chantal, who is a famous designer, kissed the woman.

Note that inserted information is not necessary to identify the subject. It serves only to give the reader more information about the subject. Therefore, it is separated from the rest of the sentence by commas. The commas seem to say, "By the way, . . ."—you are giving information that the reader does not really need to understand the subject of your sentence but might like to know. (See also Chapter 24, "Adjectival Clauses.") Appositive noun phrases, words that further define a prior noun phrase, are enclosed by commas. (See also Chapter 29, "Punctuation.") Sometimes dashes are used to make it even clearer that the information is additional:

My teachers—all of whom struck terror into my heart—live in my memory.

EXERCISE 4

Insert information after the subject of each sentence.

1. Students have a hard life.
2. Professors don't like to give grades.

3. My favorite professor teaches . . .
4. Professor Goldman teaches history.
5. My friend decided to drop his course.
6. The course isn't a very popular one.

2e. Adding a verb

We can expand the predicate by adding another verb.

The man kissed and hugged the woman.
The man kissed the woman and whispered something to her.
The man kissed the woman and then patted the dog.

2f. Expanding the object: direct and indirect object

We can expand a noun phrase, specifically here the object, by adding adjectives, appositives, descriptive phrases (with *-ing* or a participle), or adjective clauses. With certain verbs (*give, send, lend, tell, pay, hand, teach, buy, make,* etc.), we can add indirect objects, too, before the direct object or after it (with *to* or *for*).

STRUCTURES TO EXPAND THE OBJECT	
Structure	*Example*
Adjective(s) (See also Chapter 14.)	The man kissed the shy woman.
Appositive noun phrase	The man kissed the woman, a well-known model.
-ing phrase (See also Chapter 20.)	The man kissed the woman sitting opposite him.
Participle phrase (See also Chapter 21.)	The man kissed the woman dressed in a striped shirt.
Dependent clause (adjectival) (See also Chapter 24.)	The man kissed the woman who had just sat down opposite him.
Indirect object	The man gave the woman opposite him a big kiss. The man gave a big kiss to the woman opposite him.

Note that in the last two examples, the direct object of the verb *gave* is *a big kiss*. We can thus express the indirect object in two ways:

S	V	IO (indirect object)	DO (direct object)
She	gave	her friend	a present.

Or

S	V	DO	*to/for* IO
She	gave	a present	to her friend.

If the indirect object is a pronoun, the usual form is

S	V	IO	DO
She	gave	me	a present.

Some verbs that are followed by an indirect object use the preposition *to* when the indirect object follows the direct object; others use *for*. The most common ones are listed here.

FOLLOWED BY *to*	FOLLOWED BY *for*
give	buy
send	make
lend	bake
tell	cook
pay	
hand	
teach	

EXERCISE 5 *(oral)*

Assemble sentences from the following parts. Try out alternative positions for the indirect object. Use the past tense.

	SUBJECT	VERB	DIRECT OBJECT	INDIRECT OBJECT
1.	The woman	give	a smile	the man
2.	Her sister	lend	a sweater	her
3.	Pierre	buy	a ring	his girlfriend
4.	Marie	tell	a lie	her boyfriend
5.	He	teach	everything he knows	his students
6.	She	make	a cake	her sister

2g

2g. Adding information about the sentence at the end

We can add structures at the end of the sentence. These structures may give information about the whole sentence, similar to those that are used at the beginning of the sentence, or they may, after a comma, add information about the subject.

END STRUCTURES	
Structure	*Example*
Time phrase	The man kissed the woman yesterday.
Place phrase	The man kissed the woman in front of the restaurant.
Adverb (See also Chapter 15.)	The man kissed the woman enthusiastically.
Prepositional phrase	The man kissed the woman at her instigation.
-ing phrase (See also Chapter 20.)	The man kissed the woman, hoping she would respond.
Descriptive phrase	The man kissed the woman, enthusiastic about her beauty.
Infinitive phrase (See also Chapter 19.)	The man kissed the woman to show that he loved her.
Dependent clause (adverbial) (See also Chapter 26.)	The man kissed the woman because he felt romantic.

☆EXERCISE 6

We can add information in many of the available spaces in a sentence:

On a busy street in Paris, the man, inspired by the beautiful spring weather, kissed the woman who had just sat down opposite him, even though he was worried about her reaction.

Write three different sentences of your own in which you pack in as much information as you can about what you perceive in the scene portrayed by Cartier-Bresson.

☆EXERCISE 7

Using details from the article by Nora Ephron, "Room with View—and No People," write three sentences, each using as the independent clause the following simple sentence:

The writer didn't use the living room.

Pack each sentence with as much information as you can. Try out alternatives and take risks. See how long a sentence you can manage.

EXERCISE 8

Choose the word or phrase that best completes each sentence.

1. _____, the crowd jeered at the politician.

   a. Insulting
   b. Insulted
   c. An insult
   d. Felt insulted

2. The scientists _____ accepted the prize gratefully.

   a. the best
   b. were the best
   c. selected as the best
   d. to select

3. _____, he sounds more intelligent.

   a. Because he can make better speeches than his opponent
   b. He can make better speeches than his opponent
   c. His speeches are better than his opponent's
   d. As better speeches than his opponent

4. The New Deal, _____, shows almost no signs of life today.

   a. a program begun by Franklin D. Roosevelt
   b. the program was begun by Franklin D. Roosevelt
   c. Franklin D. Roosevelt began this program
   d. which began by Franklin D. Roosevelt

5. He gave _____ a lot of power.

   a. to his advisers
   b. trusting his advisers
   c. he trusted his advisers
   d. his advisers

2

EDIT

The following piece was written by a student after he interviewed the author of this book. In places, he writes a series of short, simple sentences. Some of these could be combined into longer sentences by packing the information around an independent clause. Play around with this paragraph, and see how many different ways you can rewrite it. Make sure that you include all the ideas that appear in the original piece.

Ann Raimes has to teach a class at 8 A.M. She wakes up at 5:50 A.M. every school day during the semester. She then has breakfast. For breakfast she has a cup of tea, toast, or cereal. She is from England. That is why she always has tea. However, she has been living in the U.S.A. about 25 years. After breakfast, she walks ten or twelve blocks to the number 4 or 5 train. She goes to 42nd Street. Then she changes to the number 6 train. She gets out of the train at Hunter College at 68th Street. She buys a cup a coffee. She takes it with her to her office. There she picks up her papers and books. She goes to her first class at 8 A.M. After that, she has another class at 9:40 A.M. This ends at 11:30. Then she has office hours from 11:30 to 12:30. She has lunch at 12:30. Usually she orders a sandwich for her lunch. Sometimes she treats herself and goes to a Japanese restaurant. Later in the afternoon, she goes home. On the way, she buys meat and vegetables for dinner. At home, she marks students' papers and writes comments on them. If she has time, she works on the textbook she is writing. She and her family eat dinner at about 8 P.M. They sit and talk over dinner for more than an hour. After dinner, she either reads or watches TV. She goes to bed around 11:30. This is her routine on weekdays. On weekends she sleeps late, goes out, and enjoys herself.

Chih Wong, China

WRITE

Use a photograph of your own choice, either a family photograph or a photograph from a magazine. You can use the same one that you used for Exercise 2. Write a description of the photograph, using as many of the sentence-packing techniques as you can. End by telling your reader why you chose this particular picture to describe. Exchange photographs and compositions with another student; read each other's compositions, and identify the independent clause or clauses of each sentence. Tell your partner if any sentences aren't clear to you. Then revise your own composition, concentrating on improving the sentence variety and structure.

1. Use a colored pencil to draw a line between the end of one sentence and the beginning of the next. That should give you a clear picture of whether you have used all short sentences or all long sentences. Try to vary your sentence length.

2. Check your sentence structure: look for the S + V structure! Underline the complete verb phrase of the independent clause, and circle its subject. What other phrases or clauses have you attached to each independent clause? Try to identify them according to the categories used in this chapter. Have you used a lot of the same type? If so, aim for more variety. If you find any structures that don't seem to fit, revise the sentence.

3. If you have written a lot of short, basic sentences, see if you can combine some by using phrase and clause types illustrated in this chapter.

4. Take a few risks! Try using some structures that you haven't used before. Then add a note to your instructor asking if they work.

3 Questions and Negatives

READ

Read the following paragraph from the article "The Doctors' Dilemma" by Sissela Bok. The entire selection, with vocabulary glosses, appears on p. 337.

> What should doctors say . . . to a 46-year-old man coming in for a routine physical checkup just before going on vacation with his family who, though he feels in perfect health, is found to have a form of cancer that will cause him to die within six months? Is it best to tell him the
> 5   truth? If he asks, should the doctors deny that he is ill, or minimize the gravity of the prognosis? Should they at least conceal the truth until after the family vacation?

ANALYZE

1. Circle the subjects in the independent clauses of the sentences in the selection.

2. Underline the complete verb phrase that goes with each subject.

3. Normal order in statements in English is S-V-O/C (subject-verb-object or complement). Write an explanation of what happens to normal S-V-O/C order in a question. Compare your explanation with another student's.

STUDY

3a. The form of questions

In writing, we signal questions with a question mark at the end and with inverted word order, that is, with V-S word order. When the statement form occurs with an auxiliary + main verb or with any form of the verb *be*, we move the first auxiliary or the *be* form to a position in front of the subject:

        They *should* tell the truth.
   Should they   tell the truth?

        He *is* lying.
    Is he   lying?

When no auxiliary occurs in the statement, a form of *do* is used as the question auxiliary, followed by the simple form of the main verb:

He *feels* in good health.
Does he *feel* in good health?

The following table uses examples to summarize question word order.

QUESTION WORD ORDER: WITH QUESTION WORDS AND WITH YES/NO QUESTIONS				
Question Word	*First Auxiliary Verb (V1)*	*Subject*	*Other Auxiliaries + Main Verb*	*Rest of Predicate*
What	should	doctors	say . . . ?	
When	do	we	leave?	
Where	are	you	going?	
	Is	it		best to . . . ?
	Should	the doctors	deny . . . or minimize . . . ?	
	Should	they	conceal . . . ?	

However, note the order when the question word itself is the subject of the sentence:

Question Word as Subject	*Complete Verb Phrase*	*Rest of Sentence*
Who	should tell	the patient?
What	happened	to him?

The question words are *who, whom, whose, what, when, where, which, why,* and *how*.

EXERCISE 1

For each of the following statements, form both a yes/no question and a question with the given question word.

EXAMPLE

They worked late. (Why)
Did they work late?
Why did they work late?

1. He tells lies. (How often)
2. She is telling the truth. (Why)

3a

3. Doctors should follow a code of ethics. (Which code)
4. Dr. Jones has concealed the truth. (Who)
5. Dr. Smith has concealed the truth, too. (Why)
6. The doctors tried to be honest. (What)

EXERCISE 2 (oral)

Imagine that you are a doctor. Prepare five questions that you would ask to find out if a patient is leading a healthy life. Vary the auxiliary verbs you use. Then ask another student your questions.

EXAMPLES

Do you smoke?
How many operations have you had?

EXERCISE 3 (oral)

Make questions from the following statements, so that the words in italics would be an appropriate answer to the question.

EXAMPLES

She went *to the doctor's office.*
    Where did she go?
She was worried about *her weight.*
    What was she worried about?

1. She went to see *Dr. Parks.*
2. She went to the doctor *because she had a very bad cold.*
3. She made the appointment *last week.*
4. He told her *that she was working too hard.*
5. She reacted *very defensively.*
6. She told the doctor about *her responsibilities.*
7. *Her boss's* plan was to increase productivity 50 percent.
8. She was working *twelve* hours a day.

☆EXERCISE 4

The reading selection by Lewis Thomas on p. 355 discusses the questions we might ask the inhabitants if we discovered life on another planet. Two of the questions Thomas suggests are "Did you think yourselves unique?" and "Do you always tell the truth?" What additional questions do you think would be important and interesting questions to ask? Write five questions.

3b. *Why?* and *what for?*

Note the alternative uses of *why?* and *what for?* "What . . . for?" is usually used when the speaker or writer is puzzled; it expresses surprise and bewilderment.

WHY? AND WHAT FOR?			
Question Word	*First Auxiliary*	*Subject*	*Verb + Rest of Predicate*
Why	is	he	lying?
What	is	he	lying for?
Why	did	she	say that?
What	did	she	say that for?
Why	was	she	fired?
What	was	she	fired for?

Note: "How come . . . ?" is often heard in conversation. Note the structure:

How come he's lying?
How come she said that?

This usage is not appropriate for formal academic purposes.

EXERCISE 5 *(oral)*

Give both a "Why?" and a "What . . . for?" response to each of the following statements.

EXAMPLE

He borrowed $100.
Why did he borrow $100?
What did he borrow $100 for?

1. The doctor told his patient a lie.
2. The doctor ordered a set of X-rays.
3. The doctor tested her reflexes.
4. The hospital employees are on strike.
5. He refused to have an operation.
6. The patients are being sent home.

3c. Negatives

The usual way to express negation is with *not* after the first auxiliary.

WORD ORDER WITH *NOT*				
Subject	*First Auxiliary*	**Not**	*Other Auxiliaries + Main Verb*	*Rest of Predicate*
Sick people	do	not	want	to know the truth.
Dying patients	can-	not	make	decisions.
The doctor	should	not	have lied.	

Note the form when *never* is used with a main verb with no auxiliaries (present or past tense).

WORD ORDER WITH *NEVER*				
Subject	*First Auxiliary*	**Never**	*Other Auxiliaries + Main Verb*	*Rest of Predicate*
They		never	tell	the truth.
He	should	never	deceive	the family.

3d. Alternative forms of negation

Alternatives to the use of *not* exist.

EXAMPLE

I don't have any spare time.
I have no spare time.

He doesn't say anything.
He says nothing.

These are the alternative ways of expressing negation:

REGULAR FORM	ALTERNATIVE FORM
not a	no
not any	no
not any	none
not anyone	no one
not anybody	nobody
not anything	nothing
not anywhere	nowhere
not ever	never
not either	neither

Standard edited English uses only one negative in a clause:

Either   The doctor has no patients.
Or   The doctor doesn't have any patients.
But not   *The doctor doesn't have no patients.

You might hear this in conversation, but it is not considered a standard form.

Alternatives exist in word order, too. You can emphasize a negative expression like *never, not a, rarely,* or *seldom* by putting it in first place in the sentence and then inverting the sentence order by putting the first auxiliary of the verb phrase before the subject:

He has never lied to a patient.
Never has he lied to a patient.

For word order with *nor* introducing an independent clause, see Chapter 22.

INVERTED ORDER FOR EMPHASIS				
Negative	*First Auxiliary*	*Subject*	*Rest of Verb*	*Rest of Predicate*
Never	have	we	told	a lie.
Not a word	did	she	utter.	

EXERCISE 6

The following sentences are based on the reading passage used in Chapter 1. Rewrite each sentence, using an alternative negative form from among those listed in section 3d.

1. I never used the living room.
2. I had a friend named Lillian who had no living-room furniture.
3. I clearly don't have a clue as to what that consists of.
4. My living room has no clear function.
5. There isn't anyone in the room.
6. There is never any activity in the room.
7. Not any of the explanations help.
8. The room offers the family nothing.

EXERCISE 7

The following sentences use emphatic word order. Make them less emphatic by removing the negative particle from first place and making any corresponding changes.

1. Never have they entertained in the living room!
2. Seldom does she use the living room!
3. Rarely do they sit and talk in that room!
4. Never would I have expected such a disaster!
5. Never could they have predicted that crisis!
6. Not a mouthful would he eat for days on end!

3e. Tag questions

We use tag questions in speech and in informal writing when we want to confirm information that we think we have or when we want to express opinions. Often we have a specific answer in mind, so we don't necessarily expect an answer to the question.

EXAMPLES

He's a doctor, isn't he? (We think he is.)
Dr. Johnson doesn't operate, does he? (We think he doesn't.)

Eight aspects of statements with tag questions are tricky.

FEATURES OF TAG QUESTIONS	
Feature	*Example*
1. Positive statement, negative tag Negative statement, positive tag	He's a doctor, isn't he? She isn't a doctor, is she?
2. Statement with auxiliary or *be* form, same form in tag	He is a specialist, isn't he? He should tell the truth, shouldn't he?
3. Statement with no auxiliary or *be* form, form of *do* in tag	He concealed the truth, didn't he? She wants to know the truth, doesn't she?
4. Noun phrase as subject, pronoun in tag	The doctor is experienced, isn't he?
5. *This, that, these,* or *those* as subject, *it* or *they* in tag	This is a problem, isn't it? Those are forceps, aren't they?
6. *There* in subject position, *there* in tag	There are moral issues here, aren't there?
7. *Am* as first or main verb in statement, *aren't* in tag	I'm healthy, aren't I?
8. *Will* in statement, *won't* in tag	You'll help me, won't you?

Note that there is no one form for a tag question as there is in some languages, such as French, German, and Japanese. Instead, the tag changes according to the auxiliary verb form and the subject that occur in the statement.

Note, too, how the abbreviated spoken form *'d* is handled in a question tag:

> They*'d* be annoyed, wouldn't they? (*'d* = would)
> He*'d* been there before, hadn't he? (*'d* = had)

EXERCISE 8 (oral)

With another student, examine these two sentences, and discuss why the tags use different auxiliaries.

> The doctor has a lot of patients, *doesn't* he?
> The doctor has had a lot of success, *hasn't* he?

3f. Tag questions: summary

The box summarizes the forms used in tag questions.

TAG QUESTIONS: SUMMARY	
Statement	*Tag*
S + V	V + S
Positive	Negative
Negative	Positive
Auxiliary or *be* form	Repeat first auxiliary or *be* form
No auxiliary: present	Use *does/do*
No auxiliary: past	Use *did*
Noun phrase	Pronoun
there	*there*
this, that	*it*
these, those	*they*

EXERCISE 9 (oral)

The expected answer to the tag question "Doctors should tell the truth, shouldn't they?" is "Yes, they should." Give the expected answer to each of the following questions.

1. He'll try to understand, won't he?
2. She's happy now, isn't she?
3. She isn't sick anymore, is she?
4. There are some problems, aren't there?
5. Doctors follow a code of ethics, don't they?
6. He wanted to be told the truth, didn't he?
7. The doctor doesn't have much time, does he?
8. They are allowed to see their X-rays, aren't they?

EXERCISE 10 (oral)

Add tag questions to the following statements, as if you were seeking confirmation of the statement.

EXAMPLE

She lives alone.
She lives alone, doesn't she?

1. I have a nice living room.
2. People never sit in the living room.
3. The room always looks neat and tidy.
4. It would not solve the problem.
5. This would not solve the problem.
6. Lillian had no living-room furniture.
7. I am too old to have a bed in the living room.
8. Her mother had chosen the pool.
9. Lies do harm to those who tell them.
10. Doctors confront such choices often and urgently.
11. There is a need to debate this issue.
12. The seriously ill do not want to know the truth.

EDIT

Read the following introductory paragraphs of two students' essays. Are the questions used effectively? Are the questions and negatives formed accurately? Edit any that are not.

1. You are going to die soon and your doctor doesn't tell you the truth because he thinks that you might be not able to handle it. What is your reaction? Don't you get furious with the person who wants to decide your life for you? Don't you get disgusted with his sympathy? Don't you think that those who try to control your life by not telling you the truth are committing a crime? You'd be angry, aren't you?

Nasim Alikhani, Iran

2. The controversy about doctors telling the truth or not is complex. In our society, some people believe that doctors should tell the truth to patients in any situation, but others don't. They think it is important to answer these questions: What kind of illness does the patient have? Is it curable or incurable? Is the patient married or single? How much time there is left? Who can look after the patient when there isn't no hope?

Kam-ta Yen, China

WRITE

Write a short letter to the editor of a newspaper about an issue that you care about deeply. Make sure that you express your point of view clearly and support it with examples to make the issue come alive for the readers. When you have written a draft, try out a new beginning using questions addressed to the readers, as Sissela Bok did. Try, also, to use one tag question at an informal point in your letter at which you seek the readers' confirmation of your statement. Experiment with alternate forms of negation—take a risk and try out something that you haven't used before!

---

1. Look at your piece of writing. Make sure that every direct question has a question mark after it.

2. Check that you have used question word order (V-S) in a question, except when a question word forms the subject of the sentence ("Who is that?").

3. With tag questions, check that you have used the correct verb form (use a form of *do* when no auxiliary is used in the statement). Check, too, that you have reversed affirmative/negative order.

4. Make sure that you have not used double negatives (*"I don't have nothing").

EDITING ADVICE

Noun Phrases

Proper Nouns

4

READ

Read the following excerpt from "The Soybean," which appears with vocabulary glosses on p. 339.

In the last half of the first millennium A.D., the Japanese upper classes became slavish Sinophiles and imported many aspects of Chinese culture—writing characters, law codes, political institutions, and, perhaps most important, Buddhism. Doufu, called *tofu* in Japan—and now
5 elsewhere—arrived as one of the things associated with the new religion.(By this time the soybean itself had been cultivated in Japan for several hundred years.)

Buddhist monks are strict vegetarians, and doufu had become an important food in Chinese monasteries. For several centuries Buddhism
10 was an upper-class region in Japan; these social associations pushed the development of tofu and its associated soy foods in a different direction than in China.

ANALYZE

1. Other than the first words of sentences, which words in the reading passage above begin with capital letters? Write them down.

2. Try to classify the words you have written down into types. Read quickly through Nora Ephron's "Room with View—and No People" on p. 334, add the capitalized words that appear there to your list, and see what new categories you can form.

STUDY

4a. Categories of proper nouns

Proper nouns include the following types of nouns:

- Names of people: Lillian, Martin, Nora Ephron

4b

- Names of places (countries, cities, oceans, rivers, lakes, mountains, parks, schools, buildings, stores, etc.): China, Beverly Hills, Atlantic Ocean, Amazon River, Lake Michigan, Mount Fuji, Central Park, Coe College, Sears Tower, Bloomingdale's
- Names of religions: Buddhism, Buddhist; Hinduism, Hindu; Christianity, Christian
- Names of courses in school and college: Philosophy, History of Science
- Historical periods and events: the Middle Ages, the Civil War
- Styles of art and architecture: Victorian, Gothic, Baroque, Expressionist, Cubist
- Nationalities, languages, and associated words: Chinese, Japanese, Sinophile, Anglophobe
- Days, months, special holidays: Christmas, Passover, New Year's Day, December, Tuesday
- Titles: Mr., Mrs., Ms., Dr.

EXERCISE 1

Form two teams of students. Your instructor will read out six items from the following list. Your task is to write sentences that give some information about as many of the six proper nouns as you can.

EXAMPLE

Mount Everest: Mount Everest is the highest mountain in the world.

the Netherlands	President Bush
the Rocky Mountains	Prime Minister Thatcher
Lake Titicaca	Central Park
Egypt	the Pacific Ocean
the North Pole	Lake Superior
the Philippines	Taiwan
South Vietnam	the People's Republic of China
the Mediterranean	Leningrad
the First World War	Seoul
the United Nations	the Louvre
New Year's Eve	Mount McKinley

4b. Article use with proper nouns: summary

Article use with proper nouns has few rules and many exceptions. Each time you come across a name, remember to learn whether it is used with *the* or not. For a very general rule of thumb (though it has a lot of exceptions), use the following guide:

ARTICLES WITH PROPER NOUNS
- Singular: Ø (zero article)   *Lake Superior*
- Plural: the   *the Great Lakes*

4c. Articles with singular proper nouns

A general guideline for the use of singular proper nouns is to use no article (Ø, the zero article form). However, you will see from the examples in the box titled "Articles with Singular Proper Nouns" (pp. 40–41) that there are a lot of exceptions. Learn all the exceptions as you come across them. Whenever you read or listen to English and find an exception, write it down and learn it.

☆*EXERCISE 2*

Write a paragraph about your country in which you explain the relationship between certain foods and religious customs and festivals. Pay attention to the use of *the* with proper nouns.

4d. Articles with plural proper nouns

Usually *the* is used with plural proper nouns:

COUNTRIES
the United States
the Netherlands

GROUPS OF LAKES
the Finger Lakes
the Great Lakes

MOUNTAIN RANGES
the Alps
the Andes
the Rockies

GROUPS OF ISLANDS
the Bahamas
the Falklands
the Philippines
the West Indies

NATIONALITIES
the French (people)
the Chinese (people)
the Americans

EXERCISE 3

In the following sentences about soybean production, insert the given noun phrases. Capitalize and add *the* where necessary. First you will have to decide whether the noun is a proper noun or not.

1. Tofu is produced in _____

ARTICLES WITH SINGULAR PROPER NOUNS

	0 *(zero article: no article)*	*the*
Names of People	Nora Ephron Fred Hapgood	
Titles of People	General Eisenhower President Harry Truman Lord Nelson	the president the prime minister the duke of York the emperor Napoleon
Continents, Parts of the Globe	Asia Central America	the South Pole the Equator the East, the West
Countries†	France Canada Greece	the United Kingdom the Soviet Union the Dominican Republic (The last word in each name is a collective noun.)
States, Cities, Districts, Regions	Mississippi Tokyo Hollywood	The Hague the Bronx the Ruhr the Riviera the South End
Buildings	Westminster Abbey Rockefeller Center North Station	the Chrysler Building the Renaissance Center the Eiffel Tower
Museums, Hotels		the Metropolitan Museum the Hilton Hotel
Schools	Washington University Ithaca College Kennedy High School	the University of Michigan
Streets, Parks	Fifth Avenue Main Street Lincoln Park	the New York Botanical Garden

†Note that nationality adjectives (*French, Canadian, Greek,* etc.) also begin with a capital letter. They refer to singular or plural, and article use follows that of common nouns: *a/the Greek, a/the Greek singer, the Greeks, Greeks,* etc.

	0 (zero article: no article)	**the**
Roadways	Route 87	the Pennsylvania Turnpike the Palisades Parkway
Lakes	Lake Superior Lake Temagami	
Seas, Oceans, Gulfs, Rivers		the Mediterranean (Sea) the Pacific (Ocean) the Seine
Deserts		the Sahara (Desert) the Mojave (Desert)
Mountains	Mount Everest Mount Vesuvius	
Islands	Trinidad Sicily	the Isle of Wight
Months, Days	December Wednesday	
Holidays	Easter Chanukah Thanksgiving Memorial Day	the Fourth of July
Languages	French Chinese	the French language the Chinese language
Religions	Buddhism Christianity Islam	
Historical Periods and Events		the Renaissance the Great Depression the October Revolution
Brand Names	Pepsi-Cola Kellogg's Raisin Bran	

_____ (china, japan, and united states of amer-

ica) in vast quantities.

2. The soybean allows _____ (chinese) to feed a

quarter of the world's population.

3. For several centuries, _____ (buddhism) was an

upper-class religion in _____ (japan).

4. Soybean agriculture is less labor-intensive than other crops, especially

_____ (cotton).

5. Soy milk is as popular as _____ (coca-cola)

in _____ (hong kong).

6. The average _____ (american) consumes al-

most six gallons of _____ (soy oil) a year.

7. Soybeans are grown in the area around _____

(mississippi), but erosion of the soil is a problem.

8. In the 1980s, _____ (south america) be-

came a serious competitor in soybean production; in fact,

_____ (brazil) now earns nearly as much from

soybeans as from _____ (coffee).

EXERCISE 4

Read the last seven paragraphs of the reading passage "The Soybean" in Part II. Note each time a proper noun appears, and fit each one into the categories outlined in sections 4c and 4d.

EXAMPLES

Cinderella: singular, name of person
The United States: plural, name of country

EXERCISE 5

Form two teams in your classroom. Each team will write five questions on five separate slips of paper, asking about the location of a place. Use a proper noun in each question.

EXAMPLES

Where is the Amazon?
Where are the Himalayas?
Where is the Louvre?
Where are the Scilly Isles?

A student on the other team will take one of the slips of paper, read out the question, and answer it. One point is scored for each correct answer.

EDIT

The student who wrote the following excerpt had some problems with proper nouns. Another student who read the composition underlined places that she thought were problematic. What do you think the writer should do now? What changes should the writer make? Did the student reader miss any places where errors occurred?

We used to have most of our school courses in Chinese, and a uniform was required for entering school. We learned the course in the Chinese language because first we were Vietnam-born <u>chinese</u> people, and we all followed <u>chinese</u> customs and traditions. Secondly, the school was only for <u>Chinese Students</u>, and so students without the uniform would not be allowed to enter. But after the Communists took over, this policy changed. The Communist government said that since we lived in Vietnam, we had to speak one language, which was Vietnamese, and the uniform was abolished, so Vietnamese students could go to the <u>chinese</u> school. After three years of living in a Communist Society, my family, ten people, decided to leave Vietnam. We decided to leave on a cold <u>tuesday</u> evening in <u>march</u>. People from my neighborhood gathered in <u>front of</u> my house, wishing us luck and crying. That night, I was so sleepy when I got on the boat that I slept right away. The next day, when I woke up, all I saw was sky and water. I was scared at first, but a day later I started to get used to it. We spent seven days and nights on a small boat before we arrived in Hong Kong.

Jimmy Chong, Hong Kong

43

4

WRITE

Write about your experience with a country or region you have visited or lived in. Tell your reader about specific features of the place that interest and attract you (where it is, language, people, government, religion, mountains, rivers, lakes, parks, buildings, agriculture, crops, food specialties, etc.). Write your description as if you were trying to persuade your readers to visit that place, too.

EDITING ADVICE

1. After you have written about this experience, look carefully at every noun that you have capitalized. Check that it is a proper noun. Check also the use of *the* with each proper noun (see sections 4c and 4d).

2. Look at all the other noun phrases. Should any of them be capitalized because they are proper nouns? Pay special attention to words that indicate nationality or language (*Italian, Greek,* etc.).

Countable and Uncountable Nouns

5

READ

Read the following paragraphs from the article "The Doctors' Dilemma" by Sissela Bok. The complete article, with vocabulary glosses, appears on p. 337.

Should doctors ever lie to benefit their patients—to speed recovery or to conceal the approach of death? In medicine as in law, government, and other lines of work, the requirements of honesty often seem dwarfed by greater needs: the need to shelter from brutal news or to uphold a
5 promise of secrecy; to expose corruption or to promote the public interest.

What should doctors say, for example, to a 46-year-old-man coming in for a routine physical checkup just before going on vacation with his family who, though he feels in perfect health, is found to have a form of cancer that will cause him to die within six months? Is it best to tell him
10 the truth? If he asks, should the doctors deny that he is ill, or minimize the gravity of the prognosis? Should they at least conceal the truth until after the family vacation?

Doctors confront such choices often and urgently. At times, they see important reasons to lie for the patient's own sake; in their eyes, such lies
15 differ sharply from self-serving ones.

ANALYZE

1. If you write down in a list the words *doctors, patients, recovery, approach,* and *death,* you are writing down the common nouns in the passage. Continue listing all the nouns throughout the rest of the passage. Do not include nouns used to modify other nouns, such as *family* in *family vacation* or *patient's* in *the patient's own sake,* and do not include any *-ing* forms.

2. You should have a list of 40 words. When you examine them, you will see that some are singular in form, and some are plural. How many of the 40 nouns are plural, and which ones are they? Take care here: the passage includes some nouns that end in *-s* but are not plural in form.

3. Which of the nouns listed are preceded by *a* or *an?* Write down the complete noun phrases in a list, for example, *a 46-year-old man.* Which of the nouns are singular in form and have no marker preceding them, that is, no words such as *a, an,* or *the* or words like *this, that, my,* or *his* (called *determiners;* see Chapter 6)? Write them down in another list. With other students, examine your two lists. Can you speculate as to why the marker *a* occurs with the nouns in one list and not the other?

STUDY

5a. Common nouns and their markers

Chapter 4 gave examples of proper nouns—nouns used for names of specific people or places and written with an initial capital letter. All other nouns are common nouns. The way we use common nouns depends first on whether a particular noun is countable or uncountable—that is, can we say "one doctor, two doctors, many doctors," and so on? Then, if we use a countable noun, we also have to determine whether it is singular or plural. So it is important to distinguish those categories whenever we use a noun phrase (a noun along with its markers and modifiers). The box shows the categories and some of the possible markers for both a countable and an uncountable noun.

MARKERS OF COMMON NOUNS		
	Countable	*Uncountable*
Singular	a ring the ring one ring each ring every ring	jewelry the jewelry some jewelry a lot of jewelry not much jewelry a little jewelry a great deal of jewelry
Plural	rings two rings some rings several rings a lot of rings not many rings a few rings a large number of rings	

EXERCISE 1

Using the list of nouns that you identified in the reading passage at the beginning of this chapter, discuss with other students which nouns you can clearly identify as countable (singular or plural). Note that *the* can precede both countable and uncountable nouns, whereas *a* or *an* can precede only countable singular nouns. *A* or *an* thus always signals a countable singular noun.

EXERCISE 2

Examine the following paragraph from the article by Nora Ephron on p. 334. Some of the nouns have been underlined. List these nouns along the left edge of a sheet of paper. Make column heads as in the example. Then, for each noun on your list, indicate whether it is a proper noun or a common noun. If it is a common noun, note whether it is countable or uncountable. If it is countable, tell whether it is used in this passage in its singular or plural form.

EXAMPLE

NOUN	COMMON/PROPER	COUNTABLE/UNCOUNTABLE	SINGULAR/PLURAL
friend	C	C	S

When I was growing up, I had a <u>friend</u> named <u>Lillian</u> who had no living-room furniture. She lived in a large <u>house</u> in <u>Beverly Hills</u>, and the <u>living room</u> was empty. I always wondered why. I always supposed it was because her <u>mother</u> was having <u>trouble</u> deciding on a color scheme. Color <u>schemes</u> were important in those <u>days</u>. I had a friend named <u>Arlene</u> whose house was famous for having a color scheme in every room, including the breakfast nook, which was charcoal gray and pink. Anyway, a few years ago, Lillian was in New York and I finally got up the nerve to ask her why her family had never had any living-room furniture. She told me that her father had given her mother a <u>choice</u> of living-room <u>furniture</u> or a <u>pool</u>, and her mother had chosen the pool. I salute my friend Lillian's mother. She obviously understood something that I am still having trouble absorbing, which is this: at least you can swim in a pool.

5b. Countable nouns

Countable nouns have both singular and plural forms. Nouns that are preceded by *a* or *an* are always countable and are always singular. In fact, a countable singular noun *must* appear with *a, an,* or *the* (or some other determiner; see Chapter 6) in front of it: it cannot stand alone. So we can say

SINGULAR

a promise (= one promise): **He made a promise.**
the promise (= one specific promise): **He made the promise I had asked
  for.**

But not   *He made promise.**

PLURAL

the promises (= some specific promises): **He made the promises I had
  asked him for.**
two promises, many promises, etc.

But not   *He made a solemn promises.**

5c. Plural forms of countable nouns

Countable nouns form the plural usually by adding *-s* or *-es*.

REGULAR PLURAL FORMS	
Singular	*Plural*
promise	promises
form	forms
doctor	doctors
requirement	requirements
month	months
test	tests
match	matches
day	days
toy	toys

(For nouns ending in consonants + *-y*, see the next chart.)

However, there are also many irregular plural forms. The following box
gives examples, but it is not a complete list. Always check in a dictionary if you
are unsure of a plural form.

IRREGULAR PLURAL FORMS

Singular Form	*Plural Form*

consonant + y
    city
    family
	consonant + ies
	    cities
	    families

-f *or* -fe
    wife
    life
    thief
	-ves
	    wives
	    lives
	    thieves
	
	Exceptions:
	    beliefs
	    chiefs
	    roofs

-o
    potato
    photo
	-oes *or* -os
	    potatoes
	    photos
	    (Use a dictionary to check.)

COMMON IRREGULAR FORMS man woman child tooth foot mouse	 men women children teeth feet mice

WORDS BORROWED FROM OTHER LANGUAGES
-is
    basis
    hypothesis
 	
-on
    criterion
 	
-us
    nucleus
    syllabus
 	
-a
    vertebra
	
	-es
	    bases
	    hypotheses
	
	-a
	    criteria
	
	-i
	    nuclei
	    syllabi
	
	-ae
	    vertebrae

EXERCISE 3

College dictionaries indicate irregular plural forms. First work out with a partner what you think the plural form is of each of the following nouns: *tomato, radio, piano, potato, hero, spy, foot, goose, ox, analysis, crisis, formula, alumnus, sheep, shelf.* Then use a dictionary to check your responses.

EXAMPLE

NOUN	POSSIBLE PLURAL	DICTIONARY PLURAL
tomato	tomatos	tomatoes

5d. Uncountable nouns

Some nouns cannot be counted in certain contexts in English. Nouns that are uncountable in their context

- Do not have a plural form
- Are never used with *a* or *an*
- Are used with a third-person singular verb (*he, she,* or *it* form; see also Chapter 17)

Sometimes, nouns that are uncountable in one context become countable in another:

I love chocolate.
Chocolate comes from the cocoa bean.

But

Would you like a chocolate? (one piece of chocolate candy)

Life is exciting.
He lived an exciting life (as opposed to a boring life).

Iron is a tough metal.
She bought an iron (utensil for pressing clothes).

The frequently used nouns that are uncountable in *most* contexts are these:

MASS NOUNS		ABSTRACT NOUNS		DISEASES	SUBJECTS OF STUDY
furniture	homework	information	honesty	measles	physics
luggage	traffic	knowledge	wealth	mumps	mathematics
money	jewelry	news	health	influenza	politics
vocabulary	scenery	happiness	secrecy	arthritis	economics
equipment		education	anger		history
machinery		advice	confidence	GAMES	biology
garbage		fun	courage	checkers	medicine
				billiards	
				baseball	
				tennis	

Collective nouns, like uncountable nouns, have no distinct singular and plural form. However, unlike uncountable nouns, they are followed by a plural form of the verb:

> people (*person* is used for the singular)
> police
> the poor (= the poor people)
> the rich
> the old
> the young

> EXAMPLE   **The police are coming soon.**

EXERCISE 4 (oral)

Work with a partner. Ask each other questions about the words in one of the lists.

EXAMPLE

milk: How often do you drink milk?

Or   **Do you like milk?**

Or   **Do people drink milk in your country?**

STUDENT A	STUDENT B
rice	furniture
wealth	sugar
food	homework
weather	rain
jewelry	music
traffic	salt

☆EXERCISE 5

Identify the common nouns in the following sentences from "The Surprise" by Russell Baker on p. 342, and categorize them as countable or uncountable. Don't include *-ing* gerunds (see Chapter 20 for that).

1. [My mother] was a magician at stretching a dollar.
2. Doris was in the kitchen when I barged into her bedroom one afternoon in search of a safety pin.
3. Since her bedroom opened onto a community hallway, she kept the door locked, but needing the pin, I took the key from its hiding place, unlocked the door, and stepped in.
4. I was overwhelmed by the discovery that she had squandered such money on me and sickened by the knowledge that, bursting into her

room like this, I had robbed her of the pleasure of seeing me astonished and delighted.
5. [It] made me feel as though I'd struck a blow against her happiness.

_____

5e. Quantity words with countable and uncountable nouns

Some quantity words can be used with both countable and uncountable nouns. Others can be used with only one of the two types. The accompanying box shows the words that can be used only with countable singular, countable plural, or uncountable nouns. It also shows the words that can be used both with countable plural and with uncountable nouns.

QUANTITY WORDS		
Countable		*Uncountable*
Sᴵɴɢᴜʟᴀʀ each every another	Pʟᴜʀᴀʟ (not) many too many a few (very) few several a great number of a large number of fewer	not much too much a little (very) little a great deal of a large amount of less
	some (some) other any a lot of lots of no not any	

EXAMPLES

She took another day off.
She has less free time than Max does.
She has fewer projects to work on, but they are all big ones.
She doesn't have many clients.
He has no clients.
He has no money.

Note that *a lot of* is more common in positive statements, while *much* is used in negatives and questions:

She has a lot of free time.
She doesn't have much free time.
Does she have much free time?

Remember to distinguish between expressions like *many* and *many of the*. They are not interchangeable.

GENERAL	SOME OF A SPECIFIC GROUP
Many children are absent from school.	Many of the children in her class are absent today.
Some doctors refuse to tell lies.	Some of the doctors I know refuse to tell lies.
A few nurses are on duty.	A few of the nurses on duty tonight are in the emergency room.

EXERCISE 6

Which of the given phrases could fit into the space in the sentence? In some cases, more than one could fit.

1. She always eats _____ chocolate.

   a. many
   b. a lot of
   c. a great deal of
   d. a large number of

2. She didn't have _____ information on her essay topic, so she went to the library.

   a. an
   b. a
   c. much
   d. many

3. I asked her to give me _____ advice.

   a. some
   b. many
   c. an
   d. a little

4. She introduced her husband to _____ of her colleagues.

   a. some   c. each
   b. many   d. a large amount

53

5. In her essay, she managed to write _____ paragraphs.

    a. a great deal of
    b. many
    c. a lot of
    d. several

_____

5f. *Few* and *a few*

The expressions *few* and *a few* cause problems for language learners. They are both used with countable nouns in the plural, but they are not interchangeable. They have different meanings and occur in different contexts. These sentences illustrate the contexts:

He has a few friends, so he goes out most weekends.
He has few friends, so he stays home most weekends.

Can you work out the difference?

Synonyms provide some help here. *He has a few friends* is the equivalent of *He has some friends;* whereas *He has few friends* is the equivalent of *He has hardly any friends.* That is, *a few* implies more than *few. Few* has more negative connotations than *a few* does. *Few* is often modified by *very:*

He has very few new ideas.

Note: *Little* and *a little* work the same way with uncountable nouns:

He has little time to spare.

It is, however, more idiomatic to use *not . . . much:*

He doesn't have much time to spare.

EXERCISE 7

The students who wrote the sentences that follow made some mistakes in the use of countable and uncountable noun phrases, singular and plural verbs, or quantity words. Identify the error in each sentence, and correct it.

1. The world surrounding us affects us in more or less direct way.
2. We are affected by our surroundings like furnitures and colors.
3. Dark and crowded room make me upset.
4. She bought many new furnitures for her room.
5. Every students like to have a quiet place to study.
6. My brother has a great deal of friends.
7. Rice is important crop in my country.

8. He bought a new pants last week.
9. That pair of gloves belong to my mother.
10. The homeworks we had last week took a very long time.
11. I have less opportunities for practice than other students in my class.
12. They don't have much possibilities for promotion.

5g. Measure words

Uncountable nouns are often found preceded by a noun phrase that serves to make them countable:

a piece of furniture	many pieces of furniture
a bit of information	numerous bits of information
a piece of advice	several pieces of advice
a bottle of wine	three bottles of wine
a carton of juice	two cartons of juice
a slice of bread	a dozen slices of bread
a drop of rain	a few drops of rain
a teaspoon of medicine	two teaspoons of medicine
a cup of sugar	three cups of sugar
a pint of milk	two pints of milk

In addition, some plural countable nouns that exist only in the plural form need the measure word of *pair* to make them countable:

a pair of pants
a pair of jeans
a pair of shorts
a pair of pajamas
a pair of scissors

EDIT

The following description of a store contains 13 errors with countable and uncountable nouns. The errors occur with singular/plural form and with the use of appropriate markers (determiners) that go with nouns. Identify the errors and correct them.

Bean's Market is filled with lots of different kinds of grocery products. It has an attractive decorations. The signs help the customers find their supplies. In the store, they sell rice, pet food, cookie, beer, salad dressing, soy sauce, oil, and many other product. A man who has apron on is busy fixing the window. He is probably the owner of this store. A man and a woman who have bought a lot are holding a full bags. In the bags, they have food piled up to their faces, including a bread and margarine. A little boy is holding ice-cream cone in his left hand and laughing. He has on a T-shirt and a short.

In front of the store is a girl, who is selling a great deal of muffins. On the table is a jar that contains some money. The table is covered with a piece of cloth. Old man is buying a muffin. He looks as if he is on his way to work: he is holding roll of papers, some varnish, an electric drill, a brush, and can of paint. A cat is sitting on the sidewalk and watching some dog food on a plate. There's another boy lying on the floor reading a magazine, and he has a hot dog in his right hand. There is real dog under the table. It is staring at the boy's hot dog. It looks better than the dog food!

Thianh Cung, Vietnam

WRITE

Sissela Bok's article "The Doctors' Dilemma" deals with the ethical dilemma of doctors concealing the truth of a diagnosis from their patients. Are there other areas of professional life in which concealing of facts could also be a particularly important ethical issue? Discuss the advantages and disadvantages of telling the truth in two areas such as law, education, government, politics, and business. Try to include examples of specific incidents that you have experienced or read about. Do you know of people who have felt it necessary to conceal the truth?

Editing Advice	1. Check your piece of writing for correct use of countable and uncountable nouns by examining every noun phrase carefully. Underline each noun, and ask yourself if it is countable or uncountable in this context and then if it is singular or plural. Check the verb to be sure that the singular form goes with a singular subject and the plural with a plural.
	2. Check in your dictionary any plural forms that you are unsure about.
	3. Make sure that you have not used *a* or *an* with an uncountable noun.
	4. Make sure that you have not used *a* or *an* with a countable plural noun.

Articles

6

READ

Read the following passage from the excerpt from Russell Baker's autobiography, which appears with vocabulary glosses on p. 342.

[My mother] was a magician at stretching a dollar. That December, with Christmas approaching, she was out to work and Doris was in the kitchen when I barged into her bedroom one afternoon in search of a safety pin. Since her bedroom opened onto a community hallway, she kept
5   the door locked, but needing the pin, I took the key from its hiding place, unlocked the door, and stepped in. Standing against the wall was a big, black bicycle with balloon tires. I recognized it instantly. It was the same second-hand bike I'd been admiring in a Baltimore shop window. I'd even asked about the price. It was horrendous. Something like $15. Somehow
10   my mother had scraped together enough for a down payment and meant to surprise me with the bicycle on Christmas morning.

ANALYZE

1. Underline all the uses of *a, an,* and *the* in the passage. List them in two columns:

a or *an* + noun	*the* + noun
a magician	

2. You will see that you have *a safety pin* as well as *the pin*. In addition, you have *a bicycle* as well as *the bicycle*. How can you account for that?

3. Examine all the words that are preceded by *the,* and discuss specifically which kitchen, which door, and so on, is meant in the context of this passage; that is, do you as the reader know which kitchen or which door the writer means? For each noun phrase preceded by *the,* write down what information you and the author share about this item.

6a

STUDY

6a. Determiners and articles

Articles *(a, an, the)* are one type of noun markers called *determiners*. The class of determiners includes these types of words:

DETERMINERS
• Indefinite articles: *a, an*
• Definite article: *the*
• Demonstratives: *this, that, these, those* (see Chapter 18)
• Possessives: adjectives (*my, his, their*, etc.; see Chapter 18); nouns (*Sally's, my mother's, the children's*, etc.; see Chapter 29)
• Quantity words: *some, many, much, a lot of, each, every*, etc. (see Chapter 5)
• Numerals: *one, two, five, seventeen*, etc.

The difficulty for language learners, especially those whose languages do not make a distinction between definite and indefinite articles, is to determine when to use an article and which article to use. The box titled "Articles with Common and Proper Nouns" summarizes article use. The categories will be explained and illustrated in the rest of the chapter.

ARTICLES WITH COMMON AND PROPER NOUNS[†]					
Meaning	*Common Nouns*			*Proper Nouns*	
	COUNTABLE		UNCOUNTABLE		
	Singular	*Plural*		*Singular*	*Plural*
Specific	the	the	the	Ø (zero article)	the
Nonspecific General or total	a/an (the)	some Ø (zero article)	some Ø (zero article)		

[†]Adapted from Marianne Celce-Murcia and Diane Larsen-Freeman, *The Grammar Book* (Rowley, Mass.: Newbury House, 1983), p. 172.

Since proper nouns refer to named people and objects, they are usually specific. However, nationality words follow the pattern for common nouns: for example, *I met a Greek; Americans like barbeques.*

6b. Specific reference: *the*

When you are trying to decide whether to use *a* or *an, the*, or no article at all, one of the crucial distinctions to make is whether the noun phrase refers to something actual and specific for both you and your reader either inside the text in front of you or outside it. The examples that follow will cover most difficult situations. Many other variations are possible, and you will come across them in your reading. When you write, however, you need to be able to choose the form that is most likely to be appropriate.

1. *Specific reference given within the text.* Use the definite article *the* when a noun phrase (a noun with its markers) makes a specific reference for your reader. The reader will know from information contained in the text what actual person, thing, or concept you are referring to.

- The information can be contained at an earlier part of the text:

  Standing against the wall was a big black bicycle. . . . She meant to surprise me with *the bicycle* on Christmas morning.

  First we read about *a big black bicycle,* so we now know that *the* (actual) bicycle she meant to surprise him with was the one that she had bought and he had discovered.

- The information can be given within the same sentence, in a phrase or clause that makes a specific identification:

  The boy <u>who wants the bike</u> is called Russell.

  Which boy is called Russell? The reader knows specifically that it is the one who wants the bike.

2. *Specific reference not given in the text: familiarity.* We can also use *the* to refer to something outside the written text when we know the reader's own *familiarity* with the context will make the reference specific:

Doris was in the kitchen.

As readers, we assume this means the kitchen of the house being described, the house that is the narrator's setting, that is, one specific kitchen.

The same is true with the sentence

She kept the door locked.

From the context, we know that this means specifically Russell Baker's mother's bedroom door.

3. *Specific reference with a superlative.* When we use a superlative (*the best, the most successful,* etc.), we always use *the*. The use of the superlative distinguishes the noun phrase and makes it actual and specific:

He is the best boss I've ever had.
Sit in the most comfortable chair.

EXERCISE 1

Read the second and third paragraphs of the excerpt from Russell Baker's autobiography on p. 342. We have listed all the specific references with *the*. Referring to the context, write down what in each case makes the reference specific for you as the reader.

EXAMPLE **the discovery—within text: refers to "that she had squandered money"**

the knowledge   the least word
the pleasure   the faintest intonation
the key   the weakest gesture
the slightest hint the happiness

6c. Nonspecific reference and generalizations

When we refer to someone or something that will not be actual and specific for the reader or listener, we do not use *the*. Instead, we use one of the following, according to meaning and type of noun phrase:

- *a* or *an*
  A countable singular noun must have a determiner. So if you are not using *the* to refer to an actual, specific living thing, object, or concept, *a* or *an* must be used.

  She bought *a bicycle*.

  You might know exactly which one, but your reader does not, since you have provided no further information.
      Similarly, in this sentence

  A bicycle should have lights or reflectors.

  the writer is not referring to one actual bicycle but to any one bicycle that represents all others.

- Zero article (∅)
  For a nonspecific reference that makes a generalization about a total class of living things, objects, or concepts, use no article (the zero article form) with countable plural and uncountable nouns:

  Bicycles provide inexpensive transportation. (all bicycles everywhere)

  Furniture is expensive. (all furniture, generally)

  Note the difference between the following:

  He achieved success. (total)
  He achieved some success. (partial)

In technical writing, we can also generalize by referring to a plant or object as a specific representative of its class:

The bicycle is a popular method of transportation in China.

As a general rule, though, if you want to make a generalization about a countable noun, use the plural form of the noun with the zero article form:

Bicycles are popular in China.

The zero article form is also used with countable plural noun phrases that occur as a complement:

His parents are wage earners.

- *some*
  To make a nonspecific reference to a countable plural noun or to an uncountable noun when you are not making a generalization, use *some:*

  She bought some lamps.
  She bought some furniture.

EXERCISE 2 *(oral)*

One of the phrases is not possible in any context. Which is it? Explain why it is not possible.

A bicycle is useful.   Bicycle is useful.
The bicycle is useful.   His bicycle is useful.
Bicycles are useful.   The boy's bicycle is useful.
That bicycle is useful.   Every bicycle is useful.

EXERCISE 3

Read the following passage from the article by Sissela Bok, which appears with vocabulary glosses in Part II. Note all the underlined noun phrases that occur with the zero article form to express a generalization. Which ones are countable plural and which are uncountable?

Sharp <u>conflicts</u> are now arising. <u>Patients</u> are learning to press for <u>answers</u>. Patients' bills of rights require that they be informed about their condition and about <u>alternatives</u> for <u>treatment</u>. Many doctors go to great lengths to provide such <u>information</u>. Yet even in <u>hospitals</u> with the most eloquent bill of rights, <u>believers</u> in benevolent <u>deception</u> continue their age-old practices.

6d

EXERCISE 4 *(oral)*

With a partner, select some nouns from the following list. Ask your partner questions about these nouns, in this form:

What can you tell me about . . . ?

Your partner will reply with a generalization, using the zero article form.

EXAMPLE

What can you tell me about examinations?
Examinations make students very nervous.

little children	babies	mathematics	bicycles
doctors	clothes	baseball	pollution
health	money	homework	drugs
poverty	education	presents	

6d. Articles with proper and common nouns: summary

The following box gives examples of article use with common nouns.

ARTICLES WITH COMMON NOUNS			
Reference	**Countable Nouns**		**Uncountable Nouns**
	SINGULAR	PLURAL	
Specific	*the* The bicycle that he saw in the room was for him.	*the* The bicycles in the store were expensive.	*the* The furniture in the living room is uncomfortable.
• Familiar	*the* He put the car in the garage.	*the* The dogs have to be fed every day.	*the* She polished the furniture.
Nonspecific	*a/an* She bought a bicycle for her son.	*some* There are some bicycles in the garage.	*some* She bought some new furniture. He has some talent.
• General or total	*[the]* The bicycle is very popular. (technical writing)	$\emptyset$ Bicycles are very popular.	$\emptyset$ Furniture is expensive. He has talent.

Because the use of articles is so complicated, it will be necessary for you to build up your own store of examples. When you read, note now articles are used—or not used. Keep a notebook, write sentences down, underline the articles, and try to classify and explain their use according to the summary chart, or note them as exceptions to a general principle.

☆EXERCISE 5

The following noun phrases are taken from the passage by Russell Baker at the beginning of this chapter. Examine each one in context, consult the chart in section 6d, and write a check mark to indicate

- whether the noun phrase is countable or uncountable
- if countable, whether it is singular or plural
- whether it makes a *specific* or *nonspecific* reference; if it is specific, explain in what way it is specific to you, the reader.

The first item is completed for you as an example.

Noun Phrase	*Countable*	*Uncountable*	*Singular*	*Plural*	*Specific*	*Nonspecific*
a magician	√		√			√
work						
the kitchen						
a safety pin						
a community hallway						
the door						
the pin						
the key						
a big, black bicycle						
a Baltimore shop window						
the price						
a down payment						
the bicycle						

6e. Important points to remember

The following are important points to remember as you write and edit.

1. A countable singular noun *must* have a determiner in front of it. It never takes the zero article form. It never stands alone:

I bought a bicycle.

Not *I bought bicycle.

2. Countable plural nouns are *never* used with *a* or *an,* except after expressions like *a lot of* or *a few.*
3. Uncountable nouns are *never* used with *a* or *an:*

We bought some new furniture.

Not *We bought a new furniture.

4. As soon as a countable or uncountable noun is modified with a clause or phrase to make it unique and specific, it needs *the.*

EXAMPLES

The bicycle in his mother's room was for him. (Which specific bicycle? The one in his mother's room.)

I was overwhelmed by *the discovery that she had squandered such money on me.* (*Discovery* is made specific by the following clause, which immediately tells us which actual discovery the writer means.)

☆*EXERCISE 6*

In the following excerpt from the reading passage about the soybean (p. 339), the articles *a, an,* and *the* have been omitted. Working with another student, consult the box in section 6d and decide which form or forms you could use. Some of the blanks may take more than one form, depending on interpretation.

Doufu, _____ Chinese name for bean curd, has been made in
            a
China, where it was invented, for about 2,000 years. It is _____ most
                                                            b
important of _____ foods prepared in _____ East from _____
             c   d   e
soybean, that remarkable vegetable that not only allows _____
                                                         f
Chinese to feed _____ quarter of _____ world's population on
                 g   h
_____ tenth of its arable land, but it is also _____ rock on which
 i   j
_____ Western diet is built and _____ major hope for averting
 k   l
world famine.

I had traveled to China in part because _____ whole story began
                                          m
here, at least 3,000 years ago, when farmers in _____ eastern half of
                                                 n

northern China started planting _____ black or brown seeds of

_____ wild recumbent vine. Why they did this is unclear; plants

that lie on _____ ground are hard to cultivate, and _____ seeds

of _____ wild soybean are tiny, hard, and, unless properly prepared,

indigestible.

EXERCISE 7

The following sentences relate to the reading passages by Nora Ephron and Sissela Bok in Part II. In each sentence, identify the one underlined word or phrase that should be rewritten. Then tell how it should be rewritten.

_____ 1. I have a nice living room, but everyone sits in the kitchen
even though the living room is prettiest room in the
apartment. _____

_____ 2. Lillian's mother, who lived in a large house, didn't buy
a furniture, because she was having trouble deciding on
a color scheme. _____

_____ 3. I know what to do in a breakfast nook, but only thing I can
think of to do in a living room is living. _____

_____ 4. The father of the family gave his wife a choice of
living-room furniture or pool. _____

_____ 5. Dying patients cannot make decisions about end of life or
about whether or not to have surgery. _____

_____ 6. Doctors see important reasons to lie for the patient's
own sake; they don't want to destroy any of hopes that a
patient may have. _____

6f. Idiomatic usage

Note the following expressions. Add to this list whenever you come across others in your reading or through any other contact with English.

NO ARTICLE	DEFINITE ARTICLE
go uptown	in the morning
go downtown	in the afternoon *(but* at night)
go to school	go to the bank
go to work	go to the store
go to church	go to the movies
go to bed	go to the beach
travel by bus	go to the park
travel by train	
at college	
at school	
at work	
at home	

EXERCISE 8

Complete the following sentences with the given noun. Use *the, a,* or *an* where appropriate.

1. advice
   a. _____ you gave me was very helpful.
   b. People like to give _____ to others.

2. school
   a. _____ on the corner is an elementary school.
   b. She goes to _____ by bus.

3. parents
   a. _____ often argue with their teenage children.
   b. _____ of the students at my school donated a lot of money to the scholarship program.

4. health
   a. The most important thing in life is _____ _____.
   b. _____ of aging people is a matter of national concern.

5. wine
   a. _____ on the table is a California chablis.
   b. _____ improves with age.

6. babies   a. _____ cry a lot.

              b. _____ in the nursery are all girls.

7. pencil   a. Use _____ to fill out the form.

              b. Use _____ that I give you to fill out the form.

8. pencils   a. _____ in my pocket don't have erasers.

              b. Students will need _____ to fill out the answer sheets.

EDIT

In the following piece of student writing telling about a surprise, some errors with the use of articles appear. Circle errors, or use an omission mark (∧) for an omitted article; write what you think the correct form should be.

Two months ago, at school, I saw that the practice room for music students was open. I really wanted to play. I walked toward the piano and carefully touched keys. Since I hadn't played for almost ten years, movement of my hands was terrible. My fingers touched the keys like the hammer hits the nails. I played a piece from Beethoven's sonatas and then I played Chopin for a few days as my fingers got smoother and softer.

One day, a student came up to me and said, "You are good player. I found out you are not a music major. I want to introduce you to the professor." I was so excited that I couldn't say anything. I just stared at her. I couldn't believe what I had heard. Next day, I met the professor and played a piece by Chopin. He said he wanted me to study music with him. I was so happy.

The next day, I found there would be an audition to choose a music performance student. My major is art. However, I wanted to test myself. I practiced whenever there was a time.

The day before the audition, I found that I would have to play four pieces. But I had only one piece ready for audition. I knew another one but I hadn't memorized it. The chairman of the music department said he would allow me to play only two pieces if I played them beautifully. So I left the room with uncertainty of possibility of memorizing the additional piece. However, by 6:30 I had managed to memorize every note.

Then it was time to play in front of the juries. When I got up on a stage, I couldn't think of anything but the waves of melody. I didn't even realize when I had finished the two pieces. One of the professors in the jury asked me for my address and phone number. A few days later, I got the letter from him. Now I have a double major. What a surprise that was! It was at first just a test of myself, to see what I could do. However, it became turning point of my life.

Soonjin Park, Korea

WRITE

Write about a surprise that you once had or one that you prepared for somebody else. Make your story as vivid as you can so that your reader can share not only the setting but also the feelings and the emotions of the event. Try to write it so that you explain the situation first and lead up to the surprise—so that your reader, too, shares in the feeling of surprise. Check your work for the use of articles before you show it to a reader.

EDITING ADVICE	

1. Examine every noun phrase you have written. Determine whether you have used a determiner in front of it, or *a, an, the,* or zero article.

2. If you have used *a, an, the,* or zero article, check to see whether your use of it fits with the categories in the chart in section 6d.

3. Remember to check for the following:

   • No *a* or *an* with plural countable or with uncountable nouns.
   • A countable singular noun needs a determiner of some kind.

Verb Phrases

7. VERB PHRASES
   a. Complete verb phrases
   b. Active and passive verb phrases
   c. The time clusters of verb phrases: present-future and past
   d. Summary of requirements for checking verb phrases

8. VERB TENSES: OVERVIEW
   a. Referring to basic time
   b. Referring to time before basic time (perfect aspect)
   c. Referring to an event or action in progress at basic time (progressive aspect)
   d. Verbs not used with progressive aspect
   e. Referring to time both before basic and in progress (perfect progressive aspect)
   f. Consistency of tenses

9. VERB TENSES: PAST
   a. Identifying and using past cluster verb phrases
   b. Basic past tense
   c. Irregular verb forms
   d. Past perfect
   e. Past progressive and past perfect progressive
   f. *Used to* and *would*

10. VERB TENSES: PRESENT AND FUTURE
   a. Present-future verb phrases
   b. Basic present for habitual action
   c. Other uses of basic present verb forms
   d. Perfect tenses: present and future
   e. Progressive tenses: present and future
   f. Perfect progressive: present and future

11. MODAL AUXILIARIES
   a. Meanings of modal auxiliaries: ability, permission, polite questions and statements
   b. Meanings of modal auxiliaries: advisability, necessity, no necessity, prohibition
   c. Meanings of modal auxiliaries: expectation, possibility, and logical deduction
   d. Simple form after the modal auxiliaries
   e. The uses of *would*
   f. Summary chart

12. ACTIVE AND PASSIVE
   a. Forms of the passive
   b. Uses of the passive
   c. Passive idioms with *get* and *have*
   d. The passive with direct and indirect objects
   e. *Been* and *being*
   f. Participle used to describe a situation

13. VERB FORMS: SUMMARY
   a. Forms of the verb
   b. Troublesome verb forms
   c. The verb system at a glance
   d. Phrasal verbs

7 Verb Phrases

READ

Read the following section from the reading, "Vincent van Gogh," which appears with vocabulary glosses on p. 343.

Van Gogh was born in Holland in 1853, the son of a vicar. He was a deeply religious man who had worked as a lay preacher in England and among Belgian miners. He had been deeply impressed by the art of Millet and its social message, and decided to become a painter himself. A
5 younger brother, Theo, who worked in an art-dealer's shop, introduced him to Impressionist painters. This brother was a remarkable man. Though he was poor himself, he always gave ungrudgingly to the older Vincent and even financed his journey to Arles in southern France. Vincent hoped that if he could work there undisturbed for a number of
10 years he might be able one day to sell his pictures and repay his generous brother. In his self-chosen solitude in Arles, Vincent set down all his ideas and hopes in his letters to Theo, which read like a continuous diary. These letters, by a humble and almost self-taught artist who had no idea of the fame he was to achieve, are among the most moving and exciting in
15 all literature. In them we can feel the artist's sense of mission, his struggle and triumphs, his desperate loneliness and longing for companionship, and we become aware of the immense strain under which he worked with feverish energy.

ANALYZE

1. Underline *was born, was,* and *had worked* in the first two sentences of the passage. Each of these functions as the complete verb phrase of a clause. Each one has a grammatical subject; each one, by its tense or its use of auxiliaries, indicates a connection with time (past, present, future), voice (active, passive), or aspect (progressive, perfect). Continue underlining all the word groups that form a complete verb phrase attached to the subject of a clause. These should add up to a total of 22 verb phrases. A verb phrase can consist of one, two, three, or more words, including the main verb. Take care with *to sell . . . and repay;* these are not complete verb phrases.

2. Each complete verb phrase will contain a main verb (the verb that carries the meaning). So in the verb phrase *had worked, worked* is the main verb, while *had* adds a dimension of tense (before past time). Sometimes, though, the main verb is the only verb in the phrase: it contains in it the idea of time or number. Underline the main verb of each clause twice:

had <u>worked</u>

3. Some of the verb phrases you have underlined consist of only one word (the main verb), while others consist of auxiliaries + the main verb. Make two lists, one of the single-word verb phrases and one of the verb phrases that contain auxiliaries.

STUDY

7a. Complete verb phrases

To be able to analyze and check your use of verbs in English, it is helpful to practice identifying and explaining the categories of verb phrases that occur in your reading. First, as you did in analyzing the passage, you need to be able to identify the main verb and any auxiliaries.

Each main verb has five forms. Three of them can be used as a complete main verb:

the *-s* form (present tense)   *she writes*
the past tense form   *he wrote*
the simple form (present tense)   *they write*

The other two forms do not, by themselves, indicate tense:

the *-ing* form   *writing*
the participle form (- *ed/-en* form)[†]   *written*

They cannot be used alone as the main verb of a clause.

FORMS OF THE VERB				
	Simple	*-s*	*- ing*	*Past*	*Participle*
Regular	walk	walks	walking	walked	walked
Irregular	see	sees	seeing	saw	seen

[†]This is often called the *past participle*. However, since it is used in structures *not* associated with past time, there is less chance for confusion if we label it simply as the *participle*.

A complete list of irregular verb forms appears in the Appendix. Note that the -*ing* and participle forms are *never* complete verb forms. So if you write an -*ing* form or a participle form with no auxiliaries attached (words like *have, is, was, might be, should have been*), check to make sure that it does not function as the complete verb phrase.

> *Not*   *The people on the beach running.
> *But*   The people on the beach are running.

Chapters 14, 20, and 21 give examples of how -*ing* and participle forms are used in descriptive phrases.

EXERCISE 1

In the following sentences based on readings in this book, underline the complete verb phrases, and underline the main verb twice.

1. The couches were recently cleaned by men with small machines.
2. Many reasons have been put forward for why we never use the living room.
3. Sharp conflicts are now arising.
4. What should doctors say to a 46-year-old man?
5. Bean curd has been made in China for 2,000 years.
6. As we talked, walking through the corridors of plane trees that line the streets of Shanghai, we would pass through the outdoor markets.

EXERCISE 2

To verify that a verb phrase is a complete verb phrase, you should be able to identify its subject. This should agree in number (singular or plural) with the first auxiliary or with the single main verb of the verb phrase. Identifying the subject is necessary if you need to check agreement of subject and verb in your own writing (see Chapter 17).

In Exercise 1, you have already identified complete verb phrases. Now circle the subject of each verb phrase.

7b. Active and passive verb phrases

To use the correct sequence of auxiliaries and main verb, you must be able to distinguish between verb phrases that indicate active or passive voice.

EXAMPLE

> *Active:*   The art of Millet had impressed him.
> *Passive:*   He had been impressed by the art of Millet.

The passive voice contains a form of the *be* auxiliary + the participle form of the main verb. It is used only with transitive verbs (verbs that can be followed by an object, as in *Art impressed him*). The agent (the performer of the action) is not the grammatical subject of a passive sentence (see Chapter 12 for more on active and passive voice).

EXERCISE 3

In the following sentences from the readings "The Basic-Nonbasic Concept" and "Economics and Scarcity" in Part II, identify the complete verb phrases, and make two lists, one of active verbs and one of passive verbs. Remember that *-ing* and participle *(-ed/-en)* forms occurring alone with no auxiliaries cannot be complete verb forms.

1. If scarcity exists, then choices must be made by individuals and societies.
2. Each tradeoff reflects the value judgment of the decision makers.
3. People living in cities are engaged in specialized activities.
4. The labor force of a city can be divided into two parts.
5. A city does not serve just those people living within its own municipal boundaries.
6. Detroit is recognized as the automobile capital of the United States.
7. Automobiles produced within that city are sold mainly outside its borders.
8. The gold vein has run out.

7c. The time clusters of verb phrases: present-future and past

Verb tenses let your reader know what period of time you are referring to. Tenses occur in clusters according to time zone. A switch from a present-future cluster to a past cluster or from past to present-future occurs with a signal (such as *last week, now,* or *soon*) or within a context that the reader will understand. Chapters 8–10 deal with verb tenses in detail. To begin with, though, concentrate on determining whether a verb phrase refers to present-future time or past time. The box on page 74 shows the forms of the first verb of a verb phrase for both past and present-future time. (For the use of *would, could, should,* and *might* in the present-future cluster, see Chapter 11 on modal auxiliaries and Chapter 27 on conditions.)

EXERCISE 4

In the passage about van Gogh at the beginning of this chapter, most of the complete verb phrases indicate past time. Only four indicate present-future. Which ones are they? Discuss with your classmates and instructor why you think the author made the switch.

PAST AND PRESENT-FUTURE FORMS OF FIRST VERB OF PHRASE	
Past	*Present-Future*
Past form wrote	*Simple or -s form* write, writes
First auxiliary was, were did had would could should might had to	*First auxiliary* am, is, are does, do has, have will (would) can (could) shall (should) may (might) must ought to

EXERCISE 5

Read the following two paragraphs from the reading "Portable Computers," which appears with vocabulary glosses in Part II.

In the early 1960's, the first minicomputers were made commercially. They were the size of a two-drawer file cabinet. The revolution was on. Less than a decade later, the microcomputer was invented. The basic unit of the microcomputer is a tiny silicon chip less than 1 cm on a side. Each chip is a miniature electronic circuit that serves the different computer functions. Amazingly, each circuit contains thousands of elements.

The great advances in microelectronics have helped achieve the moon landing, satellites, digital watches, computer games, and even computer-controlled automobile engines. Still the computer continues to evolve. One of the latest developments is bubble memory.

Make a list of the eleven complete verb phrases. Next to each one, indicate whether it refers to past or to present-future time. When there is a switch from one cluster to another, try to identify any signals in the text for the switch, and explain the writer's rationale for the switch.

7d. Summary of requirements for checking verb phrases

As an aid to identifying errors with verbs, follow these instructions after you have written a few drafts of a piece of writing and when you are ready to edit the draft for accuracy.

TO CHECK VERB PHRASES

- Identify each complete verb phrase.
- Identify its subject.
- Identify whether it is active or passive.
- Identify whether it belongs with the present-future or past cluster (check the first auxiliary or the single main verb).

You must be able to do this accurately before you can check further for correct use of verb tense and verb form (see also Chapters 8 and 13).

EXERCISE 6

Choose the one word or phrase that best completes each sentence.

1. Van Gogh was a religious man who _____ as a lay preacher in England.

   a. works
   b. worked
   c. is working
   d. working

2. He decided to become a painter because he _____ impressed by art with a social message.

   a. is
   b. had
   c. was being
   d. had been

3. Toulouse-Lautrec was a painter who _____ a lot of scenes of Parisian night life.

   a. has painted
   b. has been painting
   c. painted
   d. paint

4. Van Gogh cut off his own ear when he _____ depressed.

    a. feeling
    b. could feel
    c. had felt
    d. was feeling

5. Van Gogh _____ forever for his many spectacular works of art.

    a. will be remembered
    b. will remember
    c. has remembered
    d. will be remember

☆EXERCISE 7

Look at the first three paragraphs of the article "The Soybean," on p. 339. Write down all the complete verb phrases that occur, and then make a divided list like the one shown here. Note the subject, the verb phrase, whether it is active (A) or passive (P), and which time cluster it belongs to, present-future or past.

SUBJECT	VERB PHRASE	ACTIVE/PASSIVE	TIME CLUSTER
Doufu	has been made	P	present (until now)
it	was invented	P	past
It	is	A	present
that (vegetable)	allows	A	present

EDIT

The student who wrote the following passage in a biography of a member of her family shows some difficulties with forming verb phrases and attaching them to their subjects. Identify where problems occur. What would you advise the writer to do to fix them?

I learned that my grandfather born in 1901 in a wealthy family in Shanghai. His family possessed a lot of land in the village. He was the second child in the family. He tell me that he had ten years of education in learning Chinese characters in philosophical poems. By 1911 knew he would marry my grandmother. This marriage pre-arranged the committee in his village. It was a very traditional ceremony. My grandmother had lived in her husband's house a long time before she reach adulthood. My great-grandmother had to train my grandmother to become a perfect wife for my grandfather. Corporal punishment use a lot to let my grandmother know she was just a piece of property attached to their household. My grandparents were together for only a brief period of time because took place the Second World War. My grandfather became a seaman; he keeping the engine clean and did laundry on the ship. After many years, when the ship in an American harbor, he jump the ship and became a cook.

Ji-hong Wu, China

WRITE

Write two paragraphs either about someone you admire or about a famous person in your country. Choose someone who is still alive. You might need to go to do research at a library to gather information. In the first paragraph, tell about this person's accomplishments in the past and what made this person interesting to you. In the second paragraph, tell about this person's life at present: home, family, lifestyle, work, reputation, money, pastimes, and so on.

EDITING ADVICE

1. After you have written the two paragraphs, check your use of verbs by underlining each complete verb phrase.

2. Ask yourself whether each clause contains a complete verb phrase (main verb + any necessary and appropriate auxiliaries).

3. Circle the grammatical subject of each complete verb phrase.

4. Identify whether each complete verb phrase is active or passive and whether it fits into the past or present-future time cluster.

8 Verb Tenses: Overview

READ

Read the following selection from Anna Quindlen's article "Siblings." The complete article, with vocabulary glosses, appears on p. 345.

He actually likes babies; he even wants to bring one home, the 2-month-old brother of his friend Sonia. Eric, he thinks, is perfect: he cannot walk, cannot talk, has no interest in Maurice Sendak books, Lego blocks, the trucks, the sandbox, or any of the other things that make life
5   worth living, including—especially including—me. One day at Sonia's house he bent over Eric's bassinet to say hello, but what came out instead was a triumphant "You can't catch me!" as he sailed away from him.

His baby can't catch him yet, but it's only a matter of time. Then he will have to make a choice: a partner, an accomplice, an opponent, or,
10 perhaps most likely, a mixture of the three. At some point his fantasy of a brother may dovetail with the reality; mine did when my younger brother, the insufferable little nerd with the Coke-bottle glasses whom I loathed, turned into a good-looking teenage boy who interested my girl friends, had some interesting boy friends of his own, and was a first-rate
15 dancer.

ANALYZE

1. Underline each complete verb phrase in a clause. Underline the main verb twice.

2. List the underlined verbs in three columns: past, present, and future time. How many verbs do you have in each column?

3. Note the points in the reading where the time reference changes. Are there any signals for the change? Write an explanation for why you think the author switched to a different time reference.

STUDY

8a. Referring to basic time

In the excerpt from the article by Anna Quindlen, the writer uses tenses that refer to the basic reference points of past, present, or future. The term *basic time* means that the reference is to the basic idea of past *(she wrote)*, present *(she writes)*, or future *(she will write)*. When there is no recourse to progressive *(she is/was writing)* or perfect meaning *(she has/had/will have written)*, the time reference is to basic time, and the tenses are often called *simple past, present,* and *future* tenses. Nine of the verbs in the reading indicate basic past time, two indicate future, and eleven indicate present basic time.

This chapter gives general guidelines for tenses. Exceptions and unusual cases are dealt with in more detail in Chapters 9 and 10. In the accompanying box, the basic tense forms of the verb *write* are presented for the active voice. (Chapter 12 deals with the passive.)

ACTIVE VERB TENSES (1)			
Time Reference	*Past*	*Present*	*Future*
Basic time	wrote	writes/write	will write
	did write	do/does write	am/is/are going to write

EXAMPLES

She wrote a story yesterday. (a specified time in the past)

She writes in her journal every day. (a repeated or habitual action in present time)

I'll write the article next week. I'll meet the deadline. (stated future time; a promise)

We're going to write an article about computers. (implied future time; a plan)

In academic writing, general statements and expressions of opinion usually occur in the present tense (for example, "Siblings fight a lot"). Examples and illustrations to support the generalization often refer to a past event (as in "My brother once hit me with a baseball bat").

EXERCISE 1 (oral)

Signals like *once, last year, when I was a child,* and *a few years ago* alert us to expect the past tense. Tell a partner about an incident you remember from your childhood when you had an argument with another child. Listen carefully to your partner's story, and then write it in a paragraph beginning with, "When X was a child, one day . . ." You might want to use signals like the words *first, second, then, next,* and *finally* to indicate the sequence of the events.

8b. Referring to time before basic time (perfect aspect)

Look at the following sentences from the complete version of Anna Quindlen's article, in which the writer refers to a time before now, the basic present time of reference.

Entire minutes have passed. (up until now)

Neither has made a grab for the other's toy. (at least not yet, not up to now)

Realization has come slowly for some of them. (from some time in the past up to now)

Entire minutes have passed. (from *then*—unspecified—until now)

The forms that express a perfect aspect (that is, that an activity or event is *perfected* or completed before the basic time in the past, present, or future) are as shown in the accompanying box.

ACTIVE VERB TENSES (2)			
Time Reference	*Past*	*Present*	*Future*
Before basic time (perfect)	had written	has/have written	will have written

The important thing to remember is that when you use these tenses, you use them in reference to the basic time. So "I have written my essay" is linked in meaning to now, the basic time of the present, even though you wrote your essay in the past. The point is that you are not emphasizing when you wrote it in the past; instead, you emphasize the relationship between that action and present time.

EXAMPLES

He had already written her an angry letter when she called to apologize. (Two past events: first he wrote the letter; then she called. The first activity is completed by a stated time in the past.)

He has written a lot of angry letters. (An activity completed repeatedly or at some unspecified time before the present, but the exact time in the past is not stated. The main point is not when it happened in the past but the fact that the action has an effect on present events.)

He has just written a novel. (Exactly when he did so is not important.)

He will have written the report by noon tomorrow. (Two future events: one activity will be completed by a specified time in the future.)

EXERCISE 2

Choose the one word or phrase that best completes each sentence.

1. The little boy burst into tears when he saw that his brother _____ his jigsaw puzzle apart.

   a. breaks
   b. has broken
   c. have broken
   d. had broken

2. When the little boy saw what his brother _____ to his room, he rushed to tell his parents.

   a. had done
   b. did
   c. has done
   d. do

3. His mother was angry when she saw what _____.

   a. happens
   b. is happening
   c. had happened
   d. has happened

4. She _____ it hard to forgive her son for what he had done.

   a. finds
   b. found
   c. had found
   d. has found

5. She _____ in the same house since she was a child.

   a. has lived
   b. lived
   c. lives
   d. have lived

6. He _____ that tie ever since I first met him 20 years ago.

   a. has
   b. had
   c. has had
   d. had had

EXERCISE 3

Which tense would you use in each sentence, the basic past or the present perfect? In some cases, either one would be possible, but the meaning would change.

EXAMPLES

She lived there for two years.
She has lived there for two years.

The first sentence implies that she no longer lives there (the action was completed in the past); the second implies that she is still living there (up to now).

If both tenses are possible, explain the different meaning each would produce.

1. He _____ (be) a teacher all his life.

2. She watched TV and then she _____ (cook) dinner.

3. She _____ (buy) an apartment two years ago.

4. She _____ (own) her own apartment for two years.

5. He _____ (not find) a job since he came to this country.

6. This country _____ (make) great advances in space travel in the past twenty years.

7. Space travel _____ (suffer) a severe setback in 1986.

8. We _____ (have not) such a thrilling moment

since Armstrong _____ (walk) on the moon

in 1969.

_____

8c. Referring to an event or action in progress at basic time (progressive aspect)

Look at the following sentences:

1. **In the back room the boys are playing.**
2. **I was yelling at one of the dogs.**

Here the writer refers in sentence 1 to an action in progress in the present and in sentence 2 to an action in progress in the past.

The accompanying box presents forms indicating progressive aspect.

ACTIVE VERB TENSES (3)			
Time Reference	*Past*	*Present*	*Future*
In progress at basic time (progressive)	was/were writing	am/is/are writing	will be writing

EXAMPLES

She was writing an essay when I called her at 8 P.M. yesterday. (in progress at a *specified* time in the past)

She was writing all day yesterday. She was writing while I was cooking dinner. (in progress over a period of time in the past)

She is writing a novel. (in progress right now)

She will be writing an examination essay at 10 A.M. tomorrow, so you won't be able to contact her. (in progress at a specified time in the future)

_____

EXERCISE 4 (oral)

Examine these three sentences:

1. **When I arrived at the party, everyone was leaving.**
2. **When I arrived at the party, everyone had left.**
3. **When I arrived at the party, everyone left.**

Imagine that you arrived at the party at 10 P.M. exactly. At what time did the guests leave? For each sentence, describe the scene upon your arrival at the party.

EXERCISE 5 (oral)

Make sentences telling about the activity in progress for the following people at the following times. Use an -ing form.

EXAMPLE

your father's activity / when you were born
When I was born, my father was working as an accountant.

1. The activity of the president of the United States / probably, right now
2. You and type of work / in the year 2000
3. Your activity / this time last year
4. Your activity / at 9 P.M. last night
5. Your activity / at 9 P.M. tomorrow
6. The activity of your brother, sister, or other family member / at present

8d. Verbs not used with progressive aspect

Some verbs are not used with the progressive -ing form even when they refer to an action in progress at the time of speaking or writing. These verbs are not associated with movement and visible activity but with mental activity and attitudes.

EXAMPLES

That stew smells delicious.
Do you really think so?

You will have to assemble examples of these verbs as you read and listen to English. Some of the most commonly used ones are listed here.

MENTAL ACTIVITY VERBS NOT USED IN THE PROGRESSIVE

Senses	Possession	Preference and desire
see	have	need
hear	own	want
smell	belong	prefer
taste		like
	Inclusion	love
Thoughts	include	
think	contain	
know	comprise	Appearance
believe		seem
understand		appear
		look

84

EXERCISE 6

In each sentence, use either the basic form or the progressive form of the given verb in the appropriate tense to fit the time signal.

1. Most children _____ (seem) to enjoy having siblings.

2. As I walked past the sandbox, I saw that it _____ (contain) a lot of broken toys.

3. She _____ (wear) a winter coat today.

4. Any middle child _____ (need) a lot of attention.

5. That teddy bear _____ (belong) to him now. His brother gave it to him last week.

6. They _____ (try) to get a loan so that they can renovate their house.

7. They _____ (own) a toy train set that is 100 years old but _____ (look) new.

8. At present, the youngest child in their family _____ (prefer) to sleep in his parents' room.

_____

8e. Referring to time both before basic and in progress (perfect progressive aspect)

You can indicate by the use of verb tense that an activity is both in progress and occurring before the basic time of reference.

ACTIVE VERB TENSES (4)			
Time Reference	*Past*	*Present*	*Future*
Both in progress and before basic time (perfect progressive)	had been writing	has/have been writing	will have been writing

8e

These tenses, as opposed to the perfect tenses, emphasize the length and duration of the action.

EXAMPLES

He had been writing for three hours when I called him. (The point of reference is "when I called him" in the past. Both the length of time of the activity and the past reference point are usually stated. This is often used accompanied by a *when* clause.)

He has been writing his term paper for two weeks *or* since December 3. (Activity in progress up to and including present time; often used with *for* or *since*.)

He will have been writing this article for three weeks by this time tomorrow. (Activity in progress up to a predicted time or event in the future. Both the duration—for three weeks—and the future reference point—this time tomorrow—*must* be stated or clearly implied.)

EXERCISE 7

Fill in the appropriate progressive or perfect progressive form of the given verb. Certain signals in the sentence should help you determine whether to use a past, present, or future tense.

1. He _____ (hit) his brother when I walked into the room;

   I made him stop.

2. The twins _____ (fight) for hours before their mother

   came home.

3. They _____ (probably sleep) now.

4. Their mother _____ (try) to get some sleep since 10

   P.M.—and now it is 5 A.M.!

5. It is now 6:35 P.M. By seven o'clock, she _____ (play)

   with them for twelve hours.

6. It was obvious from the screaming and crying that they _____

   _____ (fight) for a long time.

86

8f. Consistency of tenses

Consistency of tenses is important. Usually, the verb tenses a writer uses will fit consistently into one of two time clusters, either the past or the present-future. The time relationship and the tense used may change, but there should be no switch from one time cluster to another without a clear reason. Often, too, a signal in the text is required, such as in Anna Quindlen's article: "One day [switches the reader back to the past time] at Sonia's house he *bent* over Eric's bassinet to say hello . . ."

The box summarizes the two clusters of tenses for active tense forms.

TENSE-TIME RELATIONSHIPS: ACTIVE VOICE			
Time Reference	*Past Cluster*	*Present-Future Cluster*	
		PRESENT	FUTURE
Basic	wrote	writes/write	will write am/is/are going to write
question and negative	did write	does/do write	
Perfect (before basic)	had written	has/have written	will have written
Progressive (in progress)	was/were writing	am/is/are writing	will be writing
Perfect progressive (before basic *and* in progress)	had been writing	has/have been writing	will have been writing

For additional focused practice with the past cluster and the present-future cluster, see Chapters 9 and 10. For modal auxiliaries and their forms in past and present-future clusters, see Chapter 11.

EXERCISE 8

In the following account of a relationship with another person, written by a student, the verbs have been omitted, and the simple form of the main verb is given. Fill in the appropriate verb form.

Six years ago, I _____ (meet) a wonderful person

whose name _____ (be) Mark. I _____

(meet) him at a party. We _____ (dance) and we

_____ (start) talking about ourselves. He

_____ (live) with his parents in Greenwich, Connecti-

cut, and he _____ (work) in New York City. He
_____ (use to) travel a lot, so we hardly
h
_____ (see) each other.
i

Now he _____ (live) here in Manhattan and
j
_____ (have) a new job that _____ (pay)
k
much better. He _____ (have) his own beautiful apart-
l
ment with a beautiful view of the city and of Central Park. He
m
_____ (be) married to a happy woman, who
n
_____ (be) me.
o

Sandra Pastran, Salvador

☆EXERCISE 9

Read the following fable written by Aesop in the fifth century B.C. Fables follow a consistent pattern. The first part, written in the past tense, tells a story, usually about animals and usually using the past tense cluster. The second part points out a moral (that is, it makes a generalization about human behavior), using the present-future cluster. This reading has not been glossed for you. Use a dictionary to find the meanings of words that you cannot understand from their use in the context.

A lion fell in love with a farmer's daughter and asked for her hand in marriage. The farmer could not bear to give his child to a wild beast, but he did not dare refuse. So he evaded the difficulty by telling the lion that he approved of the marriage but could not consent unless the lion would pull out his teeth and cut off his claws, because the girl was afraid of them. The lion was so much in love that he willingly made these sacrifices. But when he presented himself again, the farmer treated him rudely and clubbed him off the farm.

Moral: Do not be too quick to take advice that is offered you. If nature has given you special advantages over others, do not let yourself be deprived of them, or you will be easy prey for people who used to be awed by you.

Think of a moral that you consider important, and then think of a specific animal. With a group of students in your class, discuss possible fables to illustrate the moral you chose. Now write a fable of your own, following the format of Aesop's fable. You can make one up, or if you know of one in your own culture, write that.

EDIT

The student who wrote about his relationship with his siblings in the piece below has made several errors with verb tenses. Find the errors, fix them, and explain what was wrong.

I still remember when there was no peace in the house. Every day, my brothers and I have fights. Sometimes we fight over the littlest things. One time, my younger brother borrowed my pen without asking for my permission. I guess I was still very young. When I couldn't find my pen, I practically blow up. We had a great big fight over a stupid little pen. We didn't speak to each other for a whole week.

When you are little and have two other brothers, you do not want to share too much. Sometimes we fight over food on the dinner table. That really made my parents mad. My father always tell us that brothers should be like a pair of hands, always working together in harmony.

As I grew older, I began sharing more with my brother. Ever since I started college, my older brother and I been sharing books and notes. Sometimes we talk about our problems. For the first time in my life, I felt I could talk to my brother like a friend.

Tony Cheng, Hong Kong

WRITE

Anna Quindlen's article describes the sibling rivalry she witnessed between her two sons. Form groups with other students born in the same order as you (firstborn, second, etc.). Tell each other about your family experiences, and discuss whether you think that sibling rivalry is inevitable or even healthy. Then write an essay in which you state your point of view and, as Quindlen did, tell stories from your own experience to explain why you hold that point of view.

EDITING ADVICE

1. Underline all the complete verb phrases you have used.

2. Determine whether each verb belongs to the past or the present-future cluster. When you have made a switch, can you explain why? Will your reader be able to understand why?

3. Examine any perfect, progressive, or perfect progressive verbs you have used. Check the forms against those in the summary chart of tense-time relationships in section 8f.

9 Verb Tenses: Past

READ

Read the following selection from the reading, "Cultural Exchanges," excerpted from Mark Salzman's *Iron and Silk*. The complete reading, with vocabulary glosses, appears on p. 347.

I had walked along the river many times since meeting the fisherman that day in winter, but I did not see him again until spring. It was late afternoon, and I had bicycled to a point along the river about a mile downstream from where we had met, hoping to find a deserted spot
5   to draw a picture. I found a niche in the sloping floodwall and started drawing a junk moored not far from me. Half an hour passed, and just as I finished the drawing, I heard someone calling my Chinese name. I looked down to see Old Ding scrambling up the floodwall, his boat anchored behind him. I noticed that he limped badly, and when he got
10   up close I could see that one of his legs was shorter than the other and set at an odd angle. Such was his balance and skill in the boats that I only saw his deformity when he came ashore. He squatted down beside me and explained that he had just returned from a long fishing trip on Dong Ting, a sprawling lake in North Hunan. "Big fish up there," he said, gesturing
15   with his arms. Then he asked me what I was doing. I showed him the drawing, and his face lit up. "Just like it! Just like the boat!" He cupped his hands to his mouth and yelled something in the direction of the junk, and right away a family appeared on deck. "Let's show it to them!" he said, and dragged me down to the water.

ANALYZE

1. In the passage, underline every verb phrase that forms a complete verb phrase attached to the subject of a clause. These should add up to thirty-four verb phrases. (Note: In the first sentence, you'll underline *had walked* and *did see* but not *meeting,* since that is not a *complete* verb phrase.)

90

2. Each of the verb phrases contains a main verb (the verb that carries the meaning). Some verb phrases will include auxiliaries, too, such as *did, had, was,* or *could.* Underline the main verb of each clause twice.

3. Examine the complete verb phrases you have underlined. What time cluster dominates in this passage? Note how the same time cluster is maintained throughout all the verbs in the sentence. When you write, there is no need to switch back and forth between past and present-future unless your time reference changes and you signal that change.

STUDY

9a. Identifying and using past cluster verb phrases

To be able to analyze and check your use of verbs in English, it is helpful to practice identifying the verb phrases that occur in your reading. The box shows the active verb forms used in the past time cluster.

PAST TIME: ACTIVE VOICE	
Time Reference	*Verb (Past Cluster)*
Basic past	main verb, past tense: She left early. *did* + simple form: Did she leave early?
Past perfect (before basic past)	*had* + participle: She had left when I arrived.
Past progressive (in progress)	*was/were* + *-ing:* They were leaving when I arrived. They were going to leave when I arrived (but didn't).
Past perfect progressive (in progress and before basic past)	*had been* + *-ing:* She had been trying to call me for an hour when I arrived to pick her up.
Modal Reference	
For meaning and use, see Chapter 11.	could, should, might, had to could have, should have, ought to have, might have, must have

Note that when the first verb in a sentence is in the past cluster, the other verbs following it will also be in the past cluster:

> **He found a corner and started drawing.**
> **He explained that he had just returned.**
> **He said that he would be grateful for a simple gift.**

(See also Chapter 25, "Noun Clauses and Reported Speech.")

EXERCISE 1

For each of the complete verbs you underlined in the reading at the beginning of this chapter, identify which time it refers to—basic past, past perfect, past progressive, or past perfect progressive—or whether a past modal form is used.

EXAMPLE   **had walked—past perfect**

Note that *was set* is a passive form (see Chapter 12). There is only one present cluster form in the passage; can you find it?

EXERCISE 2

In the following paragraph written by a student, the verbs have been omitted. Using the given verbs, determine the tense and form, and insert the appropriate form of the main verb with any necessary auxiliaries. The first three have been done for you.

I _**have often exchanged**_ (exchange often) artwork
with other people. I _**remember**_ (remember)
when I _**was**_ (be) twelve years old, I
_____ (go) to a prison to see a relative.
I _____ (know not) what to do when I
_____ (get) there. They all
_____ (seem) very nice people. They
all _____ (seem) bored with nothing to
do. So I _____ (dance) for them, and
some of the old people there _____
(cry) when they _____ (see) me. When
I _____ (finish) dancing, they all
_____ (clap), and some of them
_____ (give) me little wood figures
that they _____ (make).   It
_____ (be) a real exchange of art.

Sandra Pastran, Salvador

9b. Basic past tense

The basic past tense is used when we state or imply that an event occurred at a specified time in the past:

> She met him *last week.*
> She met him *five years ago.*
> *But* She *has met* him before. (We don't know exactly when.)

This is the tense that is used when we tell a story in the past:

> He *went* on the boat. Then he *gave* the people a drawing. They *wanted* to give him their boat.

Even when we are writing to explain or to persuade, narration is used a great deal to provide vivid examples and illustrations of general concepts. We back up an opinion with an account of an event that shows the reader why we hold that opinion. In academic writing, we often find general truths and opinions expressed in the present tense; then examples and illustrations to support the opinion often tell about an incident in the past.

EXAMPLE

present

Cultural differences *can cause* problems. Mark Salzman, for example, *found* that the custom of returning a gift *was* very different in

China.

☆*EXERCISE 3*

Choose one of the following generalizations, and write a short paragraph to support it by telling a story about something that happened in the past. Begin your paragraph with the generalization.

1. People usually want to return a favor.
2. _____ is a dangerous sport.
3. Parents don't always understand their children.
4. Politicians are not necessarily free from corruption.
5. Adolescence is a painful time.
6. TV shows are often excessively violent.
7. Some people say that school days are the happiest days, but that is far from true for everyone.
8. The first two days at a new school/college are a time of great confusion.

9c. Irregular verb forms

Regular verbs form the basic past tense by adding *-d* or *-ed* to the stem of the verb. The past tense of many verbs is, however, irregular in form.

REGULAR AND IRREGULAR VERBS			
	Simple Form	*Past*	*Participle* (*-ed/-en*)
Regular	walk intend	walked intended	walked intended
Irregular	sing take	sang took	sung taken

You should make an attempt to learn the past tense form and the participle form of all the irregular verbs. First, as you read, note down all the irregular verbs you come across. Second, try to use each verb in sentences of your own using the past tense form and the participle form. Third, learn three or four verbs a day from the list in the Appendix.

EXERCISE 4

The following passages are adapted from the reading "The Basic-Nonbasic Concept" on p. 367. Imagine that you are writing about the town fifty years from now—so you will be looking back to describe the town and using the past tense. Make any changes in tense that are appropriate. Begin with "There was once a frontier mining town . . ."

1. [There is] a frontier mining town where 100 miners are employed in the town's only basic industry—gold mining. Each of the miners is married and has two children. The basic industry thus supports 400 people.
2. But the 400 people demand services: schools and churches have to be built, grocery and clothing stores and livery stables are operated, newspapers are published, professional personnel are needed, and saloons have to cater to visiting cowboys.
3. With 100 miners, this community supports 300 people in the various nonbasic service industries.
4. The basic mining industry not only supports its own 300 dependents but also economically supports the 300 nonbasic personnel and their 900 dependents, for a grand total of 1,600 people.

EXERCISE 5 (oral)

Form two teams in your classroom. One team chooses a person from the list and asks someone from the other team, "Tell me something about

. . ." That person responds by saying who the person was or what the person did. If that team member cannot respond, anyone else on the team may try. You score two points for answering if you are chosen but only one point for anyone on your team answering. The instructor and students will determine if the answer is accurate or not.

Madame Curie	Vincent van Gogh
Confucius	Mao Tse-tung
Albert Einstein	Michelangelo
Golda Meir	George Washington
Martin Luther King, Jr.	Christopher Columbus
Aristotle	Elvis Presley
Galileo	Indira Gandhi
Eleanor Roosevelt	

You may, of course, continue with people that you name. As a follow-up exercise, write five sentences about the life and achievements of a figure of historical importance in your country.

9d. Past perfect

The past perfect (*had* + participle) is used when a relationship with the basic past time exists. It indicates that an action was completed before another one in the past occurred. It is not used just to express past time. Beware of overusing the past perfect. Every time you use it, check to make sure that you have established both a basic past time and a time preceding it.

The past perfect often occurs in one of the following patterns:

When
By the time } S + V in basic past, S + V in past perfect

S + V in past perfect *when* / *by the time* } S + V in basic past

EXAMPLES

When I arrived, everyone had left.
Everyone had left when I arrived.
(two times, one before the other in the past)

By the time I arrived, everyone had left.
Everyone had left by the time I arrived.
(I arrived late. Everyone had left. There was nobody there.)

However, the same idea of sequence can be communicated by using a time word like *before, after,* or *then,* used with the basic past:

9d

Everyone left before I arrived.
I arrived after everyone left.
Everyone left; then I arrived.

If only one past action occurs, if two actions occur simultaneously with *when,* or if a sequence is signaled with a word like *after* or *before,* the basic past form is used:

Not *When I had visited my country, I had been very happy.

But When I visited my country, I was very happy. (simultaneous events)

Not *Yesterday, I had gone to the library.

But Yesterday, I went to the library. (one past time)

Not *After he had greeted Old Ding, he noticed that he limped.

But After he greeted Old Ding, he noticed that he limped. (sequence signaled with word *after*)

EXERCISE 6 *(oral)*

Make up six sentences about new experiences you have had in your life. Use the following pattern with *until:*

I had never eaten a barbecued steak until I came to the United States.

EXERCISE 7

In each sentence, insert an appropriate form of the given verb. Remember that the past perfect is used to signal that one event occurred before another in the past when no other signal is used.

1. When my friends arrived to take me out for dinner, they were disappointed to hear that I _____ (eat).

2. They really _____ (enjoy) the concert last night.

3. When he _____ (give) them the drawing, they were delighted.

4. I saw that he was limping, and I assumed that he _____ (hurt) himself while working.

96

5. When he _____ (get) up close, I could see what was wrong.

6. The fishermen wanted to give him their boat because he _____ (give) them a drawing.

_____

9e. Past progressive and past perfect progressive

The past progressive *(was/were + -ing)* is used to express an activity in progress in the past for a long time:

He was working all day yesterday.
He was working while I was playing tennis.

Note that with *while,* the progressive form occurs in both clauses.

This tense is also used to express an activity in progress at a specified point of time in the past:

He was working at midnight last night.

A *when* clause is often used to indicate the particular point in time:

He was working when I called.

The past perfect progressive occurs with two different signals: one indicates the length of the activity in progress, and the other indicates a specific point in time in the past:

He had been working for three hours by the time I woke up *or* when I woke up.

Since duration of time is important here, *since* and *for* are often used with this tense form.

_____

☆*EXERCISE 8*

Look at the picture on p. 98. This painting, by the Flemish painter Pieter Brueghel, is called *Landscape with the Fall of Icarus.* It illustrates the myth of Icarus, whose father, Daedalus, made wings from wax in order to escape from the Minotaur in Crete. Icarus, however, flew too near the sun, his wings melted, and he fell into the sea. You'll have to look carefully to see Icarus hitting the water. The picture also shows a lot of details of what was happening at the moment when Icarus fell. Write six sentences telling about things that were happening when Icarus fell into the water. In fact, Icarus's fall is not the central focus of the picture at all; it is tucked away in the lower right-hand corner.

Landscape with the Fall of Icarus, PIETER BRUEGHEL *(1558)*

EXAMPLE   **A farmer was ploughing his field when Icarus fell into the water.**

Now imagine that this is the illustration for the beginning of a story. Write the rest of the story, imagining that someone asked, "What happened next, after Icarus fell?" Use past time verbs.

9f. *Used to* and *would*

The expressions *used to* and *would* are often used to tell about something that happened more than once in the past, as a regular occurrence. They tell about customs and rituals. Frequently, a narrative about the past will begin using *used to* + the simple form of the verb and then will continue with *would*.

EXAMPLES

When I was a child, I used to visit my grandmother every day. I would have supper there, and she would help me with my homework.

EXERCISE 9

Write a paragraph about how you used to spend Sunday afternoons when you were about 12 years old. Use *used to* and *would* in your account.

EDIT

The students who wrote the following accounts of meaningful events in their past made some errors with verb tenses and forms. Underline the errors, write down what the correct form should be, and explain why.

I was born in Lebanon and lived there until I was sixteen years old, when the war broke out. I have had a bad experience with the war; something has happened that made a turning point in my life.

When I was there during the war, I got shot. Then my parents have decided to send me to another country to finish my education. That country was Switzerland.

Wassim Hatoum, Lebanon

An event that was a meaningful point in my life was moving to America. This move has change my life and made me what I am today.

99

This change took place on May 24, 1981. On May 24, I left India to come to the United States for better educational opportunities. On that day, it was raining very hard, and my friends were telling me that the airport will close because of poor visibility. I was praying so hard that my friends will be right, but unfortunately they weren't, and I left for the United States on the eight o'clock flight. This change made me into an independent, mature, and responsible woman.

Sanhita Kar, India

WRITE

Mark Salzman chose to describe certain incidents from his long stay in China because they were particularly meaningful for him. Describe an incident in your past that was particularly meaningful for you. If you have experienced different cultural customs, as Salzman did, write about an incident that reflects those cultural differences. Describe the incident in detail, so that the reader can almost see what was happening, as if he or she were watching a movie.

EDITING ADVICE	1. Look carefully at every verb phrase. If you have used past tense forms, make sure that regular verbs have the *-d* or *-ed* ending, and check irregular verbs in the Appendix or in a dictionary.
	2. If at any time you have used a verb phrase belonging to the present-future cluster, make sure that this is intentional and that there is a reason for the switch from past to present-future that your reader will understand.
	3. If you have used *had* + participle at any point, make sure that the time referred to is a time before the basic past time. That is, the past perfect tense must refer to a time preceding a basic past time that you have already established for your reader.

Verb Tenses: Present and Future

10

READ

Read the following passage from the reading selection "The Effects of Our Environment." The full selection, with vocabulary glosses, appears on p. 351.

Many business people show an understanding of how environment can influence communication. Robert Sommer, a leading environmental psychologist, described several such cases. In *Personal Space: The Behavioral Basis of Design,* he points out that dim lighting, subdued
5   noise levels, and comfortable seats encourage people to spend more time in a restaurant or bar. Knowing this fact, the management can control the amount of customer turnover. . . .

Sommer also describes how airports are designed to discourage people from spending too much time in waiting areas. The uncomfortable
10   chairs, bolted shoulder to shoulder in rows facing outward, make conversation and relaxation next to impossible. Faced with this situation, travelers are forced to move to restaurants and bars in the terminal, where they're not only more comfortable but also more likely to spend money. . . .

15   Other studies by Robert Sommer and his colleagues found that students who sit opposite the teacher talk more, and those next to the teacher avoid talking at all. Also, the middle of the first row contains the students who interact most, and as we move back and to the sides of the classroom, interaction decreases markedly.

20   With an overwhelming lack of imagination we perpetuate a seating arrangement reminiscent of a military cemetery. This type of environment communicates to students that the teacher, who can move about freely while they can't, is the one who is important in the room, is the only one to whom anyone should speak, and is the person who has all the
25   information. The most advanced curriculum has little chance of surviving without a physical environment that supports it.

101

ANALYZE

1. Underline all the complete verb phrases in the passage.

2. Determine which ones belong to the past cluster and which to the present-future cluster.

3. Which time cluster dominates in this passage? At which points does the writer switch out of it? Can you speculate as to why the writer found it appropriate to switch to another cluster at those points?

STUDY

10a. Present-future verb phrases

To help you check your own use of verbs when you write, it is good practice to examine and identify verb phrases that you come across as you read.

Present-future cluster verb forms are dealt with together since the time references often occur together. In fact, present tenses can even be used to indicate future time, as in the following:

> **The bus leaves at eight o'clock.**
> **We're going to Europe next summer.**

The box on page 103 shows the active verb forms used in the present-future cluster.

EXERCISE 1

Work with other students to write a paragraph describing the classroom that you are in now. Describe the size, color, furniture, seating arrangement, and any other details. Describe who usually sits and stands where, and comment on this. Then add another paragraph in which you tell your reader, too, where you usually choose to sit, why, and how this choice affects your interaction with your classmates and your instructor.

10b. Basic present for habitual action

The basic present tense is used when we want to indicate that an action occurs repeatedly or habitually:

> **She goes to work by train every day.**
> **They work hard.**

ACTIVE VERBS: PRESENT-FUTURE CLUSTER

Time Reference	Present	Future
Basic	*main verb: present tense* She gets up at 6 A.M. *question: do/does + simple form* Does she get up early?	*will + simple form* We will/won't leave soon. ALTERNATIVES *am/is/are going to + simple form* She's going to leave tomorrow. *main verb: basic present* We leave for France tomorrow. *main verb: progressive* I'm flying to Greece tomorrow.
Perfect (before basic time)	*has/have + participle* I have been to Europe. (at some time before now)	*will have + participle* I will have left by the time you arrive.
Progressive (in progress)	*am/is/are + -ing* He is leaving now.	*will be + -ing* She will be leaving soon.
Perfect progressive (before basic and in progress)	*has/have been + -ing* I have been living here for six years. (up until now)	*will have been + -ing* By next month, I will have been living here for exactly twenty years.
Modal Reference		
See Chapter 11.	will/would can/could shall/should may/might must ought to } + simple form	

The tenses used in association with a description of a routine or customary actions will be in the present-future cluster. Note that when you use this tense, you must pay attention to agreement of subject and verb:

> she goes   he works
> they go   we work

(See Chapter 17, "Subject-Verb Agreement.")

EXERCISE 2

The following complete verb phrases appear in the first three paragraphs of the excerpt from "The Effects of Our Environment" at the beginning of this chapter, so you have probably underlined them. In the space provided, write what the subject of each verb is in the context of the reading passage, and indicate whether it is singular (S) or plural (P). The first one is given as an example.

SUBJECT	SINGULAR/PLURAL	VERB
Many business people	P	show
		points out
		encourage
		describes
		make
		sit
		avoid
		contains
		interact
		move
		decreases

10c. Other uses of basic present verb forms

You will use basic present verb forms in the following instances:

- To refer to habitual action:

    She takes the bus to school.

- To refer to an action occurring at the present time with a "mental activity" verb (see Chapter 8):

    I think you are right.
    He understands everything.

- To refer to future action when the future time is clearly stated. This usage occurs frequently with travel plans:

    We leave for Europe tomorrow.

    The basic present form (or the present perfect) is also used in a future time clause introduced by *when, as soon as, before,* or *after:*

    When they arrive, we'll leave.
    When they have arrived, we'll leave.

    She'll start preparing dinner as soon as the children call *or* **have called.**

- To refer to what an author says, even if the author is dead:

  Shakespeare tells us about old age in *King Lear*.

  Hemingway emphasizes masculinity and maleness in his novels.

  He tells stories of fights, hunts, drinking, and displays of aggression.

- To make generalizations:

  Children like to let off energy.

  Often, a generalization will be illustrated with a specific example, for which the author may switch to the past cluster if a past event is described. In the following passages, the first one illustrates the general statement "Children like to let off energy" with a description. The second illustrates the generalization with an account of an incident in the past.

  1. Children like to let off energy. Whenever you walk past a schoolyard, you are deafened by the noise of screaming, running, fighting, and noisy play. In a swimming pool, it is even worse!
  2. Children like to let off energy. My nephew, Juan, for example, nearly destroyed my apartment when he visited me last week. He didn't sit still for a minute and managed to do a lot of damage: he broke a plate, pulled a lamp over onto the floor, and spilled grape juice on my bedroom carpet. I was quite happy to see him leave so that I could get some rest.

- Informally, to tell a story. For a narrative, the basic present tense is sometimes used in conversation. This informal usage should be avoided in writing:

  A man walks over and sits down next to the young woman.

☆*EXERCISE 3*

Write a statement that expresses an opinion you hold in the form of a generalization. Now write two short paragraphs of support for that statement, one supporting the opinion with evidence presented in the present-future cluster and one supporting your opinion statement with evidence referring to a specific past event.

10d. Perfect tenses: present and future

The present perfect is the tense that causes language learners a lot of trouble, probably because its use of the participle form (often misleadingly labeled the "past participle") makes it seem to be a past tense. It can indeed be used to refer to an event that happened in the past, but the time is not important. What is important is the effect of the event on the present and on the speaker or writer. Note the uses of the present perfect:

- To indicate something that occurred at some unspecified (and unimportant) time in the past, before now (often used with *already, just,* or *yet*):

   He has left this address.
   Have you seen that movie yet?

- To indicate that activities occurred more than once in the past:

   I've met him several times (already).
   He has changed jobs often.

- To indicate that something began in the past and continued right up to now (often used with *since* and *for*):

   We have known each other for a long time.
   She has had that coat since 1986.

Note the use of the future perfect:

- To indicate that an activity will occur and will be perfected (completed) by a certain time in the future:

   We will have completed the renovation of our house by next month *or* **in a month's time** *or* **by August** *or* **in a few weeks. (Phrases like this occur often.)**

   With this tense, the specific time in the future must be stated or implied in the context:

   His family is going to visit him next month. He will have finished his project. (by the time they arrive)

EXERCISE 4

In each sentence, insert either the present perfect or the basic past tense.

1. I _____ (leave) Burma two years ago.

2. I love animals, and I _____ (want) to have a dog all my life, but my parents won't let me.

3. My sister _____ (decide) to go to college as soon as she realized how much I was learning.

4. I can't remember how many papers I _____ (write) up to now for my English course.

5. I wanted to make my living room look brighter, so I _____ _____ (buy) some new curtains.

6. The students who _____ (complete) all their re-quirements can graduate next month.

EXERCISE 5

Choose the word or phrase that best completes each sentence.

1. By this time next year, we _____ each other for twenty-five years.

    a. know
    b. are knowing
    c. will have known
    d. will know

2. Before we _____ the house, we're going to watch our favorite TV program.

    a. clean
    b. will clean
    c. are going to clean
    d. have cleaned

3. When the rain _____, they can begin to paint the house.

    a. is going to stop
    b. will stop
    c. stops
    d. will have stopped

4. They _____ a lot of English since they started taking classes.

    a. learn
    b. have learned
    c. will have learned
    d. learned

10e

5. It _____ windy and cold for the past few days.

    a. is
    b. will be
    c. has been
    d. have been

10e. Progressive tenses: present and future

Use the present progressive (except with mental activity verbs—see Chapter 8, section 8d) in the following instances:

- To indicate that an action is occurring right now:

  She's cooking dinner.
  He's just turning the corner.

- To emphasize the idea that a state or action is not permanent, that change is involved:

  I live in New York. (No change is implied.)
  I am living in New York. (A temporary state is underscored: I might move soon.)

  She writes articles for a film magazine. (That is her job.)
  She is writing an article for a film magazine. (When she finishes it, she will probably do something else.)

- To indicate a future plan:

  We're flying to Venezuela next week.
  We're going to the theater tonight.

Use the future progressive (except with mental activity verbs) to indicate that an activity will be in progress either for a long time or at a specific time in the future:

They will be working all day on Sunday.
I'll be watching "Cheers" at nine o'clock tonight.

But don't use the future progressive in a clause introduced by *when* or *while*:

I'll be working while (*or* **when**) he is sleeping.

EXERCISE 6 (oral)

Make up six sentences about yourself; tell a partner in your class about some things that you are temporarily involved with. In your sentences, use expressions like *currently, at present,* and *right now,* and use the present progressive.

Then speculate about what your life will be like in ten years' time: where will you be living, what will you be doing, what will your living arrangements be, and so on.

10f. Perfect progressive: present and future

Perfect progressive tenses emphasize the length of time an activity is in progress. The basic reference point is either an implied *now* or a specified time in the future:

I have been waiting here for two hours. (Up until now: I am still waiting.)

By next August, we will have been living in this house for twenty-five years.

EXERCISE 7

Identify the one underlined phrase in each sentence that should be corrected or rewritten. What should it be?

_____ 1. They have been sitting in that restaurant <u>for three hours</u>, so
  _a
the manager <u>has felt</u> unhappy because he <u>needs</u> the table for
  _b   _c
other customers. _____

_____ 2. In six months' time, they <u>are married</u> for twenty-five years, so
  _a
they <u>are planning</u> a big party that they <u>will hold</u> in their
  _b   _c
daughter's house. _____

_____ 3. We <u>try</u> to finish the report by nine o'clock, but we
  _a
<u>haven't had</u> a break all day, so we <u>will probably stop</u> for
  _b   _c
dinner soon. _____

_____ 4. Some of the students <u>are studying</u> since early this morning;
  _a
even though they <u>feel</u> tired and <u>want</u> to go home, they
  _b   _c
<u>are still sitting</u> in the library. _____
  _d

109

☆*EXERCISE 8*

Look at the picture *The Luncheon of the Boating Party* by Auguste Renoir on p. 111. Write a paragraph of description, using the present-future cluster and telling a reader what is happening as you look at the picture.

EXAMPLES

A lot of people are having a party.
They have just sat down to eat.
Three people are sitting at one table.

Tell the reader about the place and occasion, what people are there, what they are doing and wearing, what they usually or often do, what you think has led up to this event, and what will happen next.

EDIT

The student who wrote the following description made a few errors with verb tenses. Find the errors, correct them, and explain why the correction is necessary.

Morgan Park on the north shore of Long Island Sound in Glen Cove is a busy place this sunny Sunday afternoon. From my position, I can see the distant foggy shore of New Rochelle and the white sails of boats in the harbor. The sun makes millions of tiny stars in the grayish waters of the sound.

As I look around, I can see people of different ages: young, middle-aged, and old. In many of the families here, three generations had gathered on the beach to enjoy the fine weather. The older people tend to prefer the shady areas under the trees, while the younger ones splash in and out of the water.

Next to us, two men play chess. My husband is looking at them curiously because he likes to play chess, too. I know he wants to join them. In fact, after a little while, he walks over to talk to them. Now he is taking one of their seats and joining in the game. Meanwhile, I am finding a comfortable position in my beach chair. To my right, a large family occupies space under a big old tree. They brought enough food and drinks to spend a whole weekend here! The men are playing cards, the

The Luncheon of the Boating Party, PIERRE-AUGUSTE RENOIR *(1881)*

women are reading newspapers and magazines, and the children are chasing a ball. In front of me, there are two women wearing long black dresses. They only thing they bring is a big radio, but to my relief, it remains silent.

Suddenly, gray hazy clouds cover the sun. It is getting darker and might even rain. People quickly pick up their belongings—blankets, beach towels, chairs, portable coolers. The path leading to the parking lot is suddenly crowded. The only people that don't know what is going on are two chess players: my husband and the other man. I'm going to have to stop writing and tell them to move.

Jadwiga Tonska, Poland

WRITE

Find a comfortable spot to sit in a public place—a library, an airport, a bus terminal, a hotel lobby, a school entrance hall, a train station, a restaurant, a coffee shop, a shopping mall, a city square, a beach, or a park. Sit there for fifteen minutes, and write about what you see, as you see it. You will therefore use present-future cluster verb forms. Describe in detail both the setting (what the space looks like, what is there) and the people (what they are doing, who comes in and leaves, what they are wearing, what they have just done, etc.). Imagine that your readers are watching a movie of the scene: capture all the details for them so that they see the scene exactly as you see it.

EDITING ADVICE	
	1. Underline every complete verb phrase.
	2. Use the box in section 10a to check that you have kept to the present-future time cluster. If you have moved out of it, there should be a good reason. Make sure that the form you have used corresponds to the time indicated in the box.
	3. Whenever you have used a present tense form of *be*, *do*, or *have* or of the main verb, check that a form with an *-s* ending has a singular third-person subject. A verb form without an *-s* ending should have a plural subject or an *I* or *you* subject.

Modal Auxiliaries 11

READ

Read the following excerpt from the reading by Lewis Thomas, which appears with vocabulary glosses on p. 355.

Let us assume that there is, indeed, sentient life in one or another part of remote space, and that we will be successful in getting in touch with it. What on earth are we going to talk about? . . . We could begin by gambling on the rightness of our technology and just send out news of
5 ourselves, like a mimeographed Christmas letter, but we would have to choose our items carefully, with durability of meaning in mind. Whatever information we provide must still make sense to us two centuries later, and must still seem important, or the conversation will be an embarrassment to all concerned. In two hundred years it is, as we have found, easy
10 to lose the thread.

Perhaps the safest thing to do at the outset, if technology permits, is to send music. This language may be the best we have for explaining what we are like to others in space, with least ambiguity. I would vote for Bach, all of Bach, streamed out into space, over and over again. We would be
15 bragging, of course, but it is surely excusable for us to put the best possible face on at the beginning of such an acquaintance. We can tell the harder truths later. And, to do ourselves justice, music would give a fairer picture of what we are really like than some of the other things we might be sending, like *Time,* say, or a history of the U.N. or Presidential
20 speeches. We could send out our science, of course, but just think of the wincing at this end when the polite comments arrive two hundred years from now. Whatever we offer as today's items of liveliest interest are bound to be out of date and irrelevant, maybe even ridiculous. I think we should stick to music.
25 Perhaps, if the technology can be adapted to it, we should send some paintings. . . .

113

11a

ANALYZE

1. Find examples of the following modal auxiliaries in the passage:

can	must	could	might
shall	have/has to	should	had better
will	ought to	would	had to
may			

2. Underline the complete verb phrase in which the auxiliary occurs.

3. What form of the main verb or auxiliary *always* directly follows the auxiliaries in the list?

4. Some of the auxiliaries listed can express a variety of meanings. Discuss, for example, what *should* means in the following sentences:

We should send some paintings.
The turn of the century should bring exciting new discoveries.

STUDY

11a. Meanings of modal auxiliaries: ability, permission, polite questions and statements

The box on page 115 shows examples of modal auxiliaries that express ideas of ability, permission, and polite questions and statements. Both past cluster and present-future clusters are shown where they exist, and forms closely related in meaning to the modals are listed also.

EXERCISE 1

Write five sentences telling about things that you couldn't do when you were a child but you can do now.

EXAMPLE

When I was a child, I couldn't skate at all, but now I can skate without falling down.

EXERCISE 2 (oral)

Form a polite question for the following situations.

EXAMPLE

You want someone to hold the door open for you.

114

MODALS: ABILITY, PERMISSION, POLITE FORMS

Meaning	*Past*	*Present-Future*
Ability	He knew he could win. She couldn't solve the problem. She was able to convince her boss to promote her. We could have won (if) . . . (but we didn't)	She can speak French. She will be able to get a job in Paris next year. We could begin (if) . . . (see Chapter 27, "Conditions")
Permission	She said I could join the class. She said we were permitted (*or* allowed) to join the class.	May I join this class? You may/may not leave. Can I join this class? (less formal than *may*) Would you mind if I joined this class? (polite)[†] Would you mind my joining this class? (polite and formal) Are we permitted (allowed) to join this class?
Polite question		Would you please help me? Could you please help me? Do you think you could help me? Would you mind helping me? (Note the standard question form: Will you/Can you help me?)
Polite statement		I would like the day off on Friday. I would appreciate your help. I wouldn't expect anything in return. I'd be delighted to write you a reference.

[†]Note that the reply to "Would you mind?"—if you want to give your consent—is "No" ("No, I wouldn't mind. It's all right.").

Would you mind holding the door open for me?
Could you please hold the door open for me?

1. You want someone to put out her cigarette.
2. You want the man sitting behind you in the movie theater to stop talking.

115

3. You want to borrow a classmate's book.
4. You want a friend to lend you $20.
5. You want a friend to play a record again for you.
6. You want to squeeze into a full bus.

EXERCISE 3

Write some questions that you would ask inhabitants of distant space. Use modal forms in your questions.

EXAMPLES

Can you see in the dark?
Would you mind if I went into your spaceship?

11b. Meanings of modal auxiliaries: advisability, necessity, no necessity, prohibition

The box on page 117 shows modal forms used to express ideas of advisability, necessity, no necessity, and prohibition. It also shows closely related idiomatic forms.

EXERCISE 4 (oral)

Work with a partner. One of you will read out the given sentence. The other will respond with some advice that fits the situation. Use *should, ought to,* or *had better* in the response.

EXAMPLE

It's raining, and I'm going out.
You should wear your raincoat.

1. There's a lot of ice on the roads, and I'm planning to drive 100 miles.
2. I have a headache and a sore throat.
3. I want to know about life on other planets.
4. I'd really like to be an astronaut.
5. I've got a terrible pain in my right side.
6. I feel faint.
7. I've been hiccupping for five minutes.
8. I wish I knew more about philosophy.

MODALS: ADVISABILITY, NECESSITY, NO NECESSITY, PROHIBITION

Meaning	*Past*	*Present-Future*
Advisability	*Advisable action didn't occur* We should have sent some paintings. (but we didn't) We shouldn't have sent science. (but we did) We ought to have sent music, too. *Advisable action might have occurred* We'd better not have made a mistake. He was supposed to be there.	We should send some paintings. We shouldn't send science. We ought to send music, too. We had better be careful. (The result will be bad otherwise.) We had better not make a mistake. He is supposed to be here.
Necessity	The information had to make sense. Last year, we were obliged to work every weekend.	The information must make sense. The information has to make sense. The information will have to make sense. I have got to leave now. (informal) I've got to leave now. (informal; pronounced "I've gotta" or "I gotta") We are obliged to work on weekends.
No necessity	You didn't have to leave so early.	You don't have to leave yet. It's still early. You won't have to leave early. You need not leave so early.
Prohibition	You weren't allowed to go in there!	You must not leave yet. There's still a lot of work to do. You're not allowed to leave yet. You won't be allowed to leave early.

EXERCISE 5 (oral)

Work with a partner. One of you will read out the given sentence. The other will respond to the statement using *should have.*

EXAMPLE

He was injured in a car accident because he wasn't wearing a seat belt.

He should have worn a seat belt. *or* He should have been wearing a seat belt.

1. He didn't send a message.
2. She didn't take her medicine.
3. They didn't write their letters.
4. He didn't drive carefully.
5. She didn't pay her credit card bills.

EXERCISE 6

Write a set of instructions for aliens arriving from another planet or solar system. Tell them what is advisable and what is necessary for them to do once they are on earth visiting your country and also what is prohibited.

EXAMPLES

You should teach us your language.
You must not frighten anybody.
You must drive on the right in the country you are in.

11c. Meanings of modal auxiliaries: expectation, possibility, and logical deduction

The box on page 119 shows the forms used to express the ideas of expectation, possibility, and logical deduction.

EXERCISE 7

Write a paragraph about what you think life will be like in the year 2050. Tell your readers what you think is possible and what your expectations are.

MODALS: EXPECTATION, POSSIBILITY, LOGICAL DEDUCTION

Meaning	Past	Present-Future
Expectation	We should have/ought to have received the signal last year.	We should/ought to receive the signal soon.
Possibility	The crew may/might have repaired the satellite already.	The crew may/might repair the satellite later this week. They might be repairing it now.
Logical deduction	They must have tried to contact us before.	There must be life on other planets.

You need to have a clear reason in mind when you use *must* in this way.

☆EXERCISE 8

Look at the picture by Renoir that appears on p. 111. What expectations, possibilities, and logical deductions can you make about the people and the situation, and what can you say about the advisability and necessity of the situation? Write at least five sentences using different modal forms.

EXAMPLE

They must be having a good time.

11d. Simple form after the modal auxiliaries

The modal auxiliaries are followed by the simple form of the verb or the second auxiliary:

might repair   ought to send
should receive   might have
must leave   should be

Note that when *be* or *have* is used as the second auxiliary, the appropriate verb form has to follow:

should *have* received   should *be* taking (active)
must *have* left   should *be* taken (passive)
ought to *have* sent

See the summary chart of verb forms in Chapter 13, section 13c.

11e. The uses of *would*

Note the variety of uses of *would*.

<table>
<tr><th colspan="3">USES OF WOULD</th></tr>
<tr><th>Meaning</th><th>Past</th><th>Present-Future</th></tr>
<tr>
<td>Polite question or statement</td>
<td></td>
<td>Would you help me?
I would like your help.</td>
</tr>
<tr>
<td>Permission</td>
<td>Would you have minded if I had left?</td>
<td>Would you mind if I leave/left now?</td>
</tr>
<tr>
<td>Past action, repeated
(See Chapter 9.)</td>
<td>Whenever I saw him, I would cry.</td>
<td></td>
</tr>
<tr>
<td>Preference</td>
<td>I would rather have gone to the theater.</td>
<td>I would rather go to the movies than the theater.
I'd rather not see that play.</td>
</tr>
<tr>
<td>Hypothetical condition
(See Chapter 27.)</td>
<td>I would have won if . . .</td>
<td>I would win if . . .</td>
</tr>
</table>

EXERCISE 9 (oral)

In one sentence, state your preference about the following pairs, using *would rather*, and explain why in a clause using *because*.

EXAMPLE

play tennis / go to the beach
I'd rather play tennis than go to the beach because it's better exercise.

1. go dancing / watch TV
2. read a novel / read a nonfiction book
3. live in the city / live in the country
4. study economics / study anthropology
5. work for myself / work for a company

11f. Summary chart

The summary chart on page 121 shows the modal forms and the related idioms. All forms are followed by the simple form of the verb, except those for which "+ participle" is indicated.

USES OF MODALS AND RELATED IDIOMS

Meaning	Past	Present-Future
Ability	*could* *could have* + participle *be able to*	*can/can't*
Permission	*could* *would have minded* *be allowed to* *be permitted to*	*can* *may* *would mind*
Advisability	*should have* + participle *ought to have* + participle *had better (not) have* + participle *be supposed to*	*should* *ought to* *had better*
Possibility	*may have* + participle *might have* + participle	*may* *might*
Necessity	*had to* *be obliged to*	*must* *has/have to* *has/have got to*
No necessity	*didn't have to* *didn't need to*	*doesn't/don't have to* *doesn't/don't need to* *won't have to/need to*
Prohibition	*(not) be allowed to* *(not) be permitted to*	*must not*
Expectation	*should have* + participle *ought to have* + participle	*should* *ought to*
Logical deduction	*must have* + participle	*must*
Polite statement or question		*could* *would* *would . . . mind*
Past action, repeated	*would*	
Preference	*would rather have* + participle	*would rather*
Hypothetical condition	*would have* + participle	*would*

☆*EXERCISE 10 (oral)*

Discuss the difference in meaning between the sentences in the following groups. Suggest a situation in which each sentence might be used.

1. a. You mustn't use the washing machine.
   b. You don't have to use the washing machine.

2. a. You should study harder.
   b. You have to study harder.

3. a. His theory might be valid.
   b. His theory must be valid.

4. a. She should have saved a lot of money.
   b. She might have saved a lot of money.
   c. She must have saved a lot of money.
   d. She didn't have to save a lot of money.
   e. She had to save a lot of money.

5. a. He will arrive on time.
   b. He should arrive on time.
   c. He might arrive on time.

6. a. She had to see a doctor.
   b. She had better see a doctor.

EDIT

The following piece of student writing, a letter to possible future grandchildren, shows a few problems with the use of modal verb phrases. Underline the problem areas, write down what the student should have written, and explain why.

My very dear grandchildren:

Life was very hard for me when I came to this huge country. I was a new bride, and I had to adapted to my new environment. I used to be alone all day in the house, looking through the window at the traffic in the street. Sometimes I would think about going out, but I didn't know how to get around the city, so I stayed home. I should have being more adventurous, I think. But I wasn't allowed to go out alone because your grandfather was scared that something may happen if I was alone.

I expect that life might be better for you. I want to remind you that studying should be the most important thing in life. Without knowledge, you couldn't fulfill your dream and become an expert in your chosen career. You should choose a career and go firmly after your goal. So you had better make up your mind to go to college. You might not think this is very original advice, but you must follow it if you want a successful and happy life. Don't let anyone discourage you. May all your dreams come true.

> With all my love,
> Grandma
> Gisèle Zuméta, Martinique

WRITE

Pretend you are a grandparent. You are going to write a letter to your grandchildren. First, tell them about life for you at a particular age, particularly about what you used to do *(would)*, what you were not allowed to do *(could not)*, what you were compelled to do *(had to)*, and any regrets and preferences you have had *(should have; would rather have)*. Second, speculate about their life: about what you expect or guess it will be like *(should, might)* and what they will be able to do. Finally, use the wisdom of your experience to give them advice *(should, ought to, had better, must)*.

1. Underline all the modal verbs you have used.	**EDITING ADVICE**

2. Check that each one is followed by the simple form of the second auxiliary or of the main verb.

3. Check that the form you have used (past or present-future) fits in with the time cluster of the passage in which it occurs. Don't switch without a reason.

4. Find the form you have used in the summary chart in section 11f, and check that the meanings listed there include the one you intend.

12 Active and Passive

READ

Read the following selection from the article "Portable Computers," which appears with vocabulary glosses on p. 357.

The first digital computer was built in 1946 at the University of Pennsylvania. It weighed 30 tons and filled a large room. It was called ENIAC. In its early days it required 18,500 vacuum tubes to store information. Obviously, a 30-ton computer had its limitations. Scientists
5   and engineers worked to make it better. The use of transistors as small amplifiers in place of the large vacuum tubes reduced the size and cost of computers. Smaller was better.

In the early 1960's, the first minicomputers were made commercially. They were the size of a two-drawer file cabinet. The revolution
10   was on. Less than a decade later, the microcomputer was invented. . . .

One of the latest developments is bubble memory. In bubble memory, the information is stored in tiny magnetic spots or islands that look like bubbles floating on the chip. One great advantage of bubble memory is that it does not lose stored information when the power is
15   turned off.

Portable computers, ranging from briefcase size down to handhelds, are the latest innovation. In the smallest of the portables, the cathode ray tube has been replaced by a flat electroluminescent display and the disk drives by bubble memory chips. In these computers,
20   information is stored on the road, at conferences, at the library, or elsewhere, and then transferred to print or conventional disk drive memory later.

ANALYZE

1. The verb phrase in the first sentence (*was built*) consists of a form of the verb *be* followed by the participle form of the main verb. Underline the eight other complete verbs in the passage that also use a form of *be* with a participle form. Note that the last sentence contains an auxiliary with two main verbs: *is stored* . . . and *[is] transferred.*

2. With passive verbs, if we want to know who or what performed the action of the verb, we won't find it in the subject of the sentence. We have to look elsewhere in the sentence or assume that the performer of the action (the *agent*) is not the focus of the information. Rewrite each of the sentences in which you have underlined verbs so that you specify the agent (the person or thing responsible for the action of the verb).

EXAMPLE

Someone (Some engineers) built the first digital computer in 1946 at the University of Pennsylvania.

For how many of the sentences could you find the agent actually specified in the sentence?

3. Look at the verb phrases you underlined. Divide them into two columns, past and present-future.

STUDY

12a. Forms of the passive

Only transitive verbs (verbs that can be followed by an object) have a passive voice form:

Mary wrote that letter.
That letter was written by Mary.

Verbs like *be, happen, seem, appear, agree, belong,* and *die* have only active forms, with no passive transformations. However, not all transitive verbs have an acceptable passive transformation:

> **He has a big house.**
> *But not* ***A big house is had by him.**

When a passive is possible with transitive verbs—verbs such as *paint, throw, eat, write, take, put off, attend to,* and *take care of*—tense and aspect in the passive are shown by the form of the verb *be* + the participle of the main verb. The forms corresponding to the active forms are shown in the box on page 126, using the regular verb *paint.*

The future progressive and the perfect progressive forms are not in common use because they are considered awkward.

Note that the participle form of the main verb is *always* used to form the passive voice, whatever the tense and aspect of the *be* auxiliary.

ACTIVE AND PASSIVE FORMS

Reference	Active	Passive
BASIC Past / Present / Future	He painted the house last year.	The house was painted last year.
	He paints the house every five years.	The house is painted every five years.
	He will paint the house next year.	The house will be painted next year.
PERFECT Past	The house looked good because he had just painted it.	The house looked good because it had just been painted.
Present	He has (just) painted the house.	The house has (just) been painted.
Future	He will have painted the house by the end of next month.	The house will have been painted by the end of next month.
PROGRESSIVE Past	He was painting the house all last week.	The house was being painted all last week.
Present	He is painting the house right now.	The house is being painted right now.
QUESTION	Did he paint the house last year?	Was the house painted last year?
NEGATIVE	He wasn't painting the house all last week.	The house wasn't being painted all last week.

The passive can be used with modal verbs, too, following the patterns used with *will*.

EXAMPLES

The house *might be sold* next week.
The kitchen *should have been cleaned* yesterday.
The house *can be seen* from the mountain.
The roof *must be repaired* soon.

EXERCISE 1

In each of the following sentences from the reading "White Lies," which appears with vocabulary glosses on p. 365, fill in the appropriate active or passive form of the given verb.

1. White lies _____ (define) as being unmali-

cious.

2. In one study, 130 subjects _____ (ask) to

126

keep track of the truthfulness of their everyday statements.

3. Sometimes a face-saving lie _____

(prevent) embarrassment for the recipient.

4. "You didn't receive the check? It must _____

(delay) in the mail."

5. Sometimes we _____ (lie) to escape an un-

pleasant situation.

6. "I really have to go. I should _____ (study)

for a test tomorrow."

_____

12b. Uses of the passive

There are four main uses for the passive:

1. Use the passive when it is not necessary to mention the agent (the person or thing doing the action) because the agent is obvious, not known, or not important. The emphasis is on the action itself or on the receiver of the action.

EXAMPLES

Passive: **The first digital computer *was built* in 1946. (no agent mentioned)**
Active: **Engineers built the first digital computer in 1946.**

The "agentless passive" occurs frequently in journalism and in scientific writing:

Jewelry worth $500,000 *was stolen* from the Hotel Eldorado late last night.

In all early attempts at biological classification, living things *were separated* into two major groups: the plant kingdom and the animal kingdom. These two groups *were* then *subdivided* in a variety of ways.

2. Use the passive when you purposely want to avoid mentioning the agent.

EXAMPLES

I *was told* to come to this office.
An error *was made* in our sales forecast for the coming year.

It *is believed* that some top executives are involved in the crime.
Some top executives *are believed* to be involved in the crime.

It *is said* that he is a spy.
He *is said* to be a spy.

Most clauses with a passive verb (about 85 percent of them) do not mention the agent. There are, however, cases where disclosing the agent is necessary.

3. Use the passive with an agent when the agent is not a person but an inanimate object.

EXAMPLES

The cathode ray tube *has been replaced* by a flat electroluminescent display.

The alarm *is triggered* by photomagnetic cells.

4. Use the passive when the structure of the sentence or the relationship between two sentences determines that the new information should come last. Often old or given information precedes new information in a sentence. (See also Chapter 28.)

EXAMPLES

The vice-president wrote a report. That report is being studied by all the company officers.
Not The company officers are studying that report.

The senator lost the election, but he was invited by the president to join the White House staff.
Not The senator lost the election, but the president invited . . .

We will never forget last winter. We were buried under three feet of snow.
Not Three feet of snow buried us.

He picked up the wallet. It had been dropped by the gangster.
Not The gangster had dropped it.

EXERCISE 2

In the following active sentences, the agent is the very general *they*. Rewrite them as passive sentences, emphasizing the receiver and the action and omitting mention of the agent.

EXAMPLE

They have translated the film into many different languages.
The film has been translated into many different languages.

1. They delivered supplies to the North Pole last week.
2. They passed new tax laws a year ago.
3. They will revise the defense budget within the next year.
4. They grow rice in China and Japan.
5. They cultivate the soybean in many parts of the world.
6. They made my sweater in Ireland.
7. They should cancel the game if it rains.
8. They might have offered that course last semester.

☆EXERCISE 3

In the following excerpts from readings in this book, sections have been omitted and two possible alternatives—active or passive—have been provided. Choose which sentence or clause, a or b, you think the author probably used. Discuss with other students why the sentence you chose seems more appropriate to you.

_____ 1. It is a cheerful room furnished in light colors. _____

_____ .

    a. The couches in it were recently cleaned by men with small machines.
    b. Men with small machines recently cleaned the couches in it.

_____ 2. Years ago, when I lived in a two-room apartment, _____

_____ .

    a. I never used the living room either.
    b. the living room was never used by me either.

_____ 3. If he asks, should the doctors deny that he is ill, or minimize the

gravity of the prognosis? _____

_____ .

    a. Should they at least conceal the truth until after the family vacation?
    b. Should the truth be concealed until at least after the family vacation?

_____ 4. You didn't receive the check? _____

_____ .

    a. It must have been delayed in the mail.
    b. They must have delayed it in the mail.

_____ 5. Sommer also describes _____.

    a. how they design airports to discourage people from spending too much time in waiting areas.

    b. how airports are designed to discourage people from spending too much time in waiting areas.

_____ 6. He was a deeply religious man who had worked as a lay

preacher in England and among Belgian miners. _____

_____.

    a. He had been deeply impressed by the art of Millet and its social message.

    b. The art of Millet and its social message had deeply impressed him.

_____ 7. Most people know some of these paintings; the sunflowers, the

empty chair, the cypresses and some of the portraits have

become popular in colored reproductions and _____

_____.

    a. we can see them in many a simple room.

    b. they can be seen in many a simple room.

_____

12c. Passive idioms with *get* and *have*

Sometimes passives can be formed with *get* or *have*. A passive formed with *get* is more common in informal, spoken English than in formal, written English.

EXAMPLES

She got fired last week. (She was fired by her boss.)

He had his article published last month. (His article was published by someone. Someone published his article.)

She had (got) her hair cut yesterday. (Her hair was cut by somebody. Somebody cut her hair.)

These two sentences differ in meaning:

She washed the car.
She had the car washed.

In the first sentence, she washed the car herself. In the second, she paid or asked someone to do it for her.

EXERCISE 4 (oral)

Write five questions on five slips of paper using the *have* + participle or *get* + participle idiom with the following verbs and the noun phrases associated with them.

EXAMPLE   **When did you last have (*or* get) your hair cut?**

cut	hair	paint	house
shine	shoes	polish	nails
make	suit	fill	tooth
bleach	hair	shorten	skirt/pants

Give the five slips to students in your class, who will read out the questions and answer them in a complete sentence.

12d. The passive with direct and indirect objects

Options are available to you when you use a passive with a direct and indirect object:

1. A long report has been given to the president.
2. The president has been given a long report.

In sentence 1, the *president* is given prominence by being place last. In sentence 2, the *report* is given prominence by being placed last.

To help you decide, you will have to consider the whole context, including what comes before and after.

EXERCISE 5

Make two different agentless passive sentences from each active sentence.

EXAMPLE

Someone sent telegrams to the employees.
The employees were sent telegrams.
Telegrams were sent to the employees.

12e

1. Someone sent the stockholders copies of the takeover bid.
2. Someone handed her a set of instructions.
3. Someone told the boss the whole story of the takeover attempt.
4. Someone gave the reporters the information.
5. Someone paid the chief executive a huge amount of money.

12e. *Been* and *being*

Language learners frequently confuse the forms *been* and *being* in writing, probably because they sound so similar in spoken English and also because *has* and *is* both contract in spoken English to sound like [z]. One way to help you sort out these two forms is to remember the following:

- *Been* is used after forms of *have*.
- *Being* is used after forms of *be*.

EXAMPLES

He has been taken to the hospital. (He's been taken . . .)
He is being examined right now. (He's being examined . . .)

They had never been arrested before.
They were being questioned when the lawyer arrived.

EXERCISE 6

In the following sentences, insert either *been* or *being*.

1. Her computer's _____ repaired right now.

2. It's _____ fixed many times before.

3. New types of computers are constantly _____ developed.

4. The old models should have _____ replaced.

5. While the first computers were _____ made, the world was changing in other ways.

6. Space travel has _____ assisted a great deal by the development of microelectronics.

12f. Participle used to describe a situation

A participle form can be used to describe a situation, not an action. In these cases, no agent is implied, and there is no equivalent active form.

EXAMPLES

The store was closed.
The doors were locked.
The radio is broken.
He is lost.
Mexico City is located in southern Mexico.
Her blouse is made of silk.

For more on participles as adjectives, see Chapter 14, "Adjectives and Noun Modifiers," and Chapter 21, "Participle Forms."

EXERCISE 7

Choose the word or phrase that best completes each sentence.

1. The first digital computer, which _____ in 1946, weighed 30 tons.

   a. built
   b. has been built
   c. was built
   d. was building

2. When computers were first invented, they _____ the amount of calculation that could be done quickly.

   a. increased
   b. were increased
   c. were increasing
   d. had been increased

3. The switch _____ on the back of the machine.

   a. locates
   b. located
   c. is located
   d. is locating

4. He can't start the computer because the disk drive _____

   _____ for the past two weeks.

   a. broken   c. was broken
   b. is broken   d. has been broken

133

5. The information we need for the meeting _____ on a hard disk.

    a. stores
    b. is stored
    c. is storing
    d. had been store

6. The information on that disk can never _____.

    a. be replace
    b. have replaced
    c. being replaced
    d. be replaced

7. The keyboard _____ right now; it should be ready tomorrow.

    a. is fixing
    b. is being fix
    c. is being fixed
    d. is been fix

EDIT

The student who wrote the following piece has used passive verbs in a few places. Which verbs are passive, and which are correctly formed? Edit any forms that are not correctly formed.

Our daily life has been significantly changed by computers. They can be seen all around us, in school, in business, and even in many homes. It seems that there is no field or aspect of life today that has not been affect by this new technology. When we go shopping, do our banking or any other business, or register for courses, the calculations are made by computers. Computers are often involve when we buy a book or order a sweater from a catalog. Children use them now for games and at least are active instead of just watching a TV show.

As this technology develops and progresses, computers will become more and more available to people. This availability is going to make the impact of the computer even more significant in the next ten years. Our lives and our children's lives will definitely be affected. What we don't know is whether the effect will be good or bad.

Shlomo Freiman, Israel

WRITE

Write a paragraph on how the world (and this generation's life) has been changed by computers. You might want to include, for example, information about what skills have been gained (and lost), what work procedures have been replaced, how people are being retrained, what toys are being marketed, what new possibilities are being developed, or how children's leisure activities have been affected.

Don't overuse the passive, but don't avoid it either. After you have written your paragraph, look closely at all your verbs.

EDITING ADVICE

1. If you have problems with the active/passive distinction and with forming passive verbs, begin by underlining all the complete verb phrases you have written.

2. Determine which verb phrases are active (Is the subject the agent, the performer of the action?) and which ones are passive (Is an agent stated or implied? Could you include in the sentence the idea of "by _____"?).

3. Wherever you have used a passive verb, check first to see that it fits the uses outlined in section 12b. Otherwise, consider whether an active form would be more appropriate.

4. Once you are sure that you want and need a passive verb in a particular place, check to see that you have used the correct auxiliaries (see section 12a) and that you have used the participle form of the main verb.

5. Check that you haven't tried to use any intransitive verbs (such as *occur, happen*) in the passive voice.

13 Verb Forms: Summary

READ

Read the following paragraphs from the reading selection "The Effects of Our Environment," which appears with vocabulary glosses on p. 351.

Physical settings, architecture, and interior design affect our communication. [Recall] for a moment the different homes you've visited lately. Were some of these homes more comfortable to be in than others? Certainly a lot of these kinds of feelings are shaped by the people you
5 were with, but there are some houses where it seems impossible to relax, no matter how friendly the hosts. We've spent what seemed like endless evenings in what Mark Knapp calls "unliving rooms," where the spotless ashtrays, furniture coverings, and plastic lamp covers seemed to send nonverbal messages telling us not to touch anything, not to put our feet
10 up, and not to be comfortable. People who live in houses like this probably wonder why nobody ever seems to relax and enjoy themselves at their parties. One thing is quite certain: They don't understand that the environment they have created can communicate discomfort to their guests.

15 There's a large amount of research that shows how the design of an environment can shape the kind of communication that takes place in it. In one experiment at Brandeis University, Maslow and Mintz found that the attractiveness of a room influenced the happiness and energy of people working in it. The experimenters set up three rooms: an "ugly"
20 one, which resembled a janitor's closet in the basement of a campus building; an "average" room, which was a professor's office; and a "beautiful" room, which was furnished with carpeting, drapes, and comfortable furniture. The subjects in the experiment were asked to rate a series of pictures as a way of measuring their energy and feelings of
25 well-being while at work. Results of the experiment showed that while in the ugly room, the subjects became tired and bored more quickly and took longer to complete their task. Subjects who were in the beautiful room, however, rated the faces they were judging more positively, showed a

136

greater desire to work, and expressed feelings of importance, comfort, and
30 enjoyment. The results teach a lesson that isn't surprising: Workers
generally feel better and do a better job when they're in an attractive
environment.

ANALYZE

1. Underline all the complete verb phrases in the passage.

2. Underline each main verb (the verb carrying the meaning of the verb phrase) twice.

3. You'll see that you have underlined phrases like these:

have visited	calls	have communicated
were	seemed	can create
are shaped	don't understand	were judging

From the phrases that you underlined in the reading passage, discuss with other students what you can say about the following:

1. The form of the verb used after *do/does/did*
2. The form of the verb used after modal verbs *(will/would; can/could; shall/should; may/might; must; ought to)*
3. The form of the present tense main verb used with a singular or *he/she/it* subject
4. The form of the present tense main verb used with a plural or *I/you/we/they* subject
5. The form of past tense main verb, both regular and irregular
6. The form of the verb used after *has/have/had*
7. The forms of the verb that are possible after *am/is/are/was/were*

STUDY

13a. Forms of the verb

The box shows the five forms of a verb that are used in complete verb phrases.

FORMS OF THE VERB				
	Simple (no -s)	*-s*	*-ing*	*Past*	*Participle*
Regular	paint	paints	painting	painted	painted
Irregular	sing	sings	singing	sang	sung
	take	takes	taking	took	taken

137

13b

Both *-ing* and participle forms *must* occur with auxiliaries to form a complete verb phrase. In contrast, the *-s* form and the past form always stand alone and are never used with preceding auxiliaries. The simple form can stand alone to form a present tense with a plural or an *I/you/we/they* subject, or it can occur after certain auxiliaries or as part of an infinitive phrase after *to.*

EXAMPLES

They paint.
They may paint.
They like to paint.

We sing.
We can sing.
We want to sing.

Note the irregular forms of *be,* the only verb to have a "no *-s*" form different from the simple form and to show a singular/plural distinction in the past tense.

FORMS OF *BE*					
Simple	*No -s*	*-s*	*-ing*	*Past*	*Participle*
be	am/are	is	being	was/were	been

EXERCISE 1

In the reading passage at the beginning of this chapter, identify all the forms of *be* that occur. In which instances does a form of *be* occur as a main verb, and in which instances does it occur as an auxiliary (with a main verb)? When it is used as an auxiliary, what verb forms follow?

13b. Troublesome verb forms

The verbs in the box titled "Troublesome Verb Forms" on page 139 often cause trouble for students. Work with a partner to determine the meaning of each one. Use a dictionary if you need help.

TROUBLESOME VERB FORMS

Simple (no -s)	-s	-ing	Past	Participle
lie	lies	lying	lied	lied
lie	lies	lying	lay	lain
lay	lays	laying	laid	laid
raise	raises	raising	raised	raised
rise	rises	rising	rose	risen
arise	arises	arising	arose	arisen
arouse	arouses	arousing	aroused	aroused
feel	feels	feeling	felt	felt
fall	falls	falling	fell	fallen

13c. The verb system at a glance

The chart on p. 140 shows the complete verb system of English. If you begin a sentence with the auxiliary or auxiliaries listed in the left-hand column, only the form of the main verb indicated by shading is possible.

Note that the *will* list consists of the following verbs. They all follow the same pattern.

will	may
would	might
can	must
could	ought to
shall	has/have/had to
should	

Whenever *will* begins a sequence in the chart, any of these other verbs may be used in its place, according to meaning. The structure, though, remains the same.

Note that in only *one* instance do you have to make any decisions: after *be* forms, you have to decide whether you need the active or passive voice. Otherwise, the forms you can use are fixed. So this really does constitute a system.

THE VERB SYSTEM

Auxiliary Verbs +	Simple (no -s)	-s	-ing	Past	Participle
Do does/do did					
Will will/would can/could shall/should may/might must/ought to has to/have to/had to					
Have has/have had will have, would have, etc. (+ rest of **will** list)					
Be am/is/are was/were has been/have been had been will be, etc. (+ rest of **will** list) will have been, etc. (+ rest of **will** list)					Passive
Being am/is/are being was/were being					Passive
No Auxiliary	Simple (no -s)	-s	-ing	Past	Participle
1. Past time					
2. *He, she, it* forms as subject, present tense					
3. *I, you, we, they* forms as subject, present tense					

EXERCISE 2

In the following passages from readings in this book, underline each complete verb phrase. Then look at the chart titled "The Verb System" and note where each verb phrase fits on to the chart.

1. I had walked along the river many times since meeting the fisherman that day in winter, but I did not see him again until spring. It was late afternoon, and I had bicycled to a point along the river about a mile downstream from where we had met, hoping to find a deserted spot to draw a picture. I found a niche in the sloping floodwall and started drawing a junk. (p. 348)

2. In the winter of 1888, while Seurat was attracting attention in Paris and Cézanne was working in his seclusion in Aix, a young earnest Dutchman left Paris for southern France. (p. 343)

3. Forty years ago, I was told, the major crop in Lauderdale County was cotton, though a lot of corn and other vegetables were grown as well. A fair amount of livestock was raised, and there was a good lumber industry. Soybeans were attended to only when the cash crops had been taken care of. (p. 340)

4. Many reasons have been put forward for why we never use the living room. Last year, I came to believe that the main reason was the lamps. So I got new lamps. They are much more attractive than the old lamps. Also, they make the room much brighter. . . . It is now even possible to read in the living room. Still, we don't use the living room. Sometimes, in the evening, when we are feeling particularly melancholy about not using the living room, we wander into it and admire the new lamps. (p. 334)

EXERCISE 3

In the passage in Exercise 2, you have underlined all the complete verb phrases. Copy them onto a chart with headings as in the example. Indicate whether each verb phrase belongs to the past or the present-future cluster and whether it is in the active or the passive voice.

EXAMPLE

VERB PHRASE	PAST	PRESENT-FUTURE	ACTIVE	PASSIVE
had walked	√		√	

13c

EXERCISE 4

In the following excerpt from "Artificial Intelligence," which appears with vocabulary glosses on p. 359, fill in each blank with the correct form of the given verb.

There are about three million computers in use in the world now. But not millions or thousands, or even hundreds of them, are _____ (dedicate) to the sophisticated work of artifi-

a
cial intelligence. Though there has _____ (be) much

b
celebration of the coming of the computer revolution, it can hardly be _____ (say) to apply to our current use of these ma-

c
chines: They _____ (do) little beyond arithmetic and

d
alphabetical sorting. . . .

The one tiny academic discipline in which the limits of computers are being _____ (test) is the field of artificial or machine

e
intelligence. Of the hundreds of thousands of computer programmers in the nation, only a few hundred have _____ (devote)

f
themselves to the question of what computers are finally capable of.

EXERCISE 5 (oral)

Work with another student to identify the one underlined word or phrase in the sentence that should be corrected or rewritten. Discuss how it should be corrected or rewritten.

_____ 1. Subjects who <u>were</u> in the beautiful room <u>rated</u> the faces they

 a   b
<u>were judge</u> more positively and <u>showed</u> a greater desire to

 c   d
work. _____

_____ 2. The lamp that <u>is standing</u> in the middle of the room <u>sheds</u>

 a   b
more light than the lamp that <u>was giving</u> to me for

 c
Christmas. _____

_____ 3. The lawyers were surprised when the architect registered the
$\overline{}$
a
plans before his clients had approved the design and even
b
before they had sign the contract. _____
c
_____
d

_____ 4. The builders ordered the materials, cleared the site, and
a   b
began the work, but they didn't remembered to get a permit.
c   d
_____

_____ 5. After a table is occupy by one reader, a new reader
a
will choose a seat on the opposite side especially if that seat
b
is facing a window. _____
c

_____ 6. The people who are sitting at those small tables have
a
probably been sitting there for a while, though some
b
might have move there from where they were sitting before.
c   d
_____

_____

13d. Phrasal verbs

English, particularly spoken English, uses a lot of phrasal verbs: a verb
is used with a preposition or an adverb and takes on a new meaning. Such
verbs are highly idiomatic. The examples that follow show a few of the
complexities of these verbs.

> She *put off* her visit to the doctor. (**Put off takes on the meaning of**
> *postpone.*)
> They *put* the party *off* until April. (Note the word order: some phrasal
> verbs are separable when the direct object is short!)
> They *put* it *off* until April. (A pronoun object will always be inserted
> between the parts of a separable phrasal verb: *not* *They put off it
> until April.)
> The party *was put off* until April. (Transitive phrasal verbs can be
> used in the passive.)

The best way to learn such verbs (and there are many of them) is to watch
out for them carefully in your contact with written and spoken English, to
make a note of them in their context, and to try to use them.

You can use a dictionary to check the meaning of expressions you come across as you read or hear English (*come across* is itself a phrasal verb). Here is one dictionary's entries under *put*. You can see the number and variety of the associated phrasal verbs.

put (po͝ot) *v.* **put, put·ting, puts.**—*tr.* **1.** To place in a specified location; set. **2.** To cause to be in a specified condition: *put one's room in order.* **3.** To cause to undergo something; subject: *put a prisoner to torture.* **4.** To assign; attribute: *put a false interpretation on events.* **5.** To estimate: *He put the time at five o'clock.* **6.** To impose or levy: *put a tax on cigarettes.* **7.** To wager (a stake); bet: *put $10 on a horse.* **8.** To hurl with an overhand pushing motion: *put the shot.* **9.** To bring up for consideration or judgment: *put a question to the judge.* **10.** To express; state: *putting it bluntly.* **11.** To render in a specified language or literary form: *put prose into verse.* **12.** To adapt: *lyrics put to music.* **13.** To urge or force to some action: *put an outlaw to flight.* **14.** To apply: *We must put our minds to it.*—*intr.* **1.** To begin to move, esp. in a hurry. **2.** *Naut.* To proceed: *The ship put into the harbor.*—**phrasal verbs. put about.** *Naut.* To change or cause to change direction; go or cause to go from one tack to another. **put across. 1.** To state so as to be understood clearly or accepted readily. **2.** To attain or carry through by deceit or trickery. **put away. 1.** To renounce; discard: *put all negative thoughts away.* **2.** *Informal.* To consume (food or drink) readily and quickly. **3. a.** *Informal.* To confine to a mental institution. **b.** *Informal.* To kill. **c.** To bury. **put by.** To save for later use: *put by supplies for the winter.* **put down. 1. a.** To write down. **b.** To enter in a list. **2. a.** To bring to an end; repress: *put down a rebellion.* **b.** To render ineffective: *put down rumors.* **3.** *Slang.* To criticize: *put her down for being late.* **b.** To belittle; disparage: *She put down her attempts to ski.* **c.** To humiliate: *The teacher put the student down with a caustic retort.* **4. a.** To assign to a category: *Just put him down as a sneak.* **b.** To attribute: *Let's put this down to experience.* **5.** To consume (food or drink) readily; put away. **put forth. 1.** To grow: *The plant put forth leaves.* **2.** To exert; bring to bear. **3.** To offer for consideration. **put forward.** To propose for consideration: *put forward an idea.* **put in. 1.** To make a formal offer of: *put in a plea of guilty.* **2.** To interpose: *He put in a word for me with the boss.* **3.** To spend (time) at a given location or at a job: *a convict who had put in six years at hard labor; put in eight hours behind a desk.* **4.** To plant: *We put in 20 apple trees.* **5.** *Naut:* To enter a port or harbor: *The freighter puts in at noon.* **6.** To enter a request, application, or order: *put in for a day off.* **put off. 1. a.** To delay; postpone: *put off paying the bills.* **b.** To persuade to wait: *managed to put off the creditors for another week.* **2.** To discard; take off. **3.** To repel or repulse, as from bad manners: *His attitude put us off.* **4.** To pass (money) or sell (merchandise) fraudulently. **put on. 1.** To clothe oneself with; don. **2.** To

apply; activate: *put on the brake.* **3.** To assume affectedly: *put on an English accent.* **4.** *Slang.* To tease or mislead (another): *You're putting me on!* **5.** To add: *put on weight.* **6.** To produce; perform: *put on a variety show.* **put out. 1.** To extinguish: *put out a fire.* **2.** *Naut.* To leave, as a port or harbor; depart. **3.** To expel: *put out a drunk.* **4.** To publish: *put out a book.* **5.** To inconvenience: *Did our early arrival put you out?* **6.** To irritate: *I was put out by his sloppiness.* **7.** *Baseball.* To retire (a runner). **put over. 1.** To postpone; delay. **2.** To put across, esp. to deceive: *put a lie over on me.* **put through. 1.** To bring to a successful end: *put the project through on time.* **2.** To cause to undergo: *He put me through a lot of trouble.* **3. a.** To make a telephone connection for: *She put me through on the office line.* **b.** To obtain a connection for (a telephone call). **puʻ to.** *Naut.* To head for shore. **put together. 1.** To construct; build. **2.** To add; combine. **put up. 1.** To erect; build. **2.** To preserve; can: *put up jam.* **3.** To nominate. **4.** To provide (funds) in advance. **5.** To provide lodgings for: *put someone up for the night.* **6.** To incite to an action: *put the child up to a prank.* **7.** To start (game animals) from cover: *put up grouse.* **8.** To offer for sale: *put up his antiques at auction.* **9. a.** To make a display or the appearance of: *put up a bluff.* **b.** To engage in; carry on: *put up a good fight.* **put upon.** To impose on; overburden: *He was put upon by his friends.*—*n.* **1.** An act of putting the shot. **2.** An option to sell a stipulated amount of stock or securities within a specified time and at a fixed price.—*adj. Informal.* Fixed; stationary: *stay put.* —**Idioms. put down roots.** To establish a permanent residence. **put in mind.** To remind. **put (one's) finger on.** To identify. **put (one's) foot down.** To take a firm stand. **put (one's) foot in (one's) mouth.** To make a tactless remark. **put (one's) house in order.** To organize one's affairs. **put on the dog.** *Slang.* To give oneself airs. **put the arm (or bite) on.** *Slang.* To ask (someone) for money. **put the finger on.** *Slang.* To inform on; snitch on. **put the make on.** *Slang.* To make sexual advances to. **put the screws to (or on).** To pressure (another) in an extreme manner. **put to bed.** To make final preparations for the printing of (a newspaper, for example). **put to it.** To give extreme difficulty to: *was put to it to finish on time.* **put two and two together.** To draw the proper conclusion from given evidence or indications. **put up or shut up.** *Slang.* To endure (something unpleasant) without complaining. **put up to.** To instigate; incite. **put up with.** To endure without complaint: *had to put up with the inconvenience.* [ME putten.]

Source: American Heritage Dictionary, Second College Edition, 1985.

EXERCISE 6

With another student, look up the words *give* and *make* in your dictionary to see how many phrasal verbs are listed. Which ones did you know before, and which ones are new to you? Make a note of any new ones.

☆EXERCISE 7

With a group of students in your class, try to fit the following phrasal verbs into sentences, and discuss what you think the phrasal verbs mean. If you cannot determine the meaning, look them up in a dictionary. (*Look up* is itself a phrasal verb.) The phrasal verbs that are separable are indicated by ellipsis points (. . .) in the middle.

take . . . over	look . . . over	put up with
take . . . off	look after	get along with
take after	look into	get away with
take . . . up	look . . . up	come up with
	look for	catch up with
call . . . off		keep up with
call on	think of	look in on
call . . . up	think . . . over	check up on
	think . . . up	cut down on
pick . . . up		
pick . . . out	turn . . . in	
pick on	turn into	
	turn . . . on/off	
	turn out	

EDIT

The student who wrote this piece made a few errors in verb form. Use the chart in section 13c to help you find and correct them.

The performance of my meals has a lot to do with the way my kitchen is decorated and design.

When I first moved into a place of my own, I found myself in what was suppose to be a kitchen but in my view it was not. I was depress most of the time and my meals were affected by my moods. The steaks were often burnded and my rice looked like soup. I was not concerned with the food as much as with the broken ceiling. There was a big hole over the kitchen sink where the top floor neighbors spilled water every time they washed dishes. Who can look at rice when the wallpaper right in front of the stove look like glue from all the past grease mixed with the orange color of the paper?

So I said that if the kitchen was not fix, I would not cooked another meal there. That worked. The kitchen has been redecorated, and since

145

then my mood, attitude, and performance have change. If that hadn't happen, I might never have cook again!

Milagros Valle, Puerto Rico

WRITE

Discuss the following topic with other students: "In what ways do you think that physical settings, architecture, and interior design affect our feelings and our communication?" Make notes of ideas and examples that other students provide. Organize your notes, and make a rough plan for an essay. Then write an essay in which you express your own point of view, and support it with evidence from events you have experienced or heard or read about. Try to write one paragraph for each piece of evidence you present, and develop each paragraph with specific examples.

EDITING ADVICE	1. Underline every complete verb phrase you have used. Underline the main verb twice.

2. Look at each complete verb phrase, and find its corresponding place on the chart in section 13c. If you have written something like this:

   *He would had chose something different.

   you will look at *would* in the chart, and you will see that it is always followed by a simple form. *Had* is not the simple form. Once you have corrected that to *would have,* you will look to see what form of the verb follows *would have*. There is only one option: the participle. Check the participle form of *choose* in Appendix A—you will find *chosen*. So you will correct your verb form to *would have chosen*.

3. If your verb phrase consists only of the main verb (simple present or simple past), check the past form of irregular verbs in the Appendix, or if you have used a present tense, check that the verb agrees with its subject. That is, ask yourself, Does the verb need an *-s* ending or not?

Modifiers

14 Adjectives and Noun Modifiers

READ

Read this passage from "Artificial Intelligence" by Philip J. Hilts. The complete reading, with vocabulary glosses, appears on p. 359.

On a <u>hot</u> June afternoon I met the lab's director, John McCarthy. I had driven up from the main campus of Stanford University to his outpost in the hills. He was <u>late</u>, so I waited in his office. It was the head of a <u>long</u> snake of a building which sat coiled on the hot hilltop. Two walls
5   of the office were glass, and through them I could see the hills outside, which were the color of straw. The short, yellow bristles of grass made the hills look like the scalp of a marine recruit. With the wiry dark hair of bushes and trees shaved off, the bumps and scars of contour were <u>visible</u>. The few trees out the window were eucalyptus, and they look dusty and
10   dry as fence posts.

John McCarthy's appearance, when he finally strode into the office, struck me as extraordinary. He is about average height, five feet nine inches. His build is average, with a little age trying to collect itself around his middle. But his hair encircles his head and his face with a
15   great cloud of silver needles. Amid this prickly gray mist his eyes are two dark rocks.

ANALYZE

1. Some words in the passage have been underlined. Underline other words that serve a similar function. Do not underline determiners: articles, demonstratives, possessives, numerals, or quantity words.

2. The underlined words are adjectives, words that modify (give more details about) noun phrases. If you look closely at the adjectives in the passage, you will probably see that some come before the noun phrase they describe and others come after a linking verb like *be, look, see, appear,* or *feel.* Make a list of each type.

EXAMPLE

BEFORE NOUN PHRASE   **AFTER LINKING VERB**
<u>hot</u> <u>June</u> afternoon   he was <u>late</u>

3. Think of a way to rewrite the sentence "through them I could see the hills outside, which were the color of straw" according to this pattern: "I could see the _____ hills outside."

STUDY

14a. Form and position of adjectives

Note the following three features of adjectives.

1. *No plural form.* English differs from some other languages in that adjectives do not agree with nouns; so adjectives do not add plural endings:

> **a dark rock**
> **some dark rocks**
> *Not*   *some darks rocks

2. *Occasional -ly ending.* Although *-ly* is usually an adverb ending, a few adjectives end in *-ly:*

> **friendly**
> **lovely**
> **lively**

3. *Position before nouns or after linking verbs.* Some adjectives can occur either before a noun or after a verb, usually a linking verb such as *be, seem, look,* or *feel:*

> Her *happy* face . . .
> She is *happy.*
> He feels *happy.*

A few adjectives, however, are limited to one or the other position and function. The most frequently used ones are these:

ONLY BEFORE A NOUN   **ONLY AFTER A VERB**
her *main* ambition   She is *awake.*
a *medical* doctor   She fell *asleep.*
   He is *alone.*

EXERCISE 1

In the reading passage, did you find more adjectives occurring before a noun or after a linking verb? What can you infer about the frequency of occurrence of these types? Did you find any adjectives ending in *-ly?*

EXERCISE 2

The cartoon called "Roget's Brontosaurus" (with its word play on the words *thesaurus* and *brontosaurus*) shows a lot of adjectives that express variations on the idea of *big.* What adjectives might appear in a similar cartoon about a fictional creature called an *ant-osaurus?* (You can use a dictionary or *Roget's Thesaurus* to find synonyms.) What adjectives might occur to an animal renowned for its speed, say, a jaguar? Or one renowned for its slowness, such as a tortoise?

ROGET'S BRONTOSAURUS

EXERCISE 3 (oral)

Using adjectives in your writing gives you a way of adding details, of painting a fuller picture with your words. For example, the sentence "Margaret flung herself down on the bed" gives us only the outline of the action. The addition of an adjective adds another perspective: "Margaret flung herself down on the unmade bed." Now the reader wants to know why the bed is unmade, what that tells us about Margaret, and so on.

In van Gogh's picture of his room in Arles on p. 6, he shows us a bed, a table, two chairs, and not much else. Discuss with other students what adjectives you can use to describe each of the items you can see in the picture so that a listener or reader would know more about what kind of bed, table, chairs, and other objects van Gogh had. What color, for instance, do you think each item is? What else can you tell your audience about it, so that people who cannot see the picture get an accurate impression? Make a list, and compare your list with other students' lists.

14b. Nouns used to modify nouns

Nouns can be used to modify other nouns, functioning like adjectives, and like adjectives, they add no plural endings. In the reading passage at the beginning of this chapter, the following occurred:

> a June afternoon
> fence posts (posts used for fences)

OTHER EXAMPLES

coffee shop   kitchen floor
college students   evening gown
course requirements   file cabinet
hair spray

Even when the sense of the noun modifier is plural (a cabinet for *files:* posts used in *fences;* requirements for the college *courses*), the noun modifier remains singular: *file cabinet, fence posts, course requirements*. But when a noun occurs only in the plural form, it retains that plural form when it is used as a modifier, as in *clothes closet*.

☆EXERCISE 4

The American novelist Edith Wharton reported fellow novelist Henry James (1843–1916) as saying, "Summer afternoon—summer

151

afternoon; to me those have always been the two most beautiful words in the English language." Write five phrases, consisting of modifier + noun or noun + noun, that for you are evocative of pleasure and beauty.

EXERCISE 5 (oral)

Convert each of the following expressions into a noun phrase with a noun as modifier. It is not appropriate to use a possessive form (with an apostrophe) for the name of a building, an object, or a piece of furniture (see also Chapter 29, "Punctuation").

EXAMPLE

the handle of the door
        the door handle
  Not **the door's handle*

1. the top of the table
2. the wipers for the windshield
3. the locks on the doors   *the door locks*
4. (a) cart for shopping
5. a box for jewelry
6. a jar for cookies
7. a case for pencils
8. a purse for change
9. a bed of flowers
10. a book on economics
11. the peel of oranges
12. a tray for desserts

14c. Compound adjectives

In the readings in this book, the following forms occur:

a two-drawer file cabinet
hand-held computers

The hyphen is necessary to connect the adjective parts into one unit of description. Note the use of singular forms in the transformations:

She gave me five dollars.
She gave me (a) five-dollar <u>bill</u>.

Her son is six years old.
She has (a) six-year-old son.

She is reading a novel written in the nineteenth century.
She is reading a nineteenth-century novel.

He always looks good.
He is a good-looking man.

The boxing champion hits hard and often wins.
The hard-hitting boxing champion often wins.

And with physical description, note the form derived from a noun + *-ed:*

He plays tennis with his left hand.
He is a left-handed tennis player.

Here are some common compound adjectives using the *-ed* form:

broad-shouldered, narrow-shouldered
bow-legged
dark-haired, fair-haired
empty-headed
level-headed
flat-chested
mean-spirited

Add to this list as you find more.

EXERCISE 6

Rewrite the following sentences by making a compound adjective out of each underlined phrase.

1. He made a request <u>at the last minute</u>.
2. She has a daughter <u>with blue eyes</u> and <u>fair hair</u>.
3. There will be a delay <u>of twenty minutes</u>.
4. She wrote a report <u>of ten pages</u>.
5. They want to hire a secretary <u>who works hard</u>.
6. They bought a house <u>that is sixty years old</u>.
7. She has a cat <u>with three legs</u>.
8. He provided a meal <u>that was cooked well</u>.
9. They bought a car <u>at a high price</u>.
10. We needed a rope <u>that was ten feet long</u> to get the cat out of the tree.

14d. Adjectives formed from the *-ing* form or the participle *(-ed/-en)* form

Adjectives can be formed from the participle form of verbs:

a *locked* door
a *stamped, addressed* envelope
specialized goods and services

153

Adjectives can also be formed from the *-ing* form of verbs:

> a *fluttering* insect
> her *trembling* hand
> a *charming* restaurant

Language learners sometimes have difficulty choosing between an adjective formed from the participle and an adjective formed from the *-ing* form, particularly with adjectives expressing emotion, such as *exciting/excited, surprising/surprised*. The participle form expresses the idea that the noun it modifies is *acted on* rather than acting; it has a passive meaning.

> **The game was exciting.**
> **I was excited (by the game).**
> **They could see from my excited face that I was enjoying the game.**

Section 21b in Chapter 21, "Participle Forms," gives more explanations, examples, and exercises.

EXERCISE 7

Complete each of the following sentences with the adjective formed from the *-ing* form or the participle of the given verb.

ed/en

1. Artificial intelligence is something that is quite ___*puzzling*___

   _____ (puzzle) to me.

2. I am ___*puzzled*___ (puzzle) whenever I read about artificial

   intelligence.

3. Many people would be ___*excited*___ (excite) by the idea of

   having a robot to do the housework.

4. Robots could, however, be ___*frightening*___ (frighten) to little

   children at first.

5. I think I would find it ___*annoying*___ (annoy) to have a robot

   moving around my living room.

6. Future research on robotics could provide ___*exciting*___ (ex-

   cite) new developments in automation.

14e. Position of adjectives in a series

Adjectives in a series tend to occur in a certain order, though there may be many exceptions. As a rule, avoid long strings of adjectives. Two or, at the most, three adjectives modifying one noun phrase seem to be the limit in English.

The accompanying box shows an acceptable scheme of adjective order. You will find exceptions, but you can use this framework for guidance in your own writing. You can choose to use a comma between two adjectives only if the adjectives belong to the same category. If you want to use a comma, test to see if you could use the word *and* between adjectives. If you can, a comma would be acceptable.

the short, yellow bristles of grass (two adjectives of physical description)

a delicious, expensive French meal (no comma between *expensive* and *French*)

When three adjectives of the same category are used in a series with *and,* use commas between the items in the series:

a messy, dirty, and depressing room

But *never* use a comma between the last adjective and the noun it modifies.

ORDER OF ADJECTIVES

Determiner	Observation	Physical Description				Origin	Material	Qualifier	Head Noun
		Size	Shape	Age	Color				
four	lovely			old					trees
her			short		black		silk	business	suit
some	delicious, inexpensive					Chinese			food
our		big		old		English	oak	dining	table
that	comfortable	little				Mexican		rocking	chair
several		little	round				ivory		beads
	beautiful		broad		white	San Francisco			clouds
		big			blue	Golden Gate			ocean

EXERCISE 8

In these noun phrases, taken from the readings in this book, determine which category in the box each word belongs to. Which ones follow the order portrayed in the box and which ones do not?

EXAMPLE

long wooden table
long: physical description (shape)
wooden: material

qualifier

minute electronic packages	empty rectangular tables
plastic lamp covers	bare cement floor
subdued noise levels	big, black bicycle
absorbent building materials	

☆*EXERCISE 9*

Philip J. Hilts, in the excerpt at the beginning of this chapter, describes John McCarthy and uses metaphoric language to compare his hair to "silver needles" and "prickly gray mist" and his eyes to "two dark rocks." Look around your classroom, and write three sentences of description of three different people (students or instructor). Use metaphor to help you describe the person's appearance. Call the person X. Then show your sentences to another student, who will try to figure out which three people you chose.

14f. Adjectives + prepositions

Certain adjectives are often used with prepositions when they occur after a linking verb.

EXAMPLE

The man is proud of his achievements.

The following list contains some of the commonly used adjective + preposition combinations. You will come across many more. Remember to use your dictionary to check which preposition is commonly used with an adjective. At the same time, add to this list as you encounter more examples in your reading.

proud of	happy about	superior to
guilty of	nervous about	inferior to
tired of	anxious about	friendly to
envious of		
jealous of	different from	content with
afraid of	safe from	familiar with
capable of	sorry for	dependent on
fond of	suitable for	
full of	eager for	
aware of		

Some of the adjectives that can be used with more than one preposition are listed next. As you read and find others, make a note of them, and learn them in their context.

kind (unkind) of: It was *unkind of* you to ignore him.
kind (unkind) to: Why were you so *unkind* to your cousin?
good at: He is *good at* tennis.
good to: She is *good to* her neighbor's children.
good for: Eat your spinach. It is *good for* you.
angry about: He is *angry about* his new work schedule.
angry with/at: He is *angry at/with* his boss.
grateful to . . . for: I am *grateful to* you *for* helping me.

EXERCISE 10 (oral)

Write five questions that you could ask another student in your class. Use the adjective + preposition combinations listed in section 14f. Work with a partner; ask each other your questions, and answer them.

14g. Adjectives introducing reduced clauses

An adjective can be used to introduce a reduced clause.

EXAMPLE

The person responsible for the research is Dr. McCarthy. (The person who is responsible for the research is Dr. McCarthy.)

Proud of his daughter, he decided to buy her a car. (Because he was proud of his daughter . . .)

A fuller discussion can be found in Chapter 24, "Adjectival Clauses."

EXERCISE 11

Rewrite each of the following sentences using a reduced clause in place of the underlined clause and making other changes as needed.

1. The data that were stolen from the computer lab were being used in a medical experiment.
2. The footprints that were found in the dust gave the police a clue.
3. They collected new data that would be suitable for use in the experiment.
4. The only door that was open was the metal security door.
5. The only person who seemed agile enough to climb over the fence was the chief engineer.

6. The young police detective, <u>who was eager for promotion</u>, asked to take over the case.
7. <u>Because the detective was dissatisfied with the evidence</u>, he recalled the two key witnesses.
8. <u>Since the witnesses were called to the witness stand</u>, they had to testify.

EDIT

The following piece of student writing describes a person and her workplace. Underline any noun phrases with adjective modifiers. Are they all formed and used correctly? Change any that are not.

Ketly is a beautiful young Haitian woman who is working as a bilingual secretary. She is about 5′4″ tall. She has smooth, light skin. Her face is oval, and she has big black eyes dominating a small nose and charming little mouth. Her curly dark hair is arranged in an attractive, tidy style.

Ketly's office is really very small; however, it has just enough space to hold the necessary furniture and her personal belongings. The office is painted pale beige; there are three ivory large wall cabinets where she keeps all the important office supplies. Right near the cabinets there is a dark sturdy wood table holding an old large gray Smith Corona typewriter. On one side, you will see a paper clips box, a gray telephone, and a small file box containing doctors' and patients' phone numbers and addresses. On the other, there is a small candies box full of Italian delicious chocolates.

Patria Rojas, Dominican Republic

WRITE

The reading passage on p. 359 by Philip J. Hilts tells us about a famous scientist and introduces him by showing us where he works and what he looks like. That is, Hilts gives us the human side of the man as well as the scientific, professional side. Write about a person you know who is good in his or her chosen line of work, and tell how that person feels about the job. Describe what the work entails, but first give the reader details about what the person looks like and what the workplace looks like.

1. Read through your piece of writing. As you read, ask yourself "What kind of . . . ?" with every noun phrase you have used. Are there any places where you think the reader would get a fuller picture if you added details? Would adjectives be appropriate?

2. Adjectives like *nice, good, bad, pretty, big,* and *little* are used in so many situations that they don't give a reader a very clear or detailed picture. Try to use adjectives that specify what you mean more exactly. Use your dictionary or a thesaurus for synonyms.

3. Check the following:

   • That there is no plural *-s* ending on an adjective
   • That adjectives of nationality have a capital letter
   • That a series of adjectives occurs in an appropriate order (see the box in section 14e)
   • That *-ing* adjectives are used in active contexts and *-ed/-en* adjectives are used in passive contexts

15 Adverbs and Frequency Adverbs

READ

Read the following passage from "The Culture of 'Lead Time,'" excerpted from *The Silent Language,* by Edward Hall, which appears with vocabulary glosses on p. 361.

> Advance notice is often referred to in America as "lead time," an expression which is significant in a culture where schedules are important. While it is learned informally, most of us are familiar with how it works in our own culture, even though we cannot state the rules
> 5   technically. The rules for lead time in other cultures, however, have rarely been analyzed. At the most they are known by experience to those who lived abroad for some time. Yet think how important it is to know how much time is required to prepare people, or for them to prepare themselves, for things to come. Sometimes lead time would seem to be
> 10 very extended. At other times, in the Middle East, any period longer than a week may be too long.

ANALYZE

1. In the passage, underline all words ending in *-ly.*

2. One of the *-ly* words is *rarely.* Which other words are there in the passage, not ending in *-ly,* that tell us how frequently something occurs? What is their position in the sentence?

3. What inferences can you make about the position in a sentence of words that give information about *how* and *how often* things occur?

STUDY

15a. Form and meaning of adverbs

Adverbs give information about verb phrases. They usually answer questions like *how? how often? when? where?* and *why?* They are usually

160

different from the adjective form. The regular form has *-ly* added to the adjective, but there are also irregular forms.

ADJECTIVE AND ADVERB FORMS

	Adjective	*Adverb*
Regular	informal	informally
	technical	technically
	careful	carefully
	sincere	sincerely
	precise	precisely
	gentle	gently
	comfortable	comfortably
	tight	tightly
	coy	coyly
	lucky	luckily
Irregular	good	well
	fast	fast
	hard	hard

Hardly is unrelated to *hard*. It has a negative connotation. (I'd hardly describe that vase as beautiful! = I wouldn't describe that vase as beautiful.) It is often used in the phrase *hardly ever*. Do not mix it up with *hard*.

EXAMPLES

She works hard.
He hardly works at all!
He hardly ever (almost never) arrives on time.

Note that some adverbs are not derived from an adjective form. A few examples are *often, there, here, early, late,* and *yesterday.*

EXERCISE 1

From the examples in the box in section 15a, what spelling rules can you infer for the following situations?

1. Adding *-ly* to an adjective that ends in - *al*
2. Adding *-ly* to an adjective that ends in silent *-e*
3. Adding *-ly* to an adjective that ends in *-le*
4. Adding *-ly* to two-syllable adjectives that end in *-y*

15b. Position of adverbs and adverbial phrases

There are certain conventions associated with the position of adverbial phrases of time, manner, location, and direction in a sentence. The sentences in the box illustrate the conventions. Note that time adverbials generally occur at the beginning of the sentence or at the end, last in a series of adverbial expressions.

POSITION OF ADVERBS	
Example	*Principle*
She worked quickly.	Adverbial expression at end of sentence.
She did her work very quickly. (*Not* *She did very quickly her work.)	Adverbial expression never separates verb from object.
Yesterday, she ran fast in the marathon.	Time, manner, location
She ran fast in the marathon yesterday.	Manner, location, time
She ran home quickly.	Direction, manner
She ran home quickly yesterday.	Direction, manner, time

EXERCISE 2 (oral)

Put each set of sentence parts into an acceptable order.

1. arrive / punctually / the students / every day
2. make / quickly / every day / breakfast / her teenage daughters
3. yesterday afternoon / the architect / to his office / didn't go
4. in the library / works / she / every day
5. her father / to the beach / she / last weekend / drove
6. next month / they / to Mexico / are planning to go

15c. Adverbs modifying specific constructions in a sentence

Adverbs can be used to modify not only verbs but also adjectives or other constructions. They are positioned immediately before the construction they modify:

She is extremely rich.
He was badly hurt.
They bought a beautifully shaped vase.
That is exactly the car I want!

162

This is precisely the way the minister registered the protestations!
He almost missed the meeting.

EXERCISE 3 (oral)

The following example has been used in language-teaching class-
rooms for many years. The scene is a bus that has been in an accident. In
which positions in the following sentence could you place the word *only* as
an adjective or an adverb?

The passenger hurt his arm.

What does the sentence tell us in each case about the nature and extent
of the injuries, the number of people on the bus, or the characteristics of
the people on the bus? Discuss this with other students. Five different
meanings are possible for the six positions within the sentence.

1. ___*Only*___ the passenger hurt his arm.

2. The ___*Only*___ passenger hurt his arm. *driver*

3. The passenger ___*only*___ hurt his arm.

4. The passenger hurt ___*only*___ his arm.

5. The passenger hurt his ___*only*___ arm.

6. The passenger hurt his arm ___*only*___ .

EXERCISE 4

Place *even* in various positions in the following sentences (but not at
the end) to change the meaning of the sentence. Some instructors and
editors do not like to split infinitives, so if you can, avoid putting an
adverb between *to* and the simple form.

1. Margaret *even* offered to clean the oven.
2. The boss worked *even* on the weekend.
3. During the lesson, *even* Jack didn't ask a question. *even one question.*

15d. Very, too, enough

Very, too, and *enough* modify adjectives or other adverbs.

Very and *too* occur before the word they modify, but their meanings are
different. *Very* is an intensifier:

163

15d

- *Very* + adjective

  They are very poor. (= extremely poor)

- *Very* + adverb

  He walks very quickly.

Too, by contrast, implies excess:

- *Too* + adjective

  The suit was too expensive (= excessively expensive, so expensive that it was impossible for him to buy it)
  She eats too much.

- *Too* + adverb *or* adjective + infinitive (*to* + verb)

  They are too poor to go away on vacation.
  He walks too quickly for me to keep up with him.
  It is too hot to play tennis.

Enough means "sufficient or sufficiently." It can modify adjectives, adverbs, or nouns. With adjectives and adverbs, it follows the word it modifies. It is often followed by an infinitive or *for* . . . + infinitive:

She is well enough to leave the hospital. (She is sufficiently well.)
That apartment is big enough for us to live in.
She swims well enough to be on her school team.

When *enough* modifies a noun, it frequently precedes the noun:

They had enough time to write the essay. (They had sufficient time.)

EXERCISE 5

Write sentences using the following expressions. Relate your sentences to the idea of people's attitudes toward time.

EXAMPLE

too unpunctual   The mail carrier was too unpunctual to be promoted.

1. very punctual	4. too early
2. too late	5. very annoyed
3. early enough	6. too annoyed

164

7. annoyed enough   9. reliable enough

8. very reliable   10. too unreliable

15e. Adverbs of frequency in middle positions

Adverbial phrases of frequency can sometimes occur at the beginning of a clause, as in this sentence from the reading at the beginning of the chapter:

Sometimes lead time would seem to be very extended.

More often, though, adverbs of frequency occur in fixed order in a sentence relative to the verb phrase. The box shows the positions in the sentence.

POSITION OF FREQUENCY WORDS						
	Subject	*First Auxiliary*	*Frequency Word*	*Other Auxiliaries*	*Main Verb*	*Rest of Sentence*
After *be*	Their boss	is	always			late.
Before main verb	Their boss		always		arrives	late.
After first auxiliary	Their boss	has	never	been	reprimanded.	

Frequency words maintain their position in questions if the first auxiliary has been moved:

Has their boss ever arrived early?
Does their boss always arrive late?
Is their boss always late?

Note that *ever* is used in a question.
The frequency adverbs that follow this pattern are listed here according to meaning, from least frequent to most frequent:

NEGATIVE	POSITIVE
never (0 percent of the time)	occasionally
almost never	sometimes
rarely	generally
scarcely ever	frequently
hardly ever	often
seldom	usually
	almost always
	always (100 percent of the time)

Note the *-s* ending on *sometimes* and *always*. This ending does not affect any *-s* ending you might need to add to a verb:

He always wants to leave early.

Note, too, that there is a difference between the frequency word *sometimes,* with its meaning of *occasionally,* and the expression *some time:*

I will call you some time.
At some time in the future, I want to go to China.
She sometimes (occasionally) arrives late.

EXERCISE 6

The following sentences are from the readings. In each, the author used a frequency word. Insert the given frequency word in an appropriate position.

1. The rules have been analyzed. (rarely)
2. Lying of this sort is given the approving label of "tact." (often)
3. A face-saving lie prevents embarrassment for the recipient. (sometimes)
4. Do you tell the truth? (always)
5. The computer displays are more than a single short line in length. (rarely)
6. Workers feel better and do a better job when they're in an attractive environment. (generally)
7. Tenants have more contacts with immediate neighbors than with people even a few doors away. (generally)
8. While the library was uncrowded, students chose corner seats at one of the empty rectangular tables. (almost always)

15f. Adverbs of frequency in other positions: beginning and end

The position in the middle of the sentence is the most common one for frequency words. However, some may occur at the beginning and some at the end of a sentence. The following positive frequency words can occur at the beginning of a sentence:

occasionally
sometimes
frequently
usually
generally

EXAMPLES

Sometimes lead time would seem to be extended.
Occasionally culture interferes with business.

The following positive frequency words can occur at the end of the sentence:

occasionally
sometimes
often
frequently

EXAMPLES

He keeps people waiting often.
He types his own letters occasionally.

When you read, you might find negative frequency words occurring at the beginning of a sentence in order to give emphasis. When the negative frequency words occur at the beginning of a sentence, subject and auxiliary are inverted. Inversion conveys astonishment; it is quite formal and stylized. Don't try to use this structure unless you feel a real need to do so.

INVERSION WITH FREQUENCY WORDS			
Frequency Word	*First Auxiliary*	*Subject*	*Rest of Sentence*
Never	have	I	heard such a terrible story!
Rarely	would	anyone	believe such a story!

☆*EXERCISE 7*

Write sentences about customs in your country, things that happen usually, often, rarely, and so on. Use the following adverbs, and for each sentence that you write, write another version with the adverb in a different (but appropriate) position in the sentence.

frequently   occasionally
seldom   generally
usually   never

15g. Time adverbs and verb tense

Certain adverbs of time are regularly associated with specific verb tenses. Those adverbs are *just, already, soon, yet, still,* and *not . . . anymore.*

15g

With *just, already,* and *yet,* British English uses the present perfect:

Have you finished the project yet?
She has already moved on to the next report.

American English sometimes uses the simple past:

Did you finish the project yet?
She already moved on to the next report.

Soon is used with verb tenses indicating future time:

She'll arrive soon.
She'll be arriving soon.
She is going to write the report next week.

Still and *not . . . anymore* are used with present tenses, basic or continuous:

She is still trying to finish on time.
She is not working there anymore.
She doesn't work there anymore.

EXERCISE 8

Identify the one underlined word or phrase that should be corrected or rewritten. How should it be changed?

_____ 1. Hui Ping, an <u>excellent</u> student who <u>almost</u> won a scholarship,
         $\quad\quad$ a $\quad\quad\quad\quad\quad\quad$ b
         has <u>always</u> worked <u>very hardly</u>. _____
         $\quad\quad$ c $\quad\quad\quad\quad\quad$ d

_____ 2. She <u>sometime</u> sits in the <u>drafty</u> old library for an <u>incredible</u>
         $\quad\quad\quad$ a $\quad\quad\quad\quad\quad$ b $\quad\quad\quad\quad\quad\quad\quad$ c
         amount of time, working <u>steadily</u> on her assignments. _____
         $\quad\quad\quad\quad\quad\quad\quad\quad\quad\quad$ d

_____ 3. She arrives <u>never</u> late at her job; she works in a <u>busy</u>
         $\quad\quad\quad\quad\quad\quad$ a $\quad\quad\quad\quad\quad\quad\quad\quad\quad\quad\quad\quad$ b
         <u>Chinese</u> restaurant that is run by her <u>twenty-year-old</u>
         $\quad$ c $\quad\quad\quad\quad\quad\quad\quad\quad\quad\quad\quad\quad\quad\quad\quad$ d
         brother. _____

_____ 4. He expects all his staff to do <u>satisfactory</u> work: he wants them
         $\quad\quad\quad\quad\quad\quad\quad\quad\quad\quad$ a
         to work <u>hard</u> and <u>quick</u> and to be as <u>polite</u> as possible. _____
         $\quad\quad\quad$ b $\quad\quad\quad$ c $\quad\quad\quad\quad\quad$ d

168

_____ 5. If they do very efficiently their work, they'll get a
           a
substantial bonus at the end of the year. _____
   b   c

_____

_____ 6. The boss is an efficient, health man, who plans extremely
                          a   b   c
carefully for any emergency. _____
   d

_____

_____ 7. Hui Ping arrives usually early and sets each table carefully
                           a   b   c
with sparkling blue Chinese plates. _____
   d

_____

_____

EDIT

The following sentences are from students' essays. They contain errors in
the use of adverbs. Identify and fix the errors.

1. I always had been very protected throughout my life.
2. When I saw all the blood, I told myself that I never could become a
   nurse.
3. I have two brothers; always we play together.
4. We bought usually ice cream every day in the park.
5. She was being successfully in her new job.
6. Siblings should always be responsible and independently.
7. I got sick easy so I went often to the hospital.
8. My sister is at the University of Thessaloniki, and she is doing pretty
   good.
9. She acted always like a small adult. She seldom played with us.
10. I liked that job because the people who worked there were very nice
    to me and always were helpful and understanding.

WRITE

Discuss with other students how people in your country regard time. How
much lead time would be acceptable for arriving at a job interview, a dinner
party, a get-together of a group of friends, a business meeting, a birthday
party, and other events? For example, if people were invited to a party (or to
dinner) at 8 P.M., what time would you expect them to arrive? How are daily

15

schedules handled in your country? At what point do people get annoyed when they think someone is late? Have you noticed differences in the way people handle time in two different countries or regions of a country?

As you listen to other students discuss this, makes notes about the features of other countries. Then write two paragraphs about the way different cultures handle lead time. In one paragraph, write about your own country. In the other, write what you know or have just learned about other countries. Then add a short paragraph at the beginning that introduces the idea of lead time and prepares your reader to read about differences.

Use adverbs of time, location, and manner to provide details for your reader; in addition, use a few adverbs of frequency so that your readers will know how often a particular activity occurs.

EDITING ADVICE	1. Read your piece of writing through, and underline all adverbs and adverbial phrases. Check the position of the adverbs according to the guidelines in sections 15b and 15c.
	2. If you have used a frequency word, note its position in the sentence, and check to see if that fits with the advice given in sections 15e and 15f.
	3. Check the spelling of each adverb: remember the *-s* on *always* and *sometimes,* and check in your dictionary if you have any doubts about the adverb as distinct from the adjective form.

170

Comparisons

16

READ

Read the following excerpt from "Sizing Up Human Intelligence" by Stephen Jay Gould, which appears with vocabulary glosses on p. 363.

The range of cell size among organisms is incomparably smaller than the range in body size. Small animals simply have far fewer cells than large animals. The human brain contains several billion neurons; an ant is constrained by its small size to have many hundreds of times fewer

5   neurons. . . .

Our skills and behavior are finely attuned to our size. We could not be twice as tall as we are, for the kinetic energy of a fall would then be 16 to 32 times as great, and our sheer weight (increased eightfold) would be more than our legs could support. Human giants of eight to nine feet have

10   either died young or been crippled early by failure of joints and bones. At half our size, we could not wield a club with sufficient force to hunt large animals (for kinetic energy would decrease 16 to 32-fold); we could not impart sufficient momentum to spears and arrows; we could not cut or split wood with primitive tools or mine minerals with picks and chisels.

15   Since all these were essential activities in our historical development, we must conclude that the path of evolution could only have been followed by a creature very close to our own size. I do not argue that we inhabit the best of all possible worlds, only that our size has limited our activities and, to a great extent, shaped our evolution.

ANALYZE

1. Underline any parts of the reading where the writer makes a comparison involving two people, things, or concepts or compares three or more and makes an evaluation.

2. Write down what you notice about the form used for comparison and any associated words or structures.

3. In the first two sentences, the forms *small* and *smaller* occur. What other form is derived from *small* to compare more than two people or things?

STUDY

16a. Forms for comparison of adjectives and adverbs

When adjectives and adverbs are used to make comparisons, they follow certain patterns. To compare two people, things, concepts, or actions, the comparative form is used. To compare three or more, the superlative form with *the* is used.

COMPARISON OF ADJECTIVES AND ADVERBS		
Adjective or Adverb	*Comparative*	*Superlative*
ONE-SYLLABLE ADJECTIVE OR ADVERB		
small	smaller	(the) smallest
big	bigger	(the) biggest
fast	faster	(the) fastest
ADJECTIVE ENDING IN -Y OR -LE		
busy	busier	(the) busiest
simple	simpler	(the) simplest
ADVERB WITH -LY		
slowly	more slowly	(the) most slowly
ADJECTIVE WITH TWO OR MORE SYLLABLES		
famous	more famous	(the) most famous
comfortable	more comfortable	(the) most comfortable
ALTERNATIVES WITH TWO-SYLLABLE ADJECTIVES[†]		
clever	cleverer	(the) cleverest
	more clever	(the) most clever
polite	politer	(the) politest
	more polite	(the) most polite

[†]If you can't decide between the *-er, -est* form and the *more, most* form, it is always safer to use the *more* and *most* forms. They will be more generally acceptable.

Note that the word *than* is frequently used with comparatives. Even when it is not stated, it is implied:

. . . **many hundreds of times fewer neurons [than a human being has]**

16b. Irregular forms

Note the following irregular forms.

IRREGULAR FORMS OF COMPARISON		
Adjective or Adverb	*Comparative*	*Superlative*
good (adj.) well (adv.)	better	(the) best
bad (adj.) badly (adv.)	worse	(the) worst
far	farther further	(the) farthest (the) furthest
much many a lot	more	(the) most
(a) little	less	(the) least
(a) few	fewer	(the) fewest

Language learners often find the distinction between *worse* and *worst* tricky, probably because the two sound very similar in conversation. Remember to check the forms when you write.

Spelling tip: Note that one-syllable adjectives ending in a vowel + consonant double the final consonant before adding *-er* and *-est:*

big bigger biggest
hot hotter hottest

EXERCISE 1

The following sentences are based on the readings. Work with another student to insert an appropriate comparative or superlative form of the given adjective or adverb.

1. In the Middle East, any period _____ _longer_ _____ (long) than a week may be too long.

2. If you value good grades _____ _more_ _____ (a lot) than a good time, you may choose the book.

3. If society chooses to increase its population, there will be _____ _less_ _____ (little) space and _____ _fewer_ _____ (few) resources for each person.

4. According to the survey, the _____ _more frequent_ _____ (frequent) motive for lying was to save face.

5. Scientists and engineers worked to make the 30-ton computer _____ _better_ _____ (good).

6. The use of transistors as small amplifiers in place of the large vacuum tubes reduced the size and cost of computers. _____ _smaller_ _____ (small) was _____ _better_ _____ (good).

✓ 7. In the _____ _smaller_ _____ (small) of the portable computers, the cathode ray tube has been replaced by a flat electroluminescent display.

8. The state stores sold a _____ _cheaper_ _____ (cheap), _____ _more tasty_ _____ (tasty) version of doufu.

9. The soybean was found to have an even _____ _higher_ _____ _____ (high) protein content than lean beef.

10. Truthful information helps patients cope with illness: helps them tolerate pain _____ _better_ _____ (well), need _____ _less_ _____ (little) medication, and even recover _____ _faster_ _____ (fast) after surgery.

16c. Comparative structures

Note the following structures used to express comparison. Both sentences in the pairs are acceptable, with almost no difference in meaning. The choice you make is thus a stylistic one.

Tyson is heavier than Spinks.
Tyson is heavier than Spinks is.

Tyson weighs more than Spinks.
Tyson weighs more than Spinks does.

I am taller than he is.
I am taller than he. (*Informal:* I am taller than him.)

My house is bigger than your house (is). (*is* is optional)
My house is bigger than yours (is).

My bedroom is tidier than my sister's bedroom (is).
My bedroom is tidier than my sister's (is).

The intensifier used with comparative structures is *much:*

Tyson is much heavier than Spinks (is).
Tyson is much more aggressive than Spinks (is).

EXERCISE 2

You could convey the wrong meaning if you weren't careful. What do the following sentences mean as they stand, and how could they be rewritten to change their meaning?

1. She likes ice cream better than her husband. *does*
2. My computer is bigger than Mary's.
3. I admire the president more than my father. *does*

EXERCISE 3

Write a sentence of comparison for each of the following. Remember to use *than* and, if you want to use an intensifier, use *much.*

EXAMPLES

tennis, squash
  Squash is much more demanding than tennis.
  Tennis needs a (much) larger space than squash (does).
  Tennis is much more fun than squash.

1. a bicycle, a motorcycle
2. the city, the country

175

3. a typewriter, a word processor
4. a liberal arts degree, a science degree
5. business school, law school
6. high school, college
7. living at home, living with a roommate
8. drinking, smoking
9. football, baseball
10. bankers, teachers

16d. Other comparative structures: *(not) as . . . as, like, but, however, whereas*, etc.

Apart from the comparative forms of adjectives and adverbs, there are other ways to express the concepts of difference and similarity.

- *(not) as . . . as*
  To express similarity, the *as . . . as* structure is used:

  She is as strong as I (am). (*Informal:* as me)
  She plays tennis as well as I (do). (*Informal:* as me)
  He works as hard as she (does). (*Informal:* as her)
  He does as much work as Sally (does).

    To express contrast, the *not as . . . as* structure is used:

  Spinks is not as heavy as Tyson (is).

  This last sentence has the same meaning as:

  Tyson is heavier than Spinks (is).

    Similarly,

  Spinks does not weigh as much as Tyson (does).
  = Tyson weighs more than Spinks (does).

  Sometimes, *so* replaces the first *as* in the negative structure:

  Spinks does not weigh so much as Tyson does.

- *like*
  To show similarity, we can use *like* + noun phrase:

  He acts like a grown-up.
  She has been sitting in the sun so long, she looks like a lobster.

    In formal usage, *like* is not used with a clause following it, though you might hear and read something like this: *She looks like she's been boiled. Use *as* instead:

  She looks as if she has been boiled.
  She looks as if she sat outside for too long.

- *but, however, in contrast, on the other hand, whereas*

    The following sentences show ways of expressing contrast in two clauses or two complete sentences. Note the punctuation used in each case. Chapters 22, 23, and 26 contain more examples and exercises of these uses.

EXAMPLES

Argentina has a 94 percent literacy rate, *but* Bolivia, its neighbor, has only a 75 percent rate.

Argentina has a 94 percent literacy rate; *however,* Bolivia, its neighbor, has only a 75 percent rate.

Argentina has a 94 percent literacy rate; *in contrast,* Bolivia, its neighbor, has only a 75 percent rate.

(On the one hand,) Argentina has a 94 percent literacy rate; *on the other hand,* Bolivia, its neighbor, has only a 75 percent rate.

Argentina has a 94 percent literacy rate, *whereas* Bolivia, its neighbor, has only a 75 percent rate.

EXERCISE 4 (oral)

    Make up two sentences for each pair, emphasizing contrast or similarity.

EXAMPLE

Skiing is dangerous. Skating isn't.
    Skiing is more dangerous than skating (is).
    Skating isn't as dangerous as skiing (is).

Car racing is dangerous. So is motorcycle racing.
    Car racing, like motorcycle racing, is dangerous.
    Car racing is as dangerous as motorcycle racing.

1. The couch is comfortable. The chair isn't.
2. I do a lot of work. You don't.
3. You speak English well. He doesn't.
4. The governor's expertise is impressive. So is the mayor's.
5. Sarah's dress is pretty. Jane's dress isn't.
6. They often sleep late. Their children do, too.
7. He likes chocolate. His wife doesn't.
8. My father drives well. My brother doesn't.

Then write down four pairs of sentences like these, about yourself or something or someone you know about. Give your sentences to a partner, who will rewrite each one in two ways.

☆EXERCISE 5

Read the information about two countries, Ecuador and Uruguay. Working with a small group of students, write sentences about the two countries that point out to a reader their similarities and contrasts. Use comparative forms of adjectives and adverbs as well as other structures that express similarity and contrast.

ECUADOR

PEOPLE
Population (1986 est.): 9,647,000
Population density: 92 per square mile
Urban (1986): 52 percent
Ethnic groups: Indians, 25 percent; mestizo (mixed European and Indian ancestry), 55 percent; Spanish, 10 percent; African, 10 percent
Religion: predominantly Roman Catholic

GEOGRAPHY
Area: 109,483 square miles
Location: northwestern South America, on the Pacific coast, astride the equator

ECONOMY
Industries: food processing, wood products, textiles
Chief crops: bananas (largest exporter), coffee, rice, sugar, corn
Minerals: oil, copper, iron, lead, silver, sulfur
Arable land: 9 percent
Labor force: 34 percent in agriculture, 12 percent in industry, 35 percent in services

HEALTH
Life expectancy at birth (1981): male, 59.8; females, 63.6

URUGUAY

PEOPLE
Population (1986 est.): 2,947,000
Population density: 45 per square mile
Urban (1983): 83 percent
Ethnic groups: Caucasians (Iberians, Italians), 89 percent; mestizos, 10 percent; mulattos and blacks, 1 percent
Religion: predominantly Roman Catholic

GEOGRAPHY
Area: 68,037 square miles
Location: southern South America, on the Atlantic Ocean

ECONOMY
Industries: meatpacking, metals, textiles, wine, cement, oil products
Chief crops: corn, wheat, citrus fruits, rice, oats, linseed

Arable land: 12 percent

Labor force: 16 percent in agriculture, 31 percent in industry and commerce, 12 percent in services, 19 percent in government

HEALTH

Life expectancy at birth (1983): males, 61.1; females, 73.7

SOURCE: *The World Almanac and Book of Facts: 1988* (New York: World Almanac, 1987).

Discuss how you could organize all your information into an essay comparing the two countries. What alternative is there to simply writing about Ecuador first and then Uruguay? Discuss other ways of organizing the material. Then write an essay comparing and contrasting the two countries, from the information you have here.

16e. *Most, the most,* and *most of*

Structures with *most* often cause difficulties for language learners. The following examples show the most common uses.

- *most* + noun
  When *most* is used as a quantity word, followed by a noun, it makes a generalization, meaning simply "almost all" and certainly "more than half":

  Most children like ice cream.
  Most computers are expensive.

- *most* + adjective
  Most can also be used to intensify an adjective, in the same way as *very:*

  It was most kind of you to offer to help me.
  It was a most difficult lesson.
  I am most interested in that book.

- *the most* + noun or adjective
  We express a real comparison when we use *the most:*

  She does the most work of anyone in the class.
  He chose the most difficult assignment of all.

- *most of* + noun phrase or noun clause
  We use *most of* when we refer to a large number of a specific noun phrase: *most of my friends, most of those apples, most of the books on the table,* and so on:

  Most of the students in this class still haven't bought their books. (*Most of the* points ahead to the phrase that completes the thought: *students in this class.* Note how this differs from "*Most students* spend a lot on books.")

179

Note the difference between these two sentences:

> **Most Norwegians have fair hair. (generalization)**
> **Most of the Norwegians I've seen have fair hair. (limited)**

Most of can also be followed by a noun clause:

> **I liked most of what I saw.**
> **Most of what he said was nonsense.**

EXERCISE 6

In each of the following sentences based on the readings, insert an appropriate phrase—*most, the most,* or *most of*—along with any other necessary words.

1. _____ steel produced in Pittsburgh and Gary is sold outside those cities.

2. _____ people would agree that lying to gain advantage over an unknowing subject is wrong.

3. According to the study, _____ frequent motive for lying was to save face.

4. _____ people nowadays know some of van Gogh's paintings.

5. Doufu is _____ important of the foods prepared in the East from the soybean.

6. The Chinese have developed dozens of different ways of reprocessing doufu, _____ of which change the texture and/or the taste of the food radically.

16f. Idiom: *the more, the merrier*

Comparative forms are used in idiomatic expressions according to the following patterns:

> **The more, the merrier. (a common saying)**
> **The faster she ran, the worse she felt.**
> **The more work she did, the less satisfied she felt with it.**

16g. Figures of speech

Figures of speech are often used to help explain a concept by comparing it to something else. The poet Langston Hughes wrote that a deferred dream dries up "like a raisin in the sun." The image of a raisin in the sun was so powerful that it has since been used as the title of a play by Lorraine Hansberry. An occasional figure of speech will provide a strong image and make your point more vivid.

Students of English wrote the following similes (stated comparisons) and metaphors (implied comparisons) in their essays.

SIMILES

Every day in the morning, I would take the crowded bus with a heavy school bag; the ride was *like a life contest.* (Youn Kim, Korea)

Just as leaves return to their roots and water flows back to the sea, I will always remember that I am Chinese. (Huey-fen Song, China)

METAPHORS

I felt the threatening *floodwaters of tears* when I heard her voice again. (The tears were like a flood.) (Yolanda Perez, Colombia)

☆*EXERCISE 7*

The following similes and metaphors occur in the reading passage "Artificial Intelligence" on p. 359.

1. It was the head of a long snake of a building.
2. The short yellow bristles of grass made the hills look like the scalp of a marine recruit.
3. With the wiry dark hair of bushes and trees shaved off, the bumps and scars of contour were visible.
4. The few trees . . . looked [as] dusty and dry as fence posts.
5. His hair encircles his head and his face with a great cloud of silver needles. Amid this prickly gray mist his eyes are two dark rocks.

What comparisons are being made in each sentence? What can you say about how the comparisons help your understanding of the image the writer wants to convey to the reader?

☆*EXERCISE 8*

In the next day or so, keep your eyes open for a person who looks unusual. Write a description of that person and his or her surroundings. Include a few figures of speech to help your reader see precisely what you saw. For example, in "Siblings," Anna Quindlen doesn't just say that her son "shook a short index finger" in his brother's face; she makes it more vivid with an image: he shook "an index finger as short as a pencil stub."

EDIT

The following sentences from students' essays exhibit some problems with comparative forms. Where are the errors, and what should the students do to correct their sentences?

1. Some people might feel that more vitamins you take, healthier you will get.
2. People who take vitamins stay more healthier.
3. Some of the students I met when I first arrived were a lot kinder then others.
4. When food becomes scarce, living conditions get worst.
5. The city's advantages are more obvious than the country.
6. Calculus is not difficult as statistics.
7. The most of his friends were Mexican.

WRITE

In "Sizing Up Human Intelligence," Stephen Jay Gould summarizes F. W. Went's explorations of the perspectives of an ant-sized man in order to make his point that the size of human beings determines their activities and evolution. Discuss with other students how a small creature such as a 3-year-old child sees the world differently from the way we see it. For example, how do little children see people, buildings, stairs, animals, tables, and other objects? What do these objects look like to them? How do they make the children react? What would happen to us and our environment if we were all child size? Take notes during your discussion.

Then organize your ideas into sections dealing with people, animals, buildings, and furniture. Write an essay about the perspective on the world experienced by a 3-year old child, and comment on how it differs from an adult's perspective.

EDITING ADVICE	1. If you have used any comparative forms, make sure that you have used *than* and not *then*.
	2. Check the forms of comparatives and superlatives that you have used; make sure that you have made an appropriate selection of the *-er, -est* form or the *more, most* form.
	3. If you have compared two people, objects, or concepts, make sure you have used the comparative form with *than*. For comparing three or more, use the superlative form with *the*.
	4. Try out an alternative structure that you have not used before (see sections 16d, 16e, and 16f).

Agreement

17. SUBJECT-VERB AGREEMENT
   a. The *-s* ending
   b. Subjects and verbs
   c. Verbs in a sequence
   d. Tricky singular and plural subjects
   e. Proximity and ellipsis
   f. Agreement with adjectival clauses
   g. *There* and *one of*

18. PRONOUNS AND PRONOUN REFERENCE
   a. Personal pronouns
   b. Demonstrative pronouns and adjectives
   c. Pronoun agreement: gender and number
   d. Pronoun reference and faulty pronoun reference
   e. Pronouns and sentence structure
   f. Possessive pronouns and adjectives

17 Subject-Verb Agreement

READ

Read the following sections of the article "Siblings" by Anna Quindlen. The complete article appears with vocabulary glosses on p. 345.

In the back room the boys are playing, a study in brotherly love. The younger one has the fire engine and the older one has the tow truck and although entire minutes have passed, neither has made a grab for the other's toy. The younger one is babbling to himself in pidgin English and
5　the older one is singing ceaselessly, tonelessly, as though chanting a mantra. It is not until I move closer to the two of them, toe to toe on the tile floor, that I catch the lyrics to the melody: "Get out of here. Get out of here. Get out of here." . . .

My son loves his brother, who is immensely lovable; at the same
10　time he dislikes his brother intensely. He wants him to be around, but only sometimes, and only on his terms. He is no different from a lot of us who have fantasies about the things we want and who are surprised by the realities when we get them.

ANALYZE

1. In those two paragraphs, underline all the complete verb forms that occur in independent or dependent clauses. Then circle the subjects of the verbs.

2. Make two lists of these subjects + verbs: one list containing subjects that are or could be replaced with *I, you, we,* or *they,* the other list containing subjects that are or could be replaced with *he, she,* or *it.*

EXAMPLE

I, YOU, WE, THEY	HE, SHE, IT
the boys are playing	The younger one has

3. With other students, discuss what you notice about the verb forms used in each column. What can you say is the distinctive feature common to all present tense verbs, except modals, used after a *he, she,* or *it* subject?

184

STUDY

17a. The -*s* ending

The -*s* ending is used for different signals:

Noun + -*s* = plural (one student, two students)
Verb + -*s* = singular (third person singular: he/she buys)

SUBJECT-VERB AGREEMENT		
Subject	*Present Tense Verb*	*Example*
I, you, we, they he, she it	Simple form -*s*	Students (= they) buy a lot of books. A student (= he/she) buys a lot of books.

The -*s* form is never used on a main verb after a first auxiliary.

EXAMPLES

He *doesn't like* ice cream.
She *will buy* her son a present.
She *might have* another child.

The -*s* form is used only with present tense verbs.

EXERCISE 1

In each of the following sentences adapted from Anna Quindlen's article, insert the correct form of the verb. Some occur with relative clauses; if you cannot figure them out, refer to section 17f.

1. But when there is a tussle over the fire engine, his baby

   _____ (develop/develops) a name, an identity, a reality

   that _____ (are/is) infuriating.

2. He _____ (have/has) no interest in the sandbox or any

   of the other things that _____ (make/makes) life worth

   living.

3. In his bones, my elder son probably _____ (know/

   knows) the awful truth.

185

4. Realization _____ (have/has) come slowly for some of them.

5. The look that passed over his face _____ (were/was) the one I imagine usually _____ (accompany/accompanies) the discovery of a dead body.

6. Imagine that one night your husband _____ (come/comes) home and _____ (tell/tells) you that he _____ (have/has) decided to have a second wife.

_____

17b. Subjects and verbs

The subjects and verbs from the passage at the beginning of this chapter are listed in the following chart. For the first one, the corresponding singular form has been added. Add the corresponding singular or plural form for the other entries.

I, YOU, WE, THEY	HE, SHE, IT
the boys are playing	the boy is playing
	my son loves his brother
	he dislikes his brother
entire minutes have passed	
	neither has made a grab for the toy

Note that all the verb forms in the *he, she, it* column include a present tense *-s* form: *is, loves, dislikes, has*. The subject of each one is a third person singular *(he, she, it)* subject.

Sometimes, though, it is not enough to be able to identify the complete subject. Sometimes you need to be able to identify the head word (the word that carries the weight of the meaning) of the subject to determine whether the whole subject is a *he, she, it* subject or not.

EXAMPLE **The boy with the trucks is having fun.**

The complete subject is *the boy with the trucks*. The head word of the subject is *boy* (Who is having fun? The boy is). The fact that the word *trucks* in the prepositional phrase is plural does not affect the form of the verb at all.

Some nouns may look plural in form but are always used with the singular *(he, she, it)* form of the verb:

The news was **bad yesterday.**
The United States has **a large budget deficit.**
Economics is **an important field of study for politicians.**
The lecture series sounds **interesting.**

Other nouns might look singular but need a plural verb:

The *people* **in the park** *look* **happy.**
The *police have captured* **the criminal.**

When there are two subjects, the verb form must reflect the plural form:

My brother and my sister want **to stay home. (= they)**

EXERCISE 2

The student whose writing appears below used the present tense and so had to pay attention to subject-verb agreement. She used eleven complete verb phrases. <u>Seven</u> of these she used accurately. Which ones? The other four posed problems for her. Can you correct the errors and speculate as to why the student made the errors originally?

The way Colombian teenagers act and behave differ a lot from teenagers in the United States. In my country, young people is very respectful with the elderly. We are taught from a very early age to respect our elders.
Young people in the United States, on the other hand, is very cold and independent. They don't worry about older people. They don't mind if an old woman is tired or need help; they just live their lives.

Yolanda Perez, Colombia

EXERCISE 3

The following sentences are from students' writing. Indicate which sentences have accurate subject-verb agreement (OK). Mark incorrect sentences (X), and write correct versions.

_____ 1. The best years of my life was the time that I spent at home.

_____ 2. Sharing among brothers and sisters are great.

_____ 3. The second one is my older sister; she always share everything with my younger sister and me.

_____ 4. I think that it depend on the way the parents raise their children.

187

_____ 5. His wife's advice was very useful to him.

_____ 6. When she was born, all my toys was given to her, even my favorite ones.

_____ 7. Everybody wants to be successful, and Sandra wants that more than anything.

_____ 8. When it is spring, beautiful flowers appears over all the trees.

_____ 9. When my parents are supportive and encouraging, my school grades goes up.

_____ 10. If they don't behave, their father will be the one who have the most authority to discipline them.

17c. Verbs in a sequence

The *-s* ending is needed on all the third person present tense verbs that appear in a sequence, not just on the first verb of the sequence.

EXAMPLE

He *picks* up the toy, *throws* it across the room, and *screams*.

EXERCISE 4

The following sentences are from students' writing. In each, underline the verbs, circle the head word of the subject, and make any necessary corrections to make subjects and verbs agree.

1. My brother Julio talks to everybody, ask for favors, and try to get as much as possible from people.

2. My mother is a very strict lady and she always try to maintain discipline among her children.

3. My sister hates school and avoid work whenever possible.

4. In my country, the government has rules and only allow a young couple to have one child.

5. The head of the family takes control and always order his children to do jobs in the house.

_____

17d. Tricky singular and plural subjects

Some pronouns that express the idea of quantity cause problems for language learners. The box on page 190 shows some of these problematic quantifiers. It indicates whether they are regarded as singular (S) or plural (PL). Some of them, you will see, take a plural verb when used with a countable plural noun and a singular verb when used with an uncountable noun. (See also Chapter 5.)

17e. Proximity and ellipsis

When the subject is formed with *either . . . or* or *neither . . . nor,* the verb agrees with the noun phrase nearest to it.

EXAMPLES

Either my boss or my colleagues *deserve* the blame.
Neither my boss nor my colleagues *deserve* the blame.
Either my colleagues or my boss *deserves* the blame.
Neither my colleagues nor my boss *deserves* the blame.

A word omitted from the subject but understood from a previous reference (ellipsis) will determine the form of the present tense verb:

Western ferrets *are* cuter, but the eastern *make* better pets.

The omitted word also determines the form if a possessive pronoun is used:

Her parents *are* Chinese, but mine *are* Korean.
Her father *is* Chinese, but mine *is* Korean.

_____

☆EXERCISE 5 (oral)

Work with a group of students. Your instructor will assign some of the following expressions to your group. Make up a sentence for each one, using the given expression as the subject of the sentence. When you hear another group's sentences, determine whether the subjects and verbs agree.

all the people in my family   each person in my family
all my information   living with brothers and sisters

all my information is useful.

AGREEMENT WITH QUANTIFIERS

Subject	Verb S	PL	Example
every	√		Every child *likes* toys.
each	√		Each child *has* a teddy bear.
each of	√		Each of the toys *needs* repair.
everyone/everybody	√		Everyone *wants* to travel.
someone/somebody	√		Somebody *wants* to see you.
anyone/anybody	√		Anyone who *wants* to can come.
no one/nobody	√		No one *has* any time.
one	√		One of the boys *wants* to leave.
neither	√		Neither of the boys *wants* to leave.
both		√	Both of the boys *want* to go.
all (of)	√	√	All American boys *play* baseball. All of the furniture *looks* old.
a lot of	√	√	A lot of girls *play* soccer. A lot of the furniture *looks* uncomfortable.
some (of)	√	√	Some parents *are* strict. Some of the furniture *looks* shabby.
no	√	√	No children *dislike* ice cream. No child *dislikes* ice cream. No furniture *costs* that much!
none of	√	√	None of the boys *is* playing. *or* None of the boys *are* playing. None of the furniture *is* old.

(handwritten note:) most / several / few } always plural.

Note the singular verb forms with the following subjects:			
-ing form	√		Choosing furniture *is* difficult.
Infinitive	√		To furnish a room *takes* time.
Clause	√		Why we never use the room *is* a mystery.

what she wants to do	every child
everybody in this room	each decision
nobody I know	one of the reasons
to succeed in life	neither my sister nor my parents
one of my friends	neither my parents nor my sister

everybody in this room is a foreigner.

17f. Agreement with adjectival clauses

When an adjectival (relative) clause begins with *who, which,* or *that* as the subject, look back in the sentence to see what it refers to (its referent). The referent will determine whether the verb in the relative clause should be the standard form or the *-s* form. (See also Chapter 24.)

EXAMPLES

My son loves his brothers, who *are* immensely lovable.

My son loves his brother, who *is* immensely lovable.

The word *who, which,* or *that* by itself can be either singular or plural. You can only determine which it is by looking back to find the word the relative pronoun refers to.

When a relative clause comes between the subject and the verb of the independent clause, it does not affect subject-verb agreement:

The problems [that] the student encountered *were* very troubling.

The politician [whom] the journalists want to interview *runs* a

construction company.

EXERCISE 6

The following sentences from students' essays show some problems with agreement in sentences that contain relative clauses. Underline each error, correct it, and explain why the correction is necessary.

1. The Iranian New Year has special traditions which is different from *are*

   others.

2. These are traditional acts that influences us.

3. She has a full-time job, which require *s* a lot of energy.

4. These are some of the things that happens among siblings.

17g

5. The cousin they visit every weekend always want to go swimming.

6. A family should always be considered as one unit. That means that everybody who belongs to the same family should live together and stick together.

7. The relatives that she lives with gives her a lot of freedom.

8. The family is considered to be the basic structure in our society that influence the individual's behavior.

17g. *There* and *one of*

When we use *there is, there are, there was,* or *there were,* the form of the verb is determined by the head noun of the following subject.

EXAMPLES

There *are* no *closets* near the living room.
There *is* no *furniture* in the room.
There *is* some *rivalry* between the brothers.
There *are* some *toys* on the couch.

In informal speech, you might hear sentences like "There's a lot of unanswered questions about that issue." This probably occurs because of the relative difficulty of pronouncing the contraction *There're.* In writing, though, use *there are* with a following plural subject.

One of causes difficulties because it is used with a third person singular *(he, she, it)* verb form, agreeing with *one,* yet it has to be directly followed by a plural noun:

One of the boys is playing with a truck.

One of the parents works at home.

EXERCISE 7 (oral)

Complete each of the following sentences.

1. One of the best meals . . .

2. One of the nicest . . .

192

3. One of the best ways . . .

4. One of my best friends . . . is a movie-star

5. One of the greatest . . .

6. One of the most interesting . . .

EXERCISE 8

Insert an appropriate form of *be* into each sentence.

1. There _____are_____ some apples in the bowl on the table.

2. There _____is_____ a lot of money in my wallet.

3. There _____are_____ several people absent.

4. There _____is_____ no furniture in the room.

5. There _____ no news about the trial.

6. There _____ a lot of voters in rural districts.

7. There _____ a box of books in the basement.

8. There _____ no cookies in the bag.

EXERCISE 9

Which word or phrase best completes each sentence?

1. _____ people in the room have applied for the job.

    a. One of the
    b. All of the
    c. Neither of the
    d. Every

2. The problem that is facing some business executives _____

    _____ their profits.

    a. threaten   c. threatens
    b. are threatening   d. have threatened

3. She has no interest in any of the things that _____ her boss.

    a. interest
    b. interests
    c. interesting
    d. is interesting

4. The woman carrying two large green bags _____ history.

    a. teach
    b. have taught
    c. has taught
    d. were taught

5. The drum and the guitar _____ good together.

    a. sound
    b. sounds
    c. is sounding
    d. sounding

6. Everybody _____ to earn a lot of money.

    a. is wanting
    b. are wanting
    c. have wanted
    d. wants

EXERCISE 10

In the following passage from the reading "The Basic-Nonbasic Concept," which appears with vocabulary glosses in Part II, insert appropriate present tense verb forms of the given verbs or auxiliaries.

Consider a frontier mining town where 100 miners _____ (be) employed in the town's only basic
_a
industry—gold mining. Assume that each of the 100 miners _____ (be) married and _____ (have)
_b _c
two children. The basic industry thus _____ (support)
_d
400 people. But the 400 people _____ (demand) services:
_e
schools and churches _____ (have to) be built, grocery
_f

and clothing stores and livery stables _____ (be) operated, newspapers _____ (be) published, professional personnel _____ (be) needed, and saloons _____ (have to) cater to visiting cowboys. It _____ (have) been suggested that there _____ (be) an average basic/nonbasic ratio of 1:3; that is, for every miner employed in the town's basic industry, three people _____ (may) be employed in a nonbasic industry. Thus, with 100 miners our community _____ (support) 300 people employed in the various nonbasic service industries listed above.

EDIT

Can you find the five subject-verb agreement errors in the following excerpt from a student's essay? What should Carlos do to fix the errors?

> Consuelo and Drago seems to have been born for each other. They are very young in spirit. Her ancestors are German and Portuguese and his parents are Spanish. They are both about to finish college and have plans to move to Lebanon, where they have a cousin.
> Consuelo looks very young even though she wears a lot of makeup. She has a very delicate voice, which impress everyone. When she speaks, she always give the impression of being very well educated because she says words and phrases in Latin, Spanish, German, and even Arabic. She maintains that certain words, phrases, passages, and poems should be said in the language in which they originated. When we talk, she will often refer to books she have read, and she will use foreign languages to make comments on her experiences. There is no subjects she isn't interested in.
>
> Carlos Gomariz, Argentina

WRITE

Write about two people that you know who live or work closely with each other. Tell your reader about each one of them: occupation, lifestyle, values, appearance, and behavior. Conclude by writing a paragraph that tells your reader about them both: what they have in common, how they are similar, what values and activities they share. Use the present tense to describe these people as they are now and as they usually are.

EDITING ADVICE	1. To check subject-verb agreement, circle the subject of each clause. Ask yourself if it is a third person singular *(he, she, it)* form. Then check each verb to make sure that is agrees with its subject.
	2. Remember that you have to be concerned about subject-verb agreement only if you are using present tense verbs or the auxiliaries *is, are, was, were, does, do, has, have.*
	3. Remember, too, that uncountable nouns are singular in form (The *furniture is* comfortable).

Pronouns and Pronoun Reference

18

READ

Read the following excerpts from Anna Quindlen's "Siblings." The full selection, with vocabulary glosses, appears on p. 345.

> I cannot remember which of my books described sibling rivalry thus: Imagine that one night your husband comes home and tells you that he has decided to have a second wife. She will be younger than you, cuter than you and will demand much more of his time and attention. That
> 5   doesn't mean, however, that he will love you any less. . . .
>
> My son loves his brother, who is immensely lovable; at the same time, he dislikes his brother intensely. He wants him to be around, but only sometimes, and only on his terms. He is no different from a lot of us who have fantasies about the things we want and who are surprised by
> 10   the realities when we get them. . . .
>
> At some point, his fantasy of a brother may dovetail with the reality; mine did when my younger brother . . . turned into a good-looking teenage boy.

ANALYZE

1. In the passage, underline all the pronoun forms and possessive adjectives (forms like *I, we, us, our, he, him, his, mine, themselves, this, those*). You should underline 15 words. *I* refers to the writer. Whom does *you* refer to?

2. Now draw lines in the text to connect the pronouns and possessive adjectives you have underlined with the noun phrases they refer to.

EXAMPLE

My son loves *his* brother

18a

STUDY

18a. Personal pronouns

The box provides an overview of the forms of personal pronouns.

PERSONAL PRONOUNS				
Subject Pronoun	*Object Pronoun*	*Possessive Adjective (+ noun)*	*Possessive Pronoun*	*Reflexive Pronoun*
I	me	my	mine	myself
we	us	our	ours	ourselves
you (sing.)	you	your	yours	yourself
you (plur.)	you	your	yours	yourselves
he	him	his	his	himself
she	her	her	hers	herself
it	it	its	—	itself
they	them	their	theirs	themselves
one	one	one's	—	oneself

Two problem areas are common.

- Subject and object pronouns when two subjects or objects occur
  The following are not standard English:

  *Me and Lucy are going shopping. (Lucy and I . . .)
  *They gave that cake to Emily and I. (. . . to Emily and me)

  To test your sentences, just omit the noun phrase and see which pronoun form fits when it stands alone:

  I am going shopping.
  They gave that cake to me.

  After prepositions, the object form is always used:

  He sat in front of my sister and me.
  He kept staring at my friend and me.

- Possessive pronoun used as the subject
  Subject-verb agreement is determined by the noun phrase that the pronoun refers to:

  We each have a winter jacket. Mine is warmer than hers.

  We each have two bathing suits. Mine are prettier than hers.

But **They gave us two beach balls. His was red, and mine was blue.**

(His beach ball, my beach ball)

EXERCISE 1 (oral)

With a partner, choose which pronouns to use in the following sentences, and discuss the reasons for your choice. Some of the options given are not acceptable forms in standard edited English; however, they are used in some spoken dialects, so you might come across them.

1. The children ran up to _____ (he and I/him and me).

2. The little boy was singing to _____ (himself/hisself).

3. The girls remembered their schoolbooks. The boys forgot _____ (their/theirs/their's).

4. She wrote the article for _____ (you and me/you and I).

5. The toy truck was sitting on a shelf by _____ (himself/ itself/themselves).

6. My sister and _____ (I/me) each have an ambition. _____ (Her/Hers) is to be a doctor; _____ (mine/mines) is to be a writer.

7. I wanted to take the truck away from him because it was _____ (mines/my/mine).

8. Between you and _____ (me/I), I find her extremely arrogant.

EXERCISE 2

In the following passage from the reading "Vincent van Gogh" on p. 343, fill in the appropriate pronouns.

Van Gogh was born in Holland in 1853, the son of a

vicar. _____He_____ (a) was a deeply religious man who had worked as a lay preacher in England and among Belgian miners. _____He_____ (b) had been deeply impressed by the art of Millet and _____its_____ (c) social message, and decided to become a painter _____himself_____ (d) *(emphasis) to stress*. A younger brother, Theo, who worked in an art-dealer's shop, introduced _____him_____ (e) to Impressionist painters. This brother was a remarkable man. Though _____he_____ (f) was poor himself, _____he_____ (g) always gave ungrudgingly to the older Vincent and even financed _____his_____ (h) journey to Arles in southern France. Vincent hoped that if _____he_____ (i) could work there undisturbed for a number of years _____he_____ (j) might be able one day to sell _____his_____ (k) pictures and repay _____his_____ (l) generous brother. In _____his_____ (m) self-chosen solitude in Arles, Vincent set down all _____his_____ (n) ideas and hopes in _____his_____ (o) letters to Theo, which read like a continuous diary. These letters, by a humble and almost self-taught artist who had no idea of the fame _____he_____ (p) was to achieve, are among the most moving and exciting in all literature. In _____them_____ (q) we can feel the artist's sense of mission, _____his_____ (r) struggle and triumphs, _____his_____ (s) desperate loneliness and longing for companionship, and _____we_____ (t) become aware of the immense strain under which _____he_____ (u) worked with feverish energy.

Without preposition.
1. me, too
2. Contrast to another people

18b. Demonstrative pronouns and adjectives

Demonstratives agree in number with the following noun phrase or with a previous referent:

He had a brother. This brother was a remarkable man.

She had two brothers. These brothers were remarkable men.

She had two brothers. These were remarkable men.

She wrote six poems. These were her first.

The following box shows the forms.

DEMONSTRATIVE ADJECTIVES OR PRONOUNS	
Singular	*Plural*
this	these
that	those

18c. Pronoun agreement: gender and number

A possessive adjective agrees in gender (male, female, or neuter) with the noun phrase it refers to (its referent) and not with the noun phrase following it.

POSSESSIVE ADJECTIVES: GENDER AGREEMENT			
Preceding Noun Phrase	*Possessive Adjective*		
	MALE	FEMALE	NEUTER
Countable singular	his	her	its
Uncountable			its
Countable plural		their	

EXAMPLES

The mother is playing with her son.

The father is playing with his daughter.

The dog has lost its owner.

The parents are playing with their son.

Pronouns also agree with their referent in number. To refer to uncountable nouns, use *it, this,* or *that.* To refer to countable singular nouns, use *he, she, it, this,* or *that.* To refer to countable plural nouns, use *they, these,* or *those.*

EXAMPLES

The furniture in their house is old. <u>It</u> is quite shabby.

The chairs in the living room look shabby. <u>They</u> are quite old.

☆*EXERCISE 3*

Look at the picture *The Luncheon of the Boating Party* on p. 111. With a partner, write a description of it using as many of the following pronouns as you can, in any order—but make sure the referents are clear so that your reader knows precisely whom or what you are referring to. Read your description to your class.

he	this man	it
his	him	its
she	this woman	their
her	this boating party	themselves
herself		

18d. Pronoun reference and faulty pronoun reference

When you speak or write, the referent for any pronoun should be very clear. In writing, you should usually be able to find it in the text, not far away from the pronoun.

> EXAMPLE   **Imagine that one night your husband comes home and tells you that *he* has decided to have a second wife.**

Pronouns are thus useful to help form links in what you say or write and to avoid repetition. At the beginning of the second paragraph of "Siblings," for example, you will see "this particular turn of phrase." *This* provides a link back to the preceding paragraph, to the phrase "Get out of here."

You can also use a pronoun to make a broader reference to an entire sentence or idea:

> The mother told her sons to put away their toys. *This* produced no results. *(This* refers to *the fact that she told them to put away their toys.)*

Make sure that what the pronoun refers to will be clear to a reader. Avoid ambiguity.

*My friend's father gave my friend an old motorcycle for his birthday. This caused a lot of trouble. (*This* could refer to the motorcycle or to the fact that the father gave his son a motorcycle.)

EXERCISE 4

The following student sentences cause problems for a reader because of faulty pronoun reference. Can you find what causes the problem? How should the writer fix the sentence?

1. When my brother went to visit his uncle, he told him that he wanted to quit his job. (Who told whom? The brother or the uncle?) *[his uncle]*
2. She took home a lot of homework, but she didn't have time to do them. *[it]*
3. I really believe that having siblings is a better way of adjusting to society than not having it. *[them]*
4. My brother gave me an old computer, but then her girlfriend broke its switch. *[my]*
5. The toy train fell off his tracks and broke; this made me cry. *[its]*
6. She told her parents that she was going to quit her job. This made her brother angry. *[the fact that she was— .]*

EXERCISE 5

In the fable by Aesop on p. 88 in Exercise 9, Chapter 8, a lot of third person pronouns are used in the first paragraph (*he, she, it, they, his, her,* etc.). Write a list of the pronouns used in the first paragraph and, next to each one, state which word or words in the text the pronoun refers to.

EXAMPLE

PRONOUN	REFERENT
her	a farmer's daughter

18e. Pronouns and sentence structure

A pronoun is not used to restate the subject of a sentence that is already in place. The student who wrote this sentence:

*Nowadays, a lot of people they would like to move to the country.

should have written this:

Nowadays, a lot of people would like to move to the country.

18f. Possessive pronouns and adjectives

Possessive pronouns stand alone; possessive adjectives are used with a noun phrase:

My fantasy dovetailed with reality.
Mine dovetailed with reality. (= my fantasy)

Note that possessive adjectives and pronouns do not have an apostrophe:

ours	hers
yours	his
theirs	its (*it's* means "it is")

EXERCISE 6

In the following passage from "Sizing Up Human Intelligence," by Stephen Jay Gould (p. 363), draw arrows to connect each underlined pronoun or possessive adjective to the noun phrase it refers to.

We can make a strong argument and claim that humans have to be just about the size they are in order to function as they do. In an amusing and provocative article, F. W. Went explored the impossibility of human life, as we know it, at ant dimensions. . . . Since weight increases so much faster than surface area as an object gets larger, small animals have very high ratios of surface to volume; they live in a world dominated by surface forces that affect us scarcely at all.

An ant-sized man might don some clothing, but forces of surface adhesion would preclude its removal. The lower limit of drop size would make showering impossible; each drop would hit with the force of a large boulder. If our homunculus managed to get wet, and tried to dry off with a towel, he would be stuck to it for life. He could pour no liquid, light no fire. . . . He might pound gold leaf thin enough to construct a book for his size, but surface adhesion would prevent the turning of pages.

☆*EXERCISE 7*

Look at the picture by Brueghel on p. 98. The following sentences relate to that picture, but each one makes a reference to an omitted preceding sentence by its use of a pronoun. Write a predecessor for each of the following sentences. Together, these twelve sentences plus the ones you insert will form a paragraph of twenty-four sentences.

EXAMPLE

He is looking away from the sea.

A shepherd is looking after his sheep. He is looking away from the sea.

1. Only his leg can be seen sticking out of the water.
2. It does not appear to be hurrying to help him.
3. They sail on, not varying their route.
4. This is surprising.
5. His sheep are also unconcerned about what is happening.
6. He is concentrating all his attention on it.
7. It plods steadily along, pulling the plow.
8. His fall appears to go unnoticed.
9. Even they take no notice of the event.
10. They concern themselves with their daily routine.
11. Only this one man might be in a position to notice the event.
12. His death has no dramatic impact on those around him.

EDIT

Read the following passage from a student's essay. Where do problems with pronoun use occur? What changes would you advise the student to make?

I am the youngest of three boys, and the experience of being the youngest of three made me feel like a good listener. When my brothers talked to me, they did it for a specific reason. They would call me to send me out on "important missions." The missions included the purchasing of grocery items or doing their laundry or even doing their college registration.

My brothers, by having a stronger personality and being older, they impose their point of view on me. They always think of themself that they know more than you as if that were a rule. Being the youngest definitely has it's disadvantages.

Carlos Gomariz, Argentina

WRITE

Discuss with other students what you think are the good and bad points about being the oldest or the youngest child—or one in the middle. Make a list of the advantages and disadvantages for each birth order. Once you have all provided evidence from your own experience and made as full a list as you can, use your notes to plan an essay. Choose *one* of the birth orders—first child, a middle child, youngest child—and write an essay in which you (1) explain the advantages and disadvantages a child with that birth order has and (2) express your opinion as to whether there are more advantages or disadvantages. Give examples to illustrate the points you make.

EDITING ADVICE	1. Underline all the pronouns in your piece of writing. Check to make sure that each one has a clear referent that precedes it closely in your text and agrees with it in gender.
	2. Decide whether a pronoun is singular *(he, she, it)* or plural *(we, they)* in form. Then check that a singular pronoun refers to a preceding singular or uncountable noun phrase and that a plural pronoun refers to a plural noun phrase.
	3. Check your use of *its* and *it's*. The latter means "it is." Make sure that is what you intend.
	4. Check the form and spelling of words like *himself* and *themselves*. Students sometimes have difficulties with these words.

Verbals

19. INFINITIVES
   a. Form and functions of infinitives
   b. Infinitive as subject and subject complement
   c. Infinitive as object
   d. Infinitive after verb + noun phrase
   e. Infinitive to modify adjectives
   f. Infinitive to modify nouns
   g. Infinitive to express purpose
   h. Special uses of the infinitive

20. *-ING* FORMS (GERUNDS AND MODIFIERS)
   a. The functions of *-ing* words
   b. *-ing* as subject and subject complement (gerund in a noun phrase)
   c. *-ing* as object (gerund in a noun phrase)
   d. Verbs followed by either *-ing* or infinitive (*to* + simple form)
   e. *-ing* after a preposition (gerund in a noun phrase)
   f. *-ing* after *to* as a preposition
   g. *-ing* as an adjective
   h. *-ing* in phrases substituting for clauses

21. PARTICIPLE FORMS (*-ED/-EN* FORMS)
   a. The functions of participles
   b. Participle and *-ing* forms
   c. Participle after *get*
   d. *Used to* and *get* (or *be*) *used to*
   e. Participle as clause substitute

19 Infinitives

READ

Read the following excerpt from the reading "White Lies," which appears with vocabulary glosses on p. 365.

The most frequent motive [for telling a white lie] was *to save face.* Lying of this sort is often given the approving label of "tact," and is used "when it would be unkind to be honest but dishonest to be kind." Sometimes a face-saving lie prevents embarrassment for the recipient, as

5   when you pretend to remember someone at a party whom you really don't recall ever having seen before. . . .

The second most frequent motivation for lying was *to avoid tension or conflict.* . . . Sometimes it seems worthwhile to tell a little lie to prevent a large conflict. You might, for example, compliment a friend's

10   bad work, not so much for your friend's sake but to prevent the hassle that would result if you told the truth. Likewise, you might hide feelings of irritation to avoid a fight. . . .

The fifth and last motive . . . was *to achieve personal power.* Turning down a last-minute request for a date by claiming you're busy

15   can be one way to put yourself in a one-up position, saying in effect, "Don't expect me to sit around waiting for you to call."

ANALYZE

1. Underline all the instances of the infinitive (*to* + simple form of the verb) in the passage.

2. Answer the following questions:

- How many of the instances are used directly after a form of the verb *be?*
- How many could have *in order to* as a substitute form for *to?*
- How many are used directly after a verb or after a verb + pronoun?
- How many are used directly after an adjective, and what are they?
- How many are used after a noun?

STUDY

19a. Form and functions of infinitives

All verbs have an active infinitive form, positive and negative. They also have a perfect infinitive form, indicating time before the time of the main verb. Transitive verbs (verbs that can be used with an object) have, in addition, a passive infinitive form.

FORMS OF THE INFINITIVE		
Type	*Form*	*Example*
Positive	*to* + simple form	I want *to go.*
Negative	*not to* + simple form	He decided *not to go.*
Perfect	*(not) to have* + participle	He is lucky *to have found* his wallet.
Passive	*(not) to be* + participle	She wants *to be promoted.*
Perfect passive	*(not) to have been* + participle	He is proud *to have been promoted.*

The infinitive form is used in a variety of positions in the sentence for a variety of functions. The box titled "Functions of the Infinitive" summarizes the main functions, which are then explained and illustrated in the sections that follow.

FUNCTIONS OF THE INFINITIVE	
Function	*Example*
Subject	*To succeed* is his goal, above all else.
Subject complement (after linking verb)	His aim is *not to make* one mistake.
Object of verb	He wants *to become* chief executive officer.
Following verb + noun phrase	His colleagues expect him *to succeed.*
Modifying an adjective	He is eager *to be recognized.*
Modifying a noun	He has no time *to have fun.*
Expressing purpose	He lied *to help* his career.

EXERCISE 1

Fit the 13 examples of the infinitive in the reading passage into the categories listed under "Function" in the "Functions of the Infinitive" box in section 19a.

EXAMPLE

INFINITIVE	FUNCTION
to save face	Subject complement

209

19b. Infinitive as subject and subject complement

The infinitive can be used as the subject of a sentence.

EXAMPLE **To tell the truth isn't always possible.**

Note that although the infinitive as subject is acceptable grammatically, it is neither as frequently used nor as idiomatic as the use of the filler subject *it* or the gerund (*-ing* form) as subject. (See Chapter 20, "*-ing* Forms.")

EXAMPLE

It isn't always possible to tell the truth.
Telling the truth isn't always possible.

The infinitive is also often used as a subject complement after the verbs *be, seem, appear*. It is found especially frequently when the subject of the verb is a noun like *goal, dream, aim, fear, plan, motive, object, need, desire, wish, method, job, purpose*.

EXAMPLES

The most frequent motive was to save face.
If the goal is to keep customers in a bar or restaurant for a long time, the proper technique is to lower the lighting.

Note the following idiomatic uses:

He is to blame.
He is to be envied.

Note, too, that it is more idiomatic to use the infinitive as subject complement than to use the infinitive as subject:

EXAMPLES

His job is to increase sales. (frequent)
To increase sales is his job. (less frequent)

An even more frequent variation here is the use of the filler subject *it:*

It is his job to increase sales. (See section 19f.)

EXERCISE 2

The following sentences refer to some of the ideas presented in the readings in this book. Rewrite them, moving the infinitive phrase from the subject position. Refer to the examples given at the end of section 19b.

1. To save face was the most frequent motive for lying.
2. To avoid conflict was the second most frequent motive for lying.
3. To send music to remote space is his dream.
4. To send science out into space is Thomas's aim.

[handwritten in left margin:]
1. The most frequent motive for lying was to save face.
2. The second most frequent motive for lying was to avoid—
3. His dream is to send music to remote space.
4. Thomas's aim is to send science out into space.

5. The farmers' plan is to grow soybeans.
6. A designer's job is to select comfortable furniture.

5. To grow soybeans is the farmers' plan.
6. To select comfortable furniture is a designer's job.

19c. Infinitive as object

The infinitive can be used as the object of a verb. The problem is that some verbs are followed not by an infinitive but by a gerund (*-ing* form). How can we tell whether to use an infinitive or an *-ing* form? Some systematic organizing principles have been attempted, but they are complicated and full of exceptions. Probably the best thing for a language learner to do is to memorize the verbs that are regularly followed by either the infinitive or the *-ing* form and to keep lists of verbs that can take either according to context. So whenever you come across a verb followed by one or the other, write it down as it occurs in its sentence, and learn that particular use. This chapter and the next will provide you with some examples.

Some frequently used verbs are followed by the infinitive rather than the gerund.

VERBS FOLLOWED BY AN INFINITIVE

hope	decide	pretend
want	plan	venture
expect	choose	bother
need	claim	manage
refuse	fail	

EXAMPLES

You pretend to remember someone at a party.
I expect to win.

You will see that the infinitive often expresses an idea that, in relation to the verb phrase, is in the future. Add to this list as you come across other verbs.

If you can, avoid splitting an infinitive: many English speakers object quite strongly to this practice, so it is best to avoid it.

Not   *He wants to carefully arrange all the details.
But   He wants to arrange all the details carefully.
Or   He wants carefully to arrange all the details.

EXERCISE 3 (oral)

Imagine that you are making New Year's resolutions. Tell a partner what your resolutions are. Use the following verbs, each one followed by an infinitive. Use some adverbs, too, but avoid splitting the infinitive with the adverb.

EXAMPLE **I plan to organize my room efficiently.**

want	hope	refuse
intend	plan	expect

Then imagine that you are the leader of your country. Write five New Year's resolutions that you would make.

19d. Infinitive after verb + noun phrase

Infinitives are often found after a verb + noun phrase (often a pronoun) structure.

EXAMPLES

Don't expect *me to sit around.*
They forced *their guests to stay.*
She believes *her boss to be* a genius. (She believes that her boss is a genius.)

He considers *her [to be]* an ambitious rival. (*To be* can be omitted in this sentence.)

She persuaded *us not to wait* any longer.
She urged *her students not to be late* for the exam.

EXERCISE 4 *(oral)*

With another student, discuss what you see as the difference in meaning between the two sentences in each pair. What could be a possible scenario for each sentence?

She persuaded us not to wait any longer.
She did not persuade us to wait any longer.

She urged her students not to be late for the exam.
She did not urge her students to be late for the exam.

☆EXERCISE 5

Write sentences using the verb + noun phrase + infinitive structure for five of the following verbs. Refer to your own knowledge of child rearing in your own country for the content, and write sentences that tell a reader about those practices.

EXAMPLES

Doctors advise parents to pick a baby up as soon as it cries.
School regulations force all students to wear a uniform.

advise	force	persuade
assume	want	teach
allow	expect	tell
permit	urge	warn

The teacher persuaded his students not to speak out.
My mother taught me to cook.
I permit you to play volleyball.
I assumed you to have cleaned your room.
The safeguard warned us not to go out this time.

19e. Infinitive to modify adjectives

Some adjectives can be followed by infinitives. The infinitive often expresses something that is in the future. Look at the sentence "I am anxious to finish my work." The feeling of anxiety comes before the finishing of the work.

ADJECTIVES FOLLOWED BY AN INFINITIVE

anxious	(in)advisable	foolish
eager	sorry	silly
happy	dangerous	(un)kind
proud	(im)possible	powerless
likely	right	worthwhile†
lucky	wrong	easy†
(un)necessary	(un)just	difficult†
(un)essential	(un)fair	hard†

- Filler subject *it*
  You will find that many of these adjectives are used in a structure with the filler subject *it:*

  It is essential [for you] to tell the truth.
  Sometimes it seems worthwhile to tell a little lie.
  It is now possible to see in the living room.

- *Easy* and *difficult*
  Often you will have a choice of alternate forms, and students sometimes have problems with these forms with *easy* and *difficult*. These structures are possible:

  1. It is easy [for me] to make spaghetti.
  2. [For me] to make spaghetti is easy.
  3. Making spaghetti is easy.
  4. I find it easy to make spaghetti *or* I think (*or* know) it is easy to make spaghetti.
  5. Spaghetti is easy to make.

†May also occasionally be followed by a gerund (*-ing* form).

213

But not   *I am easy to make spaghetti.

Easy and *difficult* can also be followed by the *-ing* form when simultaneous time is indicated, rather than a future event:

It's not easy being tall.
It's difficult having such big feet.

EXERCISE 6 *(oral)*

Rephrase the following sentences, beginning each with the word or words given in parentheses. Preserve the original meaning as much as possible.

1. Fixing a broken window is difficult. (It is)

2. It is difficult to understand him. (He is)

3. Trigonometry is hard for me to understand. (It)

4. Algebra is also hard for me to understand. (I)

5. Our teacher is easy to please. (It is)

6. It is difficult to open that jar. (That jar)

7. The new word processing program is hard to learn. (It is)

8. It is easy for most employees to get along with the boss. (The boss)

9. It is difficult to use a manual typewriter after an electric one. (A manual typewriter)

10. It is hard to learn statistical methods. (Statistical methods)

19f. Infinitive to modify nouns

Infinitives can be used to modify nouns in place of an adjective clause.

EXAMPLE

He is a person to trust. (= He is a person that other people can trust.)
I need a pen to write with. (= that I can write with)

The following nouns are often followed by infinitives.

NOUNS THAT MAY BE FOLLOWED BY AN INFINITIVE

way	desire	job
work	decision	motive
place	need	object
time	method	aim
turn		

EXAMPLES

Turning down a last-minute request can be one *way to put* yourself in a one-up position.

It is her *job to hire and fire* people.
Her *decision to fire* her cousin was a difficult one.
There is urgent *need to debate* this issue openly.

EXERCISE 7 *(oral)*

Complete each of the following sentences with an infinitive following and modifying the noun.

1. California is a good place . . .

2. A teacher's job is . . .

3. Most students need more time . . .

4. Being rude to your boss is one way . . .

5. The boss made a decision . . .

6. We need some games . . .

7. She couldn't find a way . . .

8. After you, it is my turn . . .

19g. Infinitive to express purpose

Often infinitives modify a verb phrase in the same way as *in order to* + verb to express purpose.

EXAMPLES

Sometimes we tell a lie (in order) *to prevent* a large conflict.
You might hide feelings of irritation (in order) *to avoid* a fight.

215

EXERCISE 8 (oral)

Work with a partner. Take turns asking each other the following questions and providing your own answers. Reply in a complete sentence, using an infinitive to express purpose.

1. Why are you studying English?
2. Why do some students have part-time jobs?
3. Why do people need health insurance?
4. Why do people tell white lies?
5. Why do some people sunbathe?
6. Why have so many people given up smoking?
7. Why do people take aspirin?
8. Why do people choose teaching as a career?

19h. Special uses of the infinitive

A few special uses of the infinitive cause difficulty for language learners.

- The infinitive is used with *too* and *enough:*

    I am too tired to go out now.
    It is too late [for me] to go out.
    He is wealthy enough to buy antiques.

(See also Chapter 15.)

- With the verbs *make, let,* and *have,* the infinitive form without *to* is used:

    He made me drive all night.
    She let me wait in her office.
    He had me change the oil, too.

But the verbs *force, cause, allow, get,* and *permit* are followed by the infinitive form with *to:*

    He forced me to drive all night.
    She allowed me to wait in her office.
    He got me to change the oil, too.

- With *help,* the infinitive form with *to* is sometimes used:

    They helped him to solve the problem.

In American usage, *to* is usually omitted:

    They helped him solve the problem.

- With the sensory verbs *see, hear, feel, notice, observe,* and *watch,* when the object is animate and when the action described has definite time boundaries, the infinitive form without *to* is used:

I heard her recite the poem. (I heard the beginning and end: there are time boundaries.)

I heard her reciting the poem. (I heard a bit of it as I was walking past: no definite time boundaries.)

I saw your report lying on the couch. (Inanimate object: *your report.*)

- After question words in a noun clause as the object of the sentence, the infinitive is used (see also Chapter 25):

  He didn't know *what to say.*
  He couldn't decide *how to behave* when he arrived late.

☆EXERCISE 9 (oral)

Make up six sentences describing your childhood, and tell a partner about how permissive or how strict members of your family were. In three of the sentences, tell about what members of your family *made* you do when you were a child, and in the other three, tell about what others *let* you do.

☆EXERCISE 10

In each of the following sentences, insert the perfect infinitive, passive infinitive, or perfect passive infinitive of the given verb.

1. A majority of patients want _____ (tell) the

   truth when they are ill.

2. It is not easy for them _____ (fool) by white

   lies.

3. I am proud _____ (invite) here for the fourth

   time.

4. I went to Singapore last year. I am delighted _____

   _____ (have) the opportunity to go to Southeast Asia.

5. Most people want _____ (notice) by their

   colleagues.

6. Her brother was in a car accident last year. He still can't walk well, but

   he is lucky _____ (survive) the crash.

   217

7. He still needs _____ (admit) to the hospital

once every three months.

8. She was in the same crash. She seems _____

_____ (recover) totally.

_____

EDIT

The following piece of student writing contains several errors in the use of the infinitive. Find the errors, and suggest ways to correct each error.

I believe that people sometimes should lie not only for their own sake but also for others. There are many instances in our life when lies are helpful. For example, when someone is sick, we have to do something to make that person to feel more cheerful. A few lies about how well he looks and how brilliantly he will play football next week could really help.

I know only too well that the truth can be more painful than lies. A few months ago, my good friend asked me if I liked the dress she had just bought. The dress in my opinion was not very nice, and I told her so. As a result, she decided not talk to me for a long time.

In another case, I lost a job when I told my employer what I thought about him and his store. I told him the truth and I was sorry later—especially when he said he was sorry to fire me. I could have told a white lie and so allowed my boss to keep me and promote me. However, my truthful tongue made it necessary for me to be punish.

White lies are not as bad as some people think. We use them when we expect keeping a friend; they may let us to keep a job, or, more simply, they may cheer people up when they most need it.

Wojtek Sokolowski, Poland

WRITE

Some people think that it is never justifiable to tell a lie of any kind, even a white lie. What do you think? Tell your reader the reasons for your opinion, and support it with examples from your own experience. Use at least three of the adjectives in section 19e and three of the nouns in section 19f to help you practice using infinitive structures. Try out one or two of the special uses of the infinitive in section 19h as well.

1. Read through what you have written, and underline all uses of the infinitive or of the infinitive form without *to* after *see, hear, watch, make, have, let.*

2. Fit each use into one of the categories in this chapter:

    Infinitive as subject or subject complement
    Infinitive as object of verb
    Infinitive after verb + noun phrase
    Infinitive as a modifier after an adjective
    Infinitive as a modifier after a noun
    Infinitive to express purpose
    Special uses

3. If you have used a passive infinitive, make sure that you have used the participle form of the main verb.

20   *-ing* Forms (Gerunds and Modifiers)

READ

Read the first paragraph of "The Surprise" by Russell Baker, which follows. The entire selection, with vocabulary glosses, appears on p. 342.

> [My mother] was a magician at stretching a dollar. That December, with Christmas approaching, she was out to work and [my sister] Doris was in the kitchen when I barged into her bedroom one afternoon in search of a safety pin. Since her bedroom opened onto a community
> 5   hallway, she kept the door locked, but needing the pin, I took the key from its hiding place, unlocked the door, and stepped in. Standing against the wall was a big, black bicycle with balloon tires. I recognized it instantly. It was the same second-hand bike I'd been admiring in a Baltimore shop window. I'd even asked about the price. It was horrendous. Something
> 10   like $15. Somehow my mother had scraped together enough for a down payment and meant to surprise me with the bicycle on Christmas morning.

ANALYZE

1. Underline all the words in the paragraph that end in *-ing*. You should have eight. For two of them, the *-ing* ending is inseparable from the rest of the word. Which ones? For two others, the *-ing* form is used as the main verb (along with an auxiliary verb to form the complete verb phrase of a clause). Which ones? (There is one unusual use of inverted word order here, so be careful.)

You should be left with four other *-ing* forms. These are all verbals (forms derived from a verb). Copy down the whole phrase in which the verbal occurs, for example, *a magician at stretching a dollar.*

2. What conclusions can you draw from examining these *-ing* verbals about when and how such forms are used?

STUDY

20a. The functions of *-ing* words

We saw in Chapters 7 through 10 that an *-ing* ending can occur on a verb, making a verb form used with auxiliaries to indicate a progressive aspect in relation to basic time. The box summarizes that use and the other main functions of *-ing* forms as gerunds (noun forms) and as noun or sentence modifiers. Note: Gerunds act like nouns, so in formal usage they take possessive forms:

His wanting a new bicycle is extravagant.
They appreciated *our helping* them.

In informal usage, however, the gerund may be preceded by an object:

They appreciated *us helping* them.

FUNCTIONS OF *-ING* WORDS	
Function of -ing	*Example*
VERB Part of complete verb phrase	He was *working* all day yesterday.
VERBAL: GERUND Subject (+ singular verb) Subject complement Object Object of preposition Noun modifying noun	*Cycling* is healthy. One of the healthiest sports is *cycling*. I enjoy *cycling*. He complained about *being* the only boy without a bike. He bought a *sleeping* bag. (= a bag used for sleeping)
VERBAL: ADJECTIVE Before noun After linking verb	She had an *exciting* vacation. Her vacation was *exciting*.
VERBAL: CLAUSE SUBSTITUTE Adjectival Adverbial	The man *sitting* outside the café is French. (= who is sitting) *Wanting* to win, she swam as fast as she could. (= Because she wanted)

EXERCISE 1

Read paragraphs 2 and 3 of "The Surprise" on p. 342. Write down all the words that end in *-ing* (you should find eight). *Nothing* occurs three times; the other five are verbals. List the five verbals and assign each to one of the functions of verbals listed in the box in section 20a.

20b. *-ing* as subject and subject complement (gerund in a noun phrase)

-ing phrases can be used as the subject of a sentence or the subject complement:

> *Stumbling* upon it like this made me feel as though I'd struck a blow against her happiness.

The subject of *made [me] feel* is *Stumbling upon it like this*. This type of *-ing* construction is known as the gerund form; it fills the position of a noun phrase. Note that a gerund is found in the subject position more frequently than an infinitive form is. So if you are not sure which one to use in the subject position, try the gerund first.

EXAMPLES

Cycling is a healthy sport. (subject)
Russell's *finding out* about the surprise was unexpected. (subject with possessive)

His *finding out* about the surprise was unexpected. (subject with possessive)

One of the healthiest sports is *cycling*. (subject complement)

EXERCISE 2 (oral)

Make up sentences that include the following gerund noun phrases as the subject of the sentence.

EXAMPLE

Just thinking of owning a new bicycle
Just thinking of owning a new bicycle made him feel excited.

1. Finding old photographs *is a surprise and present for me.*
2. Jogging every day *is good for our health.*
3. Walking in the rain *is usually experienced by people.*
4. My wanting to stay home *made me reject my friend's request*
5. Their getting married *was a surprise to their friends.*
6. His finding the bicycle *ended to a fail.*

20c. *-ing* as object (gerund in a noun phrase)

- ing phrases can be used as the object of a verb phrase:

His mother loved *preparing* surprises.

Certain verbs in English are regularly followed by *-ing* rather than *to* + simple form.

EXAMPLE

> **He enjoys riding a bike.**
> *Not*   ***He enjoys to ride a bike.**

Grammarians have attempted to establish systems to explain the use of the infinitive or *-ing* after certain verbs, but these systems are, for the most part, complex and full of loopholes and exceptions. Rather than trying to master these systems, you can save time by simply memorizing the verbs that are regularly followed by either the infinitive (see Chapter 19) or the *-ing* form. Some of the most common verbs followed by the *-ing* form are listed here.

VERBS FOLLOWED BY THE *-ING* FORM

admit	dislike	miss
appreciate	enjoy	postpone
avoid	finish	practice
can't help	give up	risk
delay	help	suggest
deny	imagine	tolerate
discuss	keep (on)	

The negative is formed with *not:*

EXAMPLES

I *enjoy not having* to go to work every day.
They *appreciate not being* required to attend the ceremony.

In addition, certain idiomatic expressions are regularly followed by a verb in the *-ing* form:

have difficulty	be busy
have fun	be worth
have a good time	go (swimming, shopping, bowling, etc.)

EXERCISE 3 (oral)

Complete the following sentences, using an *-ing* form.

1. Could you imagine not . . .
2. Children enjoy not . . .

223

3. When I am older, I will really miss not . . .
4. I can't keep on . . .
5. In business, we can't risk . . .
6. When I am excited, I can't help . . .

20d. Verbs followed by either *-ing* or infinitive (*to* + simple form)

Some verbs can be followed either by the *-ing* form of a verb or by the infinitive, sometimes with a significant change in meaning, sometimes with a shade of difference so subtle that for most purposes you don't have to worry about it. Note the following patterns.

- *Remember, forget*

   He *remembered to mail* the letter. (The remembering happened first. Then he mailed the letter: future in relation to *remembered.*)

   He *remembered mailing* the letter. (The mailing comes before the remembering. He mailed the letter first. Then he remembered doing it.)

- *Try*

   She *tried being* more forceful. (She experimented with this approach.)

   She *tried to be* more forceful. (This was her intent and aim for the future.)

- *Stop*

   Finally, she *stopped playing* and said, "Thank you very much." (She didn't play anymore.)

   Sometimes we would see a doufu seller and *stop to chat.* (= in order to chat)

- *Consider, imagine*
   Consider and *imagine* follow these patterns:

verb + *-ing*	He is *considering running* for office. I can't *imagine speaking* in front of 500 people.
verb + noun phrase + infinitive	People *consider him to be* very competent. I don't *imagine him to be* a good public speaker.

- *Hate, like, love*
   These verbs can be followed by either *-ing* or *to* + simple form with only a subtle difference in the meaning or context.

I *hate smoking.* (I hate it when people smoke.)
I *hate to smoke.* (I myself do not enjoy smoking.)
I *love watching* tennis. (generally)
I'd *love to watch* tennis tomorrow. (future event)

- *Start, begin, continue*
  These verbs, too, can be followed by either *-ing* or infinitive with hardly any difference in meaning.

  She *started writing* the report this morning.
  She *started to write* the report this morning.

  Either version would be acceptable in most situations.

- *See, hear, feel, watch, notice, observe*
  With these verbs, you can use the *-ing* form or the infinitive form without *to*—just the simple form by itself:

  I saw him *driving* away. (activity in progress)
  I saw him *drive* away. (the whole event)

(See also section 19h of Chapter 19.)

EXERCISE 4

Complete each of the following sentences with the appropriate form of the given verb (infinitive or *-ing.*).

1. I can't imagine _____ (live) in that great big house.

2. She stopped _____ (drink) at the water fountain because she was thirsty.

3. She stopped _____ (drink) on her doctor's orders.

4. I saw her _____ (drive) off the road, but I woke her up just in time to avoid an accident.

5. I saw him _____ (drive) into a tree and ran up to help immediately.

6. I last saw your report _____ (lie) on the couch.

7. Would you like _____ (go) to the theater tonight?

8. I really love _____ (go) to the movies.

9. She considered _____ (take) a trip to Venezuela.

10. She considers travel _____ (be) the best form of education.

20e. -*ing* after a preposition (gerund in a noun phrase)

-*ing* phrases, since they are noun forms, are used after prepositions (*at, about, in, on, of, by, for, with,* etc).

My mother was a magician *at stretching* a dollar.
I had robbed her of the pleasure *of seeing* me astonished.

The negative is formed with *not* after the preposition:

She was excited *about not having* to go to work.

When a verb phrase is itself regularly followed by a particular preposition, a noun phrase or an -*ing* verbal serves as the object of the preposition.

EXAMPLE

complain about

He complained about his <u>unfair treatment</u>.

He complained about [his] <u>being treated unfairly</u>.

COMMON VERBS + PREPOSITION + -*ING*	
concentrate on	be proud of
thank (someone) for	be responsible for
blame (someone) for	be aware of
apologize for	be ashamed of
insist on	be excited about
worry about	be interested in

20f. -*ing* after *to* as a preposition

Pay special attention to these expressions with *to:*

look forward to	admit to
be accustomed to	get accustomed to
be used to	get used to

You might expect to find the simple form of the verb after *to* (that is, the infinitive form). In these cases, however, *to* is a preposition, and so it is followed by a noun phrase, and thus, when appropriate, by an *-ing* verbal:

noun phrase
I am looking forward to <u>my vacation</u>.

-ing form
I am looking forward to <u>traveling around Italy</u>.

noun phrase
He is used to <u>American culture and customs</u>.

-ing form
He is used to <u>living in America</u>.

Take care not to confuse this last sentence in form or meaning with the following:

He used to live in America.

This tells us that he lived there in the past, but he doesn't live there anymore. The sentence

He is used to living in America.

tells us what he is accustomed to. It is not necessarily related to past time as *used to* + simple form is. (See also section 21d of Chapter 21.)

EXERCISE 5 *(oral)*

Complete each of the following sentences with the *-ing* or simple form, as appropriate.

1. When I was in my country, I always used to . . .
2. I can't get used to . . .
3. My family is looking forward to . . .
4. The thief admitted to . . .
5. The police managed to . . .
6. It's difficult to get accustomed to . . .
7. I would love to . . .
8. Most people would like to . . .

EXERCISE 6

In the following selections from the readings, fill in the gaps with appropriate forms of the given verbs. Add *to* when appropriate.

1. Perhaps the safest thing to do at the outset, if technology permits,

   is ___to send___ (send) music. This language may be

   the best we have for ___explaining___ (explain) what we

   are like to others in space. (p. 355)

2. We suspect that many people who are careless in ___*buying*___ _____ (buy) furniture for their homes get much the same result without ___*trying*___ (try). One environmental psychologist . . . refuses ___*to buy*___ (buy) a chair or couch without ___*sitting*___ (sit) in it for at least half an hour ___*to test*___ (test) the comfort. (p. 352)

3. We've spent . . . endless evenings in . . . "unliving rooms," where the spotless ashtrays, furniture coverings, and plastic lamp covers seemed ___*to send*___ (send) nonverbal messages telling us ___*not to touch*___ (not touch) anything. (p. 351)

4. Airports are designed ___*to discourage*___ (discourage) people from ___*spending*___ (spend) too much time in waiting areas. . . . Travelers are forced ___*to move*___ _____ (move) to restaurants and bars in the terminal. (p. 352)

5. Studies show that most doctors sincerely believe that the seriously ill do not want ___*to know*___ (know) the truth about their condition, and that ___*informing*___ (inform) them risks ___*destroying*___ (destroy) their hope. (p. 337)

6. Nurses may bitterly resent ___*having to*___ (have to) take part, day after day, in ___*deceiving*___ (deceive) patients, but feel powerless to take a stand. (p. 338)

_____

20g. *-ing* as an adjective

An *-ing* noun phrase can function as a noun modifier in an adjective position:

Christmas is an *exciting* time.

The *-ing* form used as an adjective usually has an active meaning:

> Christmas is very *exciting*. (Christmas excites most people.)
> The *exciting* moment for him was first glimpse of the tree surrounded by presents. (The moment excited him.)

(For more explanation, examples, and exercises on the forms *interested/interesting, bored/boring,* etc., see section 14d of Chapter 14 and section 21b of Chapter 21.)

20h. *-ing* in phrases substituting for clauses

-ing phrases can substitute for adjectival or adverbial clauses.

- Adjectival
    -ing phrases can substitute for a *who, which,* or *that clause:*

> His mother, *wanting* to surprise him, bought a bicycle. (= who wanted)

- Adverbial
    -ing phrases can also substitute for a full *when, while, since, before, after,* or *until* clause:

> While *admiring* the bicycle, he heard a noise. (While he was admiring . . .)
> I had walked along the river many times since *meeting* the fisherman. (since I met . . .)
> Before *opening* the door, he hesitated. (Before he opened the door, . . .)

An *-ing* phrase is often used to provide more information about the sentence. When it precedes the subject, it is set off from the main subject + predicate structure with a comma. When an *-ing* phrase is used without the introductory conjunction (like *while, when, since,* or *before*), the meaning implied is usually one of cause *(because, since)* or of simultaneity *(while, as)*.

> *Needing* the pin, I took the key from its hiding place.
> *Feeling* guilty about seeing his present, he pretended he knew nothing about it.
> *Admiring* the bicycle, he heard a noise.

☆*EXERCISE 7*

Answer the following questions, using the underlined phrases or parts of phrases in your answer.

1. What did Baker's mother hope to achieve <u>by hiding the bicycle</u>?

2. What is someone in your family a magician <u>at doing</u>?
3. How do you think Baker planned to show that he was stunned with amazement on Christmas day? (<u>by -ing</u>)
4. What did he have to <u>avoid doing</u> so as not to spoil his mother's secret?
5. What had bursting into her room robbed her of <u>the pleasure of</u>?
6. What will he have to <u>apologize</u> to his mother <u>for doing</u>?
7. How are you <u>accustomed to</u> celebrating holidays?
8. What are you <u>looking forward to owning</u> at some time in the future?

EDIT

The following passage from a student's journal contains errors with *-ing* forms. Sometimes a wrong form is used in place of *-ing,* sometimes *-ing* is used in place of the correct form, and sometimes the *-ing* form is misused in the context. Try to identify and suggest possible corrections for any errors you find.

A big part of my life was go to my grandparents' house for my vacation in the summertime. I used to go every single year without missing any. All my childhood memories were attached to that house, which I called "another world." The house was all by itself and isolated from the other houses. There was a little river one mile from the house where my grandfather and I used to go fishing. After reach home, we had a big supper. My grandparents used to tell me stories before I fell asleep. I was always exhausting at the end of the day. I was very close to them and I enjoyed to stay at their house.

Marie François, Haiti

WRITE

The excerpt at the beginning of this chapter is taken from Russell Baker's autobiography. Imagine that you are writing a part of your autobiography. Write sentences that would tell readers about yourself and your characteristics. They want to learn about your likes and dislikes, your aims, your problems, your good points, and your faults. Try to use some of the following expressions:

can't help	worry about
be afraid of	have difficulty
look forward to	get excited about
enjoy	be good at
dislike	be proud of
love	give up
avoid	ashamed of
delay	be (*or* get) used (*or* accustomed) to

Remember that these expressions are followed by a noun phrase, which means the *-ing* form if you want to use a verbal.

When you have written as much as you can, show your sentences to another student, who will ask you questions about yourself and will try to summarize your character in one sentence.

Then write a paragraph about yourself that begins by summarizing for your reader the type of person you think you are. In the rest of the paragraph, tell the reader why you have reached that conclusion by supplying details.

---

1. Check that a verbal used after any of the verbs listed in section 20c is an *-ing* verbal.

2. If you have used a preposition + verbal, that verbal should be an *-ing* form (see section 20e).

3. Did you use any *-ing* forms as subject? If so, did you remember to use a singular verb?

4. If you have used a gerund, check that you have used a possessive adjective with it, not just a personal pronoun.

EDITING ADVICE

---

21 Participle Forms (*-ed/-en* Forms)

READ

Read the following excerpt from the reading "The Basic-Nonbasic Concept," which appears in full with vocabulary glosses on p. 367.

> People living in cities are engaged in specialized activities. The activities imply that cities are centers of trade. In other words, the specialized goods and services produced by a population and not consumed by that population are exchanged for the specialized goods and
> 5 services produced by other cities and regions. . . . As we shall see, . . . the labor force of a city can be divided into two parts: (1) [workers] employed in *basic* industries, or "city forming" employment that depends upon areas outside the city for its market, and (2) the nonbasic component, the "city serving" employment activity that is
> 10 sustained from money generated within the area where it is found.

ANALYZE

1. In the passage, underline all the participle[†] forms (*-ed/-en* forms) of verbs that you can find, whether they are part of a complete verb phrase or not. Remember that the participle form of regular verbs ends in *-ed* (but the past tense form will look the same); the participle forms of irregular verbs can be found in the Appendix.

2. Make a list of the forms that occur as part of a complete verb phrase, that is, with *have* auxiliaries in the active or with *be* auxiliaries in the passive.

3. Of the remaining participle forms, which ones modify a noun phrase by occurring before it and which ones occur after it?

[†]We noted in Chapter 7 that this form is often called the past participle, but since it is used in nonpast contexts, it is less confusing to call it simply the *participle*.

STUDY

21a. The functions of participles

We have seen in other chapters that a participle (*-ed*/*-en* form) can appear with a form of *have* to form a complete active verb phrase or with a form of *be* to form a passive verb phrase.

EXAMPLES

ACTIVE
The gold vein *has run* out.
This *has happened* to thousands of contemporary cities.

PASSIVE
The excess goods *are exchanged* for other cities' excess goods.

The box summarizes verb phrase uses and the other main functions of the participle form as a modifier and as an introduction to a reduced clause:

FUNCTIONS OF PARTICIPLES	
Function	*Example*
VERB Part of complete active verb Part of complete passive verb	This has already happened. The labor force can be divided into two parts.
VERBAL: ADJECTIVE Before noun After linking verb	They sell the specialized goods. The swimmer felt exhausted.
VERBAL: CLAUSE SUBSTITUTE Adjectival Adverbial	The food prepared in that restaurant is very good. (that is prepared) Engrossed in what she was reading, she didn't hear the doorbell. (while *or* because she was engrossed)

Note also the following common idioms in which participles appear:

be concerned about   be used to
be supposed to   get used to

EXERCISE 1

Read these sentences based on "The Soybean," which appears with vocabulary glosses on p. 339. Underline all the occurrences of the participle. All of them are verbals. Which type are they? List them, and fit them into the functions illustrated in the box. The first has been done for you.

PARTICIPLE   FUNCTION
1. prepared   Clause substitute (adjectival)

1. It is the most important of the foods <u>prepared</u> in the East from the soybean.
2. These changes are sufficient to add the bean to the list of <u>domesticated</u> plants. *before grown*   *that are*
3. The bean grows well in soils too <u>depleted</u> to support other crops.
✓ 4. The Chinese consider doufu [to be] <u>valued</u> but common.
5. Doufu arrived as one of the things <u>associated</u> with the new religion.
6. Postwar affluence sent the <u>developed</u> world on a binge of meat eating.

21b. Participle and -*ing* forms

Students often have difficulty with adjectives formed from participles and from -*ing* words. Sometimes they mix them up. The point to remember is that -*ing* adjectives have more of an active flavor, while adjectives formed from participles have a passive flavor.

EXAMPLES

The swimmer was exhausted by the exercise. (passive verb)
The *exhausted* swimmer slept for three hours. (participle) (The swimmer who was exhausted by the exercise . . .)

The race exhausted the swimmer. (active verb)
The race was *exhausting*. (-*ing* adjective)
The *exhausting* race won a lot of attention.

The following pairs, all formed from verbs expressing emotion, often cause difficulties.

-ING FORM	PARTICIPLE FORM +	PREPOSITION
interesting	interested	in
boring	bored	with, by
confusing	confused	by
depressing	depressed	by

-*ING* FORM	PARTICIPLE FORM +	PREPOSITION
exciting	excited	about, by
surprising	surprised	at, by
amazing	amazed	by
amusing	amused	by
annoying	annoyed	with, by
irritating	irritated	by
disappointing	disappointed	in, by
frightening	frightened	of, by
embarrassing	embarrassed	by
satisfying	satisfied	with
worrying	worried	about, by

EXERCISE 2

In the following passages based on Mark Salzman's "Cultural Exchanges" (p. 347), insert the form derived either from the -*ing* or the participle form of the given verb.

1. He had just returned from a long fishing trip on Dong Ting, a

   _____ (sprawl) lake in North Hunan.

2. The men rowed out to meet us in one of two tiny boats _____

   _____ (lash) to the side.

3. They seemed _____ (delight) by the drawing.

4. I took off one of the boards _____ (conceal) the

   pedal mechanism of the piano.

5. I finished just before dinner. I was terribly_____

   _____ (excite) and went into the kitchen to announce my

   success.

6. We had a delicious meal of _____ (smoke) eggs

   and a whole chicken _____ (stew) in a thick yellow

   sauce.

EXERCISE 3

Write three sentences for each group, and include all the words in the group in each sentence. In each case, use (a) the verb as a verb; (b) the -ing form, and (c) the participle form of the given verb.

EXAMPLES

amaze / the fishermen / the drawing
a. **The drawing amazed the fishermen.**
b. **The drawing was amazing to the fishermen. / The fishermen thought the drawing was amazing. / The drawing was so amazing that the fishermen wanted to keep it.**
c. **The fishermen were amazed by the drawing. / Amazed by the drawing, the fishermen wanted to keep it. / The fishermen were so amazed by the drawing that they asked to keep it.**

1. annoy / Julie / the loud radio
   the radio was annoying to Julie

2. confuse / the students / the lecture

the students were confused by the lecture.
the lecture confused the students.
the lecture was confusing for the students.
(b)
more common

3. surprise / we (*or* us) / the end of the movie

4. disappoint / the students / the exam results

5. frighten / the little girl / the big dog

6. satisfy / the diners / the meal

21c. Participle after *get*

Get is often followed, particularly in spoken English, by a participle form, which makes reference to the state of the subject.

EXAMPLE **I got depressed when I heard the bad news.**

Here are some common expressions with *get* + participle:

get acquainted	get lost
get annoyed	get married (to somebody)
get bored	get paid
get confused	get scared
get divorced (from somebody)	get tired
get dressed	get used to
get drunk	get worried
get hurt	

There are many more. Add to this list as you come across other expressions.

EXERCISE 4 (oral)

Prepare five questions to ask another student in your class, using expressions with *get*.

EXAMPLES

When do you get worried?
What makes you get annoyed?
When do you expect to get married?

Ask your partner your questions. Your partner will answer each question with a complete sentence.

21d. *Used to* and *get (or be) used to*

The two expressions *used to* and *get* (or *be*) *used to* have different meanings and contexts and should not be confused.

USED TO AND *GET* (OR *BE*) *USED TO*			
	Meaning	*Followed by*	*Example*
used to	past habit	simple form of verb	We *used to live* in Chicago. (We don't now.)
get* (or *be*) *used to	become familiar with, grow accustomed to	- *ing* *or* noun phrase	We can't *get used to living* in this little village. We can't *get used to village life*.

(See also section 9f of Chapter 9 and section 20f of Chapter 20.)

EXERCISE 5

Insert the correct form of the given verb.

1. She gets up early every day, but she can't get used to

_____ (leave) her house in the dark.

2. She used to _____ (leave) for work at nine o'clock.

237

3. She has had this routine for so long now that she is used to
_____ (jump) out of bed as soon as her alarm
rings.

4. Her boss often used to _____ (reprimand) her for
being late.

5. Now her boss is used to _____ (see) her there
when he arrives.

6. When she worked in England, she couldn't get used to
_____ (drive) on the left.

EXERCISE 6

Write a few sentences about what you used to do during one period
of your life (things that you don't do now). Then write a few sentences
about what things you are finding it difficult to get used to doing in the
situation you are in now. Use patterns like these:

I can't get used to . . .
I'll never get used to . . .
I'm finding it difficult to get used to . . .

21e. Participle as clause substitute

The participle form is often used to introduce a phrase that represents a
reduced adjectival or adverbial clause.

EXAMPLES

ADJECTIVAL
The goods *produced* by a population can be exchanged. (The goods
that are produced by a population can be exchanged.)

ADVERBIAL
Embarrassed by all the attention, she left the festivities early.
(Because she was embarrassed by all the attention . . .)

Faced with this situation, travelers are forced to move to restaurants
and bars. (Whenever they are faced with this situation . . .)

The chair puts pressure on the back if occupied for more than a few minutes. (if it is occupied . . .)

☆EXERCISE 7

Read the second paragraph of "The Basic-Nonbasic Concept" on p. 367, and identify all the participle forms. List each one by line number, and state its function according to those in the box in section 21a. The first one has been done as an example.

PARTICIPLE	LINE	FUNCTION
recognized	13	Part of passive verb

EXERCISE 8

Choose one word or phrase that best completes each sentence.

1. He _____ when he heard that he had gotten a job in San Francisco.

   a. was excite
   b. was exciting
   c. was excited
   d. felt exciting

2. When the professor doesn't explain the theories clearly, the students _____.

   a. get confuse
   b. are confused
   c. feel confusing
   d. seem to be confuse

3. She looked extremely _____ when her boss pointed out all her mistakes.

   a. embarrassed
   b. embarrass
   c. embarrassment
   d. embarrassing

4. Some people _____ , so they change their jobs often.

   a. never satisfy
   b. are never satisfied
   c. are never satisfy
   d. are never satisfying

5. The accident was a _____ experience for all the passengers.

   a. terrify
   b. terrified
   c. terrifying
   d. terrifies

6. The _____ radio was found in a lot on Atlantic Avenue.

   a. stolen
   b. stealing
   c. stole
   d. robbed

7. The _____ rain forced them to pull off the road and wait for an hour.

   a. driven
   b. driving
   c. drive
   d. drove

8. She wanted _____ someone twenty years her senior, but her parents disapproved.

   a. to get marry with
   b. getting married to
   c. to marry with
   d. to get married to

EDIT

The following sentences written by students contain participle forms. Which ones are used correctly, and which are not? How should the students correct the ones that are incorrect? How would you explain to the students why they should fix those sentences in a particular way?

1. One day I got up and felt very depress and said, "It is time for a change."
2. I always try to keep my room clean and organize.
3. When occupy by more than three people, the room seems so small that I can't get use to invited anyone there.
4. A person who loses interested in his surroundings will become very sad.
5. In a restaurant we are not only concern about the food, but about the atmosphere.
6. Rooms design with taste and appropriately lit make us feel comfortable and relax.

WRITE

The last paragraph of "The Basic-Nonbasic Concept" on p. 368 presents an analogy (an example) to demonstrate the concept. Think of a concept that has been presented to you in a class in any subject (economics, accounting, business, computer science, physics, biology, history, etc.), and write an example that will show a reader clearly what that concept means. You might want to discuss your choice of concept with your classmates and instructor first to make sure that it is not too difficult.

Begin like this: "The concept of _____ is quite easy to understand when we look at an analogy to demonstrate the concept. Consider, for example, . . ." After you have written your first draft, look through it to see where you have used participles and where you might use participles. Check the form.

---

1. If you have used the participle form of a regular verb, it should end in -*ed*.

2. If you have used the participle form of an irregular verb, check the form in the Appendix or in a dictionary.

3. You should be able to place every participle you have used into one of the categories listed in the box in section 21a. Try that.

4. Sometimes, participle forms are confused with -*ing* forms. So look, too, at every -*ing* form you have used. Make sure that it is the correct form and that a participle is not required instead.

Connecting Sentences

22. COORDINATING CONJUNCTIONS
   a. Coordinating conjunctions connecting sentences
   b. Avoiding run-ons and the comma splice
   c. Conjunctions connecting phrases and other parallel structures
   d. *Not only* and *nor*
   e. Coordinate tags: *so, too, either,* and *neither*

23. TRANSITIONS
   a. Linking related sentences: the semicolon
   b. Transition words and expressions
   c. Problems with transitions: run-ons and the comma splice
   d. *In contrast* and *on the contrary*

Coordinating Conjunctions   22

READ

Read the following paragraph from Nora Ephron's article "Room with View—and No People," which appears with vocabulary glosses on p. 334.

> When I was growing up, I had a friend named Lillian who had no living-room furniture. She lived in a large house in Beverly Hills, and the living room was empty. I always wondered why. I always supposed it was because her mother was having trouble deciding on a color scheme. Color
> 5 schemes were important in those days. I had a friend named Arlene whose house was famous for having a color scheme in every room, including the breakfast nook, which was charcoal gray and pink. Anyway, a few yeas ago, Lillian was in New York and I finally got up the nerve to ask her why her family had never had any living-room furniture. She told
> 10 me that her father had given her mother a choice of living-room furniture or a pool, and her mother had chosen the pool.

ANALYZE

1. Underline each occurrence of the words *and* and *or* in the passage. These words serve to connect similar elements in a sentence. In the sentences in the passage, what do they connect?

2. In the sentences that contain the word *and,* underline all the complete verb forms.

3. Discuss with a partner how you could express the ideas that appear in the sentences with *and* without actually using the word *and.*

STUDY

22a. Coordinating conjunctions connecting sentences

Coordinating conjunctions can be used to connect two independent clauses with related content:

S + V, conjunction S + V

EXAMPLE

She lived in a large house in Beverly Hills.
The living room was empty.
> She lived in a large house in Beverly Hills, and the living room was empty.

COORDINATE SENTENCES				
Subject	*Verb . . . ,*	*Conjunction*	*Subject*	*Verb . . .*
She	lived . . . ,	and	the living room	was . . .

The comma between the sentences is sometimes omitted if there is no ambiguity for the reader. However, if you want to follow a standard procedure as you write, and one that you know will be acceptable, put a comma every time. It won't be wrong.

There are seven coordinating conjunctions: *and, but, for, nor, or, so,* and *yet.* When these conjunctions connect one sentence with another, a comma precedes the conjunction.

The following sentence is punctuated incorrectly:

*He has no free time but, he makes a lot of money.

It should look like this:

He has no free time, but he makes a lot of money.

A series of three or more independent clauses can be connected like this:

S + V, S + V, conjunction S + V

EXAMPLE

The boys are playing happily, there is music on the radio, and she feels very contented.

EXERCISE 1

Read selection 2 from Mark Salzman's "Cultural Exchanges" on p. 347. Make a list of the coordinating conjunctions that join complete sentences and their line numbers. Compare your results with another student's.

EXERCISE 2

Rewrite each of the following pairs of sentences, adapted from Anna Quindlen's article "Siblings," as one sentence each, using coordinating conjunctions.

1. The two brothers are playing happily with their own toys. Although minutes have passed, neither has made a grab for the other's toy.
2. The younger one is babbling to himself in pidgin English. The older one is singing ceaselessly.
3. His baby can't catch him yet. It's only a matter of time.
4. My brother interested my girl friends. I was interested in his boy friends.
5. He was about to say hello. What came out instead was "You can't catch me."

22b. Avoiding run-ons and the comma splice

When you write two independent clauses with related content, you need to be careful to avoid writing a run-on or a comma splice. (See also Chapters 23 and 29.) You cannot simply put one clause after another, like this:

> *She lived in a large house in Beverly Hills the living room was empty. (run-on sentence)

You also cannot use a comma by itself, without a conjunction, to separate the two independent clauses, like this:

> *She lived in a large house in Beverly Hills, the living room was empty. (comma splice)

Not   *S + V S + V

Not   *S + V, S + V

But   S + V; S + V

Or   S + V, conjunction S + V

EXERCISE 3

The structure of some of the following passages from student writing works well. Indicate which ones are well constructed (OK) and which ones contain a run-on sentence (RO) or a comma splice (CS).

_____ 1. Those people usually grow flowers there, they look very lovely, they hang down from the roofs.

_____ 2. These people furnished the outside of their homes with comfortable seats or swings and a table, and usually they have a few trees on both sides of the house.

_____ 3. The other people don't even know that their verandas exist they don't sit there.

_____ 4. Antique lanterns are on the antique tables, there are two crystal chandeliers.

_____ 5. Between the beds, there is a small night table, on the top of the night table, there is a digital clock radio.

_____ 6. Between the two windows, there is a single bed with light blue pillows that the dog likes to sleep on in the afternoon.

_____

22c. Conjunctions connecting phrases and other parallel structures

Coordinating conjunctions do more than just connect complete sentences. The conjunctions *and, but, or,* and *nor* can also connect one noun phrase with another ("Her father had given her mother a choice of living-room furniture *or* a pool") or can connect adjectives, verb phrases, prepositional phrases, infinitives, or other parallel structures. In these cases, when there are only two structures to connect, no comma is used; when three or more structures are listed in a series, a comma should be used before the final conjunction.

- Noun phrases

  It has a fireplace and moldings. (two items)
  It has a fireplace, moldings, and a view. (three or more items)

- Adjective phrases

  It always looks neat and tidy.
  It always looks neat, tidy, and cheerful.

- Verb phrases

  They probably contemplate life and have drinks before dinner.
  They probably contemplate life, have drinks before dinner, and think of themselves as civilized.

- Prepositional phrases

  She works in the kitchen and in the bedroom.
  She works in the kitchen, in the bedroom, and on the porch.

Note that the structures on each side of the coordinating conjunction must always be parallel in structure (for example, all nouns or all verb phrases).

I spent the entire weekend eating, sleeping, working, and swimming.

In that sentence, the items in the series are separated by commas, *and* is used before the last one in the series, and all the items are parallel. It would not be correct to write this:

*I spent the entire weekend eating, sleeping, working, and to swim.

EXERCISE 4

The following pairs of sentences are adapted from Anna Quindlen's "Siblings." Rewrite each pair as only one independent clause, using parallel structures with conjunctions.

EXAMPLE

She will demand more of his time.
She will demand more of his attention.
   She will demand more of his time and attention.

1. I have vivid memories of reading in a club chair.
   I have vivid memories of having my brother enter the room.
2. One night your husband comes home.
   One night your husband tells you that he has decided to have a second wife.
3. She will be younger than you.
   She will be cuter than you.
4. My younger brother turned into a good-looking teenage boy.
   He became a first-rate dancer.
5. He has no interest in the trucks.
   He has no interest in the sandbox.

22d. *Not only* and *nor*

When the *not only . . . but also* structure is used to connect two complete independent clauses, word order is inverted after *not only*. This structure provides more emphasis. *Not only* can also be used to connect structures other than complete sentences. For example, these two sentences can be connected in various ways. Each successive example is more emphatic than the preceding one.

The room is empty.
It is dark and gloomy.
   The room is empty, dark, and gloomy. (least emphatic)
   The room is not only empty but also dark and gloomy.
   The room is not only empty but dark and gloomy also (*or too or as well*).

The room is not only empty, but it is also dark and gloomy.
The room is not only empty, but it is dark and gloomy as well.
Not only is the room empty, but it is also dark and gloomy. (most emphatic)

The box shows inverted word order when *not only* begins the sentence.

INVERTED WORD ORDER				
Not only	*Verb 1*	*Subject*	*Rest of Predicate*	**but . . .**
Not only	is	the room	empty ,	but it is . . .
Not only	is	there	no furniture . . . ,	but there is . . .
Not only	does	she	avoid this room ,	but she also . . .

EXAMPLES

Not only is the room empty, but it is also dark and gloomy.
Not only is there no furniture in the living room, but there is not much light either.
Not only does she avoid this room, but she also avoided the living room in her former apartment.

When *nor* means *and not* and is used to connect two sentences, inverted word order also follows:

She hasn't bought any furniture, nor does she intend to.
She doesn't understand my feelings, nor does she try.

EXERCISE 5 (oral)

Think of someone you know, a sibling or a friend, with whom you feel rivalry. Make up five sentences about that person using *not only . . . but also* in which you criticize the person.

EXAMPLE **Not only does Martha wear too much makeup, but she also dresses badly.**

EXERCISE 6 (oral)

Work with a partner. Connect the following pairs of sentences using *nor*.

EXAMPLE

She hasn't bought any furniture.
She doesn't intend to.
She hasn't bought any furniture, nor does she intend to.

1. He doesn't earn a lot.
   He hasn't saved any money.
2. She isn't working hard.
   She isn't trying hard.
3. She can't type.
   She doesn't want to learn.
4. He won't take his father's advice.
   He won't listen to his best friends.
5. At this time, inflation can't be stopped.
   It can't be reduced.

22e. Coordinate tags: *so, too, either,* and *neither*

When you say or write tags that use words like *so, too, either,* and *neither,* you should know that alternatives exist:

She doesn't have any furniture, and Lillian doesn't either.
She doesn't have any furniture, and neither does Lillian.

She wanted a pool, and her family did too.
She wanted a pool, and so did her family.

Note that with *so* and *neither,* inverted word order is used.

COORDINATE TAGS: INVERTED WORD ORDER WITH *SO* AND *NEITHER*			
. . . and	**so *or* neither**	*First Auxiliary Verb*	*Subject*
and	neither	does	Lillian
and	so	did	her family

EXERCISE 7 *(oral)*

Rephrase the following sentences. Change each coordinate tag so that you preserve the same meaning, according to the patterns just explained.

1. She doesn't use her living room, and I don't either.
2. She wanted a pool, and I did too.
3. She had a color scheme, and so did her friend.
4. She doesn't like phones in living rooms, and neither does her sister.
5. She doesn't want a TV set in the living room, and her children don't either.
6. She worked in the bedroom, and her daughter did too.

249

☆EXERCISE 8

In the following passage from "The Basic-Nonbasic Concept," which appears in full with vocabulary glosses on p. 367, underline each occurrence of *and*. Specify what parallel structures *and* is joining.

Let us assume for a moment that the gold vein has run out. What are the consequences? The gold is gone, and the 100 miners must seek work elsewhere. The basic industry is gone, and nothing is left to support the numerous nonbasic service workers. They too will eventually leave, and our little mining community will become a ghost town. This can and has happened to thousands of contemporary cities that have lost industries that represented a portion of the town's basic industry.

EDIT

Read the following piece of student writing written in response to the writing assignment in this chapter. What feature of his friend is the writer concentrating on? What example does he give of his friend's behavior? The writer has made a few mistakes connecting sentences together. Can you find them and suggest what the writer might do to edit those passages?

When I was growing up, I had a friend named Abdel who could fix almost anything. I remember, we had a television set that lasted years and years. That TV set was dropped at least ten times. One day it just gave up, it wouldn't work. My father took it to twenty different repairmen but, none of them could fix it. He was told that the chances of getting that TV fixed were slim. One night, when Abdel was spending the weekend at our house, my brother and I wanted to go to see a movie. When we went to get Abdel, we saw that he had that TV set stripped into pieces the first thing that came to my mind was that he had no chance whatsoever. He refused to come with us, so we left without him. Four or five hours later, when we got back home, we went to see how he was doing. I couldn't believe what I saw! He was actually watching a quiz show on that TV set. Abdel not only does he fix TV sets, radios and cars, but he also knows a lot of facts. So he was answering all the quiz questions and getting them right!

Hassan el-Warari, Morocco

WRITE

Nora Ephron begins a paragraph like this:

> When I was growing up, I had a friend named Lillian who had no living room furniture.

The rest of the paragraph is devoted to explaining that situation and giving us more details. Write a paragraph beginning the same way:

When I was growing up, I had a friend named
_____ **who** _____ . . .

Use the paragraph to tell a reader more about the specific quality you have mentioned. When you have written the paragraph, read it through to see if you should edit any series of short sentences by connecting them with conjunctions. Exchange papers with a classmate. Follow the Editing Advice.

---

1. To check that sentences are connected properly, identify all the independent clauses you have written between periods. These will be clauses that stand alone, have a subject and verb, and have no subordinating word like *because, if, even if, when,* or *although.* To help you do that, first underline all the complete verbs you find; then circle the subjects. Now look at all the clauses and determine which are dependent and which are independent.

2. If you find you have two independent clauses within a sentence, check to see how they are connected. You cannot just write one clause after the other (run-on). Nor is a comma between them enough (that is a comma splice). You need one of the seven coordinating conjunctions, or you need to rewrite or repunctuate the sentence.

3. If you have used a conjunction to connect structures other than complete sentences, make sure that the structures on either side of the conjunction are parallel in form.

EDITING ADVICE

23 Transitions

READ

Read the following selection from the article "The Soybean," which appears with vocabulary glosses on p. 339.

After the Second World War two things changed. Historically, China had been the major supplier of soybeans to the world market. However, the course of postwar politics and the difficulties experienced by the Chinese in recovering from wartime devastation prevented the restora-
5 tion of prewar trade relations with the West. The world soybean market needed a new source of supply, and the American farmer successfully stepped into the position.

Second, and far more important, postwar affluence sent the developed world on a binge of meat eating. By 1973 per capita
10 consumption of chicken had increased by factors of 2, 4, and 15 in the U.S., Europe, and Japan respectively. Supplies of the traditional source of protein in livestock feed—fish meal and scraps from meat-processing plants—were inadequate to meet these increases in demand. The high food value of the soybean made it a natural candidate. The bean was
15 tested and with a few modifications and supplements met the need perfectly, not only for chickens and hogs, but also for animals as diverse as mink, foxes, shrimp, catfish, eels, trout, bears (in zoos), and even bees and silkworms.

ANALYZE

1. In the passage, underline any words or phrases that appear before the subject at the beginning of a sentence.

2. Look at the first and second sentences of the second paragraph. Those sentences are separated by a period. Could they have been separated in any other way? Could the sentences be connected to make one sentence?

3. In the third sentence of paragraph 1, could the word *however* be used in any other position in the sentence? Where? Why do you think the author chose to put it first?

STUDY

23a. Linking related sentences: the semicolon

A period is used to indicate the end of a grammatical sentence (subject + predicate along with added phrases and clauses and other independent clauses). However, when two sentences are closely linked in idea, they can be combined by placing a semicolon at the end of the first sentence and lowercasing the second sentence. Often the second sentence will add more detail, provide an explanation, point out a contrast, or contain a structure parallel to that used in the first sentence. (See also Chapter 29.)

A passage from "The Soybean" reads like this:

> Why [farmers in China began to cultivate the soybean] is unclear; plants that lie on the ground are hard to cultivate, and the seeds of the wild soybean are tiny, hard, and, unless properly prepared, indigestible.

The second half of the sentence explains to us why the reasons for beginning to cultivate the soybean were not clear. The thoughts are very closely related.

EXERCISE 1

Skim through the article by Stephen Jay Gould on p. 363. Note each occurrence of a semicolon. The author could have used a period each time. In these cases, though, he chose to use a semicolon. Discuss the connection between each pair of sentences that makes them particularly appropriate for combining into one by means of a semicolon.

23b. Transition words and expressions

Two closely related ideas can also be connected with transition words and expressions. Even if you use a transition expression that connects one sentence very closely to another in meaning, you still need to separate the two sentences with a period or a semicolon.

EXAMPLES

The Chinese grew a lot of soybeans. However, they did not export them to the West.

The Chinese grew a lot of soybeans; however, they did not export them to the West.

Expressions of transition can also be positioned at various places within their clause. They are usually set off from the rest of the clause with commas, though *thus, also,* and *next* occur without commas.

253

The Chinese grew a lot of soybeans. They did not, however, export them to the West.

The Chinese grew a lot of soybeans. They did not export them to the West, however.

Soybeans were cultivated everywhere. They thus became a staple of the diet.

The accompanying box shows some of the commonly used expressions of transition. These expressions are not necessarily interchangeable; the context and your own intentions as to meaning determine which is appropriate. Most writers use these sparingly, too. There is no need to overload your writing with excesses of *therefore, thus,* and *moreover.* Frequently, the coordinating conjunctions *and, but,* and *so* will serve your purpose. You will probably find that the transitions in the box will help you most with making a connection between two paragraphs or between two blocks of ideas.

TRANSITIONS	
Writer's Purpose	*Transitions*
To add an idea	also, in addition, furthermore, moreover, besides
To show time or sequence	meanwhile, first, second, then, next, finally
To show result	therefore, thus, consequently, as a result
To show unexpected result	however, nevertheless, still, though (usually at end of sentence), nonetheless
To show contrasting situations	however, on the other hand, in contrast, by contrast
To show similarity	similarly, likewise, in a similar way
To emphasize	in fact, of course, indeed, certainly, to be sure
To provide an example	for example, for instance
To explain	that is, in other words
To add a new topic	by the way, incidentally
To return to a topic	anyway, at any rate
To argue	on the contrary, rather
To summarize or generalize	in general, overall, in short, in conclusion, in summary, all in all

EXERCISE 2

The following passages are based on the readings. Insert an appropriate expression of transition into the sentence after the slash mark (/), and add any necessary punctuation. Discuss with other students what alternatives are possible for the position of the transitional expression.

EXAMPLE

Most of us are familiar with how lead time works in our own culture, even though we cannot state the rules technically. / The rules for lead time in other cultures have rarely been analyzed.

However, the rules for lead time . . .
The rules for lead time in other cultures, however, have . . .
The rules for lead time in other cultures have, however, rarely . . .
The rules for lead time in other cultures have rarely been analyzed, however.

1. All sorts of cues came back to the effect that the time was not yet ripe to visit the minister. / Our friend persisted. (p. 361)
2. When Detroit is recognized as the automobile capital of the United States, we realize that automobiles produced within that city are sold mainly outside its borders. The automobile industry of Detroit, then, is basic to that city. / Most of the steel produced in Pittsburgh, Pennsylvania, and Gary, Indiana, is sold outside those cities. (p. 367)
3. Consider a frontier mining town where 100 miners are employed in the town's only basic industry—gold mining. Assume that each of the 100 miners is married and has two children. / The basic industry supports 400 people. (p. 367)
4. It has been suggested that there is an average basic-nonbasic ratio of 1:3; / for every miner employed in the town's basic industry, three people may be employed in a nonbasic industry. (p. 367)
5. In some cases a lie protects the teller from embarrassment. / You might cover up your mistakes by blaming them on outside forces. (p. 365)
6. Sometimes it seems worthwhile to tell a little lie to prevent a large conflict. / You might compliment a friend's bad work, not so much for your friend's sake but to prevent the hassle that would result if you told the truth. (p. 365)
7. You might compliment a friend's bad work. / You might hide feelings of irritation to avoid a fight. (p. 365)
8. A third motive for lying is to guide social interaction. / You might pretend to be glad to see someone you actually dislike. (p. 365)
9. If the goal is to run a high-volume business that tries to move people

in and out quickly, it's necessary to keep the lights shining brightly and not worry too much about soundproofing. / If the goal is to keep customers in a bar or restaurant for a long time, the proper technique is to lower the lighting. (p. 351)

10. Watching how people use an existing environment can be a way of telling what kind of relationships they want. / Sommer watched students in a college library and found that there's a definite pattern for people who want to study alone. (p. 352)

EXERCISE 3

Write five pairs of sentences that point out a contrasting situation between the place you lived in when you were a child and the place you live in now. Use a transition expression in each pair of sentences.

EXAMPLES

In England, people drive on the left. The French, on the other hand, just across a short stretch of water, drive on the right.

In Calcutta, parents arrange marriages for their children. New Yorkers, however, choose their own partners and marry for love—or money.

23c. Problems with transitions: run-ons and the comma splice

Sentence structure errors often occur with transitions. Remember that expressions of transition serve to provide a link between two complete sentences. That means that two sentences linked in this way need end punctuation between them—a period, a question mark, an exclamation point, or, if combined into a single sentence, a semicolon (see section 23a).

The following sentences contain errors:

*Soybeans were proved to be rich in protein, therefore their cultivation spread. (comma splice)

*The soybeans grew well however erosion was a problem. (run-on)

They should be punctuated like this:

Soybeans were proved to be rich in protein. Therefore, their cultivation spread.

The soybeans grew well; however, erosion was a problem.

Chapter 29 contains more examples and exercises with run-ons and comma splices.

EXERCISE 4

Some of the following sentences contain errors in punctuation (comma splice and run-on) with transition expressions. Identify which sentences contain no error (OK), which are comma splices (CS), and which are run-ons (RO). Discuss how the writer should correct the sentences with punctuation errors.

_____ 1. I've tried tofu, however I don't like it much.

_____ 2. Bean curd doesn't have much taste, still it's good in soup.

_____ 3. He grows a lot of crops for instance he grows rice and soybeans.

_____ 4. People started to eat more meat, for example, the consumption of chicken increased.

_____ 5. Forty years ago the major crop was cotton. A lot of corn, however, was grown as well.

_____ 6. In Tennessee, they grew cotton then they grew soybeans.

_____

23d. _In contrast_ and _on the contrary_

Students sometimes confuse the uses of _in contrast_ and _on the contrary_. Their differing contexts are shown here.

- _In contrast_ points out a contrasting situation:

  The physics requirements are very demanding; the chemistry requirements, in contrast, are extremely lenient.

- _On the contrary_ is used to argue with a concept. It says that the opposite is true. This expression is often used after a negative sentence. It negates one idea in the sentence; note, though, that the second sentence actually has the same meaning as the first, but with intensification.

  She doesn't neglect her children. On the contrary, she spends a great deal of time with them.

  Here, _on the contrary_ negates the idea of _neglect_. However, the second sentence (she spends a great deal of time with her children) reinforces the meaning of the first sentence (she doesn't neglect her children).

☆EXERCISE 5

In the following sentences, which transition expressions could fill the blank in each case to show unexpected result or to contrast situations or to argue against a concept? Choose from *however, nevertheless, still, nonetheless, though, on the other hand, in contrast, on the contrary,* and *rather.*

1. Some legal procedures are not often used. They are, _____ _____, emphasized in a lawyer's training.

2. Euthanasia is illegal in most countries. There are _____ _____, a lot of advocates for it, who argue their cases with doctors, hospitals, and government officials.

3. The doctors were silent. The nurses, _____, comforted the patients a lot by talking to them.

4. The treatment was well researched and expensive. _____ _____, it was not very effective.

5. The city hospital refused to accept chronically ill patients. _____ _____, the local nursing home welcomed them.

6. The new drugs didn't help the elderly patients; _____ _____, they made them feel even sicker.

7. Raw soybeans are not appetizing. _____, they are hard and indigestible.

8. The soybean was shown to be very rich in nutrition. This caused no great demand in the Western countries, _____.
_____

EDIT

The student who wrote the following description of a process used transitions to connect ideas and establish the relationship among them. As reprinted here, the linking expressions she used have been omitted, but their position is indicated. Which transition could she have used in each place?

How to Make Scrambled Eggs

Gather all the ingredients you will need. These are eggs, butter, milk, and salt. You will _____ need a bowl, a frying pan, and a fork. Crack the eggs into the bowl, beat them until they are blended, and add the butter, milk, and salt. More or less of these ingredients can _____ be added according to your own preference. If you like your eggs soft, you will have to add a lot of milk; if you like your eggs hard, add more butter than milk. Be very careful when adding the milk because if you add too little, it will turn into an omelette instead. _____ heat your frying pan on the stove for four to five minutes. Cover its surface with butter. _____ pour your mixture of eggs, butter, milk, and salt into the pan. Keep on stirring until the eggs are cooked. Keep in mind that overcooked eggs are hard. If you like soft scrambled eggs, _____, do not leave them in the pan too long. Pay attention to the consistency, and stir! The number of eggs used depends on how many servings you want to make.

Nitasmai Tantemsapya, Thailand

WRITE

The reading passage that introduces this chapter tells us about two causes of the change in soybean production that occurred after the Second World War. Write about a time when changes took place in your country, your neighborhood, your school, or your family. Tell your reader what the changes were, and explain what caused them and what effects they had. Practice using a few transitions, especially to link paragraphs and connect ideas.

EDITING ADVICE

1. Look at the first sentence of each paragraph you have written. Is there a clear connection between that sentence and what comes before it?

2. Look at the list of transitions in the box in section 23b. Would any of them help to make your connections clearer? Have you varied the transitions that you have used?

3. Read your piece through. If you have overused words like *nevertheless, therefore, furthermore,* and *moreover,* try instead some coordinate sentences using words like *but, so,* and *and.* Too many transition words will make your writing heavy and lifeless. Use just enough to make your connections clear to your reader.

Combining Sentences

Adjectival Clauses

24

READ

Read the excerpt from the reading selection "The Effects of Our Environment." The full selection, with vocabulary glosses, appears on p. 351.

Architects have learned that the way housing projects are designed controls to a great extent the contact neighbors have with each other. People who live in apartments near stairways and mailboxes have many more neighbor contacts than do those living in less heavily traveled parts
5 of the building, and tenants generally have more contacts with immediate neighbors than with people even a few doors away. Architects now use this information to design buildings that either encourage communication or increase privacy, and house hunters can use the same knowledge to choose a home that gives them the neighborhood relationships they
10 want. . . .

Other studies . . . found that students who sit opposite the teacher talk more, and those next to the teacher avoid talking at all. Also, the middle of the first row contains the students who interact most, and as we move back and to the sides of the classroom, interaction decreases
15 markedly.

With an overwhelming lack of imagination we perpetuate a seating arrangement reminiscent of a military cemetery. This type of environment communicates to students that the teacher, who can move about freely while they can't, is the one who is important in the room, is the only
20 one to whom anyone should speak, and is the person who has all the information. The most advanced curriculum has little chance of surviving without a physical environment that supports it.

ANALYZE

1. In the passage, underline all occurrences of the words *who, whom, whose,* and *which.*

2. Then look at the uses of *that*. If you could replace *that* with *who, whom,* or *which,* underline *that.*

3. In the first sentence, the phrase *the contact neighbors have with each other* could be rewritten as *the contact that neighbors have with each other.* Find any other sentences in which a similar pattern occurs. Insert a caret ∧ at any place where *whom, which,* or *that* could be inserted.

4. Look at the clauses that the words you have underlined or inserted introduce. What similar patterns emerge? Find a way to put these clauses into groups.

STUDY

24a. Adjectival clauses: form and function

Adjectival clauses (also called *relative clauses*) give us information about a noun phrase. They always follow the noun phrase and are introduced by relative pronouns:

who	that
whom	[ ] (omitted form of *whom, which,* or *that*)
whose	where (= at which, in which)
which	when

EXAMPLES

The candidate who performs best will get the job.
The candidate that performs best will get the job.

The candidate whom I liked best got the job.
The candidate that I liked best got the job.
The candidate I liked best got the job.

The candidate whose résumé showed the most experience got the job.

The position for which the candidate applied was a managerial one.
The position [that] the candidate applied for was a managerial one.

The firm where they had worked had gone bankrupt.

The eighties was a decade when money was the sign of success.

Note that *who* refers to people and *which* to things or concepts. *That* can refer to either and is often used in preference to *who* and *which,* particularly in conversation.

Relative pronouns can serve different functions within the clause: subject, direct object, possessive, or object of a preposition. The box presents a summary.

FUNCTIONS OF RELATIVE PRONOUNS

Function in Clause	Relative Pronoun	
	PERSON	THING OR CONCEPT
Subject	who that	which that
Object	who, whom[†] that [ ]	which that [ ] (omitted pronoun)
Possessive	whose	whose of which
Object of preposition	whom [ ]	which [ ] (omitted pronoun, preposition at end of clause)

[†]Formal grammar recommends *whom* in the object position. However, in informal language you will come across *who* in the object position, as in "They hired the architect who(m) their neighbors recommended."

EXERCISE 1

The following are sentence subjects. For each, make up a sentence using a relative clause to limit and define the subject.

EXAMPLE

The student
   The student I was talking to in the hall is sitting in the corner of the room.

1. The experiment
2. The policy
3. The news
4. The information
5. The suggestion
6. The advice
7. The instructor
8. The meal
9. The person
10. The lost book

EXERCISE 2

Look at the picture *The Luncheon of the Boating Party* on p. 111. Write eight sentences to identify eight different people or objects, using adjectival clauses.

EXAMPLE

The man who is leaning against the railing has a dark beard.

24b. Relative pronoun as subject of clause

There are four important things to remember about the relative pronoun as the subject of its own clause.

1. When the relative pronoun is the subject of its own clause, it cannot be omitted.

EXAMPLES

People *who live* in apartments near stairways have many neighbor contacts.

House hunters can choose a home *that gives* them good neighborhood relationships.

2. Even when a clause comes between the subject and its verb (people . . . have), we do not insert an additonal pronoun subject:

Not *People who live in apartments near stairways they have many neighbor contacts.

3. Usually, *that* is preferable to *which, who,* and *whom* in speech and writing. However, *that* should not be used directly after a preposition (see section 24e) or to introduce a restrictive clause (see section 24g).

4. The relative pronouns *who, which,* and *that* can refer to a singular or plural noun phrase. To determine whether a present tense verb of the clause should be singular or plural in form, we have to examine the preceding noun phrase (the referent).

People who live . . . have many neighbor contacts.
A person who lives . . . has many neighbor contacts.

EXERCISE 3 (oral)

Combine each pair of sentences into one sentence by making the second sentence into a relative clause.

EXAMPLE

The student was asked to make a speech.
The student got the highest grades.
   The student who got the highest grades was asked to make a speech.

1. The girl asks a lot of questions.
   The girl is sitting in the front row.

2. I'm really annoyed with the girl.
   The girl asks a lot of questions.

3. Pass me the books.
   The books are lying on the table.

4. I paid the boy.
   The boy delivered the groceries.

5. I wrote a review of the book.
   The book impressed me so much.

6. The results teach a lesson.
   The lesson isn't surprising.

7. The journalist works for a newsmagazine.
   The journalist wants to interview you at noon tomorrow.

8. She applied for the job.
   The job was advertised in the daily newspaper.

24c. Relative pronoun as object of clause

There are two important things to know about the relative pronoun as the object of its own clause:

1. It precedes the verb.
2. It can be omitted—and, indeed, frequently is.

The box shows word order in an adjectival clause.

Independent Clause	Adjectival Clause		
	Object	Subject	Verb
Design controls the contact		neighbors	have.
Design controls the contact	that	neighbors	have.
Design controls the contact	which[†]	neighbors	have.

[†]In current American usage, *that* is preferable to *which*.

Note how two sentences are combined by using an adjectival clause. The object of one clause is transformed into the object form of the relative pronoun:

He praised the room.

He had just seen the room. = He had just seen it.

He praised the room [⌣] he had just seen.

Or   He praised the room that he had just seen.

But not *He praised the room [   ] he had just seen it.

*He praised the room that he had just seen it.

EXERCISE 4 (oral)

Combine each pair of sentences, making the second sentence into a relative clause.

EXAMPLE

I bought the suit.
My mother liked it.
  I bought the suit [that] my mother liked.

1. The environment can communicate discomfort.
   The architects have created the environment.

2. The people are from California.
   I met them at a party last night.

3. I want the TV.
   I saw it in the store window yesterday.

4. There's the house.
   I like it.

5. The couch has a high back.
   I want to buy the couch.

6. I know the furniture store.
   You want to visit it.

7. The seating arrangement was pleasant.
   The architect designed it.

8. The kitchen cabinets were too high.
   The architect designed them.

24d. Possessive relative pronoun

To form adjectival clauses expressing possession, use *whose* or sometimes, for objects and concepts, *of which*.

EXAMPLES

The man is a lawyer.
I am renting his house.
  The man whose house I am renting is a lawyer.

She bought a lamp.
Its glass shade was slightly chipped.
  She bought a lamp whose glass shade was slightly chipped.
  She bought a lamp the glass shade of which was slightly chipped.

EXERCISE 5

Compose sentences using possessive relative pronouns, according to the following pattern:

You are using a friend's book now. Tell us something about that friend.

The friend whose book I am using now isn't in school today.

1. You broke a neighbor's window. Tell us something about that neighbor.
2. You met a man's daughter last night. Tell us something about the man.
3. You read the beginning of a novel last week. Tell us something about that novel.
4. Recently in the newspaper, the curriculum of a school was praised. Tell us something about that school.
5. You respect a person's views a great deal. Tell us something about that person.
6. A doctor's patient died yesterday. Tell us something about that doctor.

24e. Relative pronoun with preposition

When you use a relative pronoun with a preposition, you have a choice of structures. There are some important things to remember:

1. Keep the preposition in the clause.
2. Don't use the relative pronoun *that* immediately after a preposition; use *which* or *whom*.
3. Don't add an extra object after the preposition.

267

Look at the following examples:

> The house was huge.
> I was living in it last summer.
>> The house   [   ]   I was living *in* last summer was huge.
>> The house   *that*   I was living *in* last summer was huge.
>> The house   *in which* I was living   last summer was huge.
>> (very formal)

> *Not*   *The house that I was living in *it* last summer was huge.
> *Not*   *The house in *that* I was living last summer was huge.
> *Not*   *The house I was living last summer was huge.

EXERCISE 6 (oral)

Work with a partner to combine the following pairs of sentences, making the second sentence the adjectival clause. Make as many possible combinations for each pair as you can.

1. House design is shaped by the family members.
   You live with them.

2. The people were late.
   We were waiting for the people.

3. The people are very generous.
   I am staying with them.

4. The woman has written a book.
   I was telling you about her.

5. The lecture was exciting.
   We were invited to the lecture last Tuesday.

6. The academic discipline is challenging.
   He is interested in the academic discipline.

24f. Idioms with *where, when, what,* and *the way*

Where, when, what, and *the way* occur in idiomatic expressions related to adjectival clauses.

- *where*
  Where can be used in place of *in which, at which, to which,* and so on. Note the possibilities of combining the two following sentences:

The restaurant is very good.
She eats there.

The restaurant *where*	she eats	is very good.
The restaurant *that*	she eats *at*	is very good.
The restaurant *at which*	she eats	is very good.
The restaurant [ ]	she eats *at*	is very good.

Don't use a preposition if you use *where*.

Not *The restaurant where she eats at is very good.

- *when*
  When can be used in place of *in which, on which,* and so on, to refer to a time expression like *year, day,* or *month:*

1971 is the year.
Emily was born then.

1971 is the year *when*	Emily was born.
1971 is the year *that*	Emily was born [*in*].
1971 is the year [ ]	Emily was born [*in*].
1971 is the year *in which*	Emily was born.

Sometimes, *where* and *when* can occur with an omitted referent, as in the following:

They announced the place where the conference would take place and the time when the invited speakers would perform.

They announced where the conference would take place and when the invited speakers would perform.

- *what*
  What is also used as a relative pronoun with an omitted referent:

Tennis is the thing that she loves more than anything.
Tennis is what she loves more than anything.

- *the way*
  Note the following alternatives:

That is *the way in which* he hits the ball.
That is *the way that* he hits the ball.
That is *the way* [ ] he hits the ball.
That is *how* he hits the ball.

The way how is not used in standard English.

EXERCISE 7 *(oral)*

Work with a partner to rephrase each of the following sentences as many different ways as you can.

EXAMPLE

I really like the town you live in.
   I really like the town where you live.
   I really like the town in which you live.
   I really like the town that you live in.

1. The corner where I was waiting was very windy.
2. Look at how she uses chopsticks!
3. Lying on a beach is the thing that I like best.
4. Even though he is 93 years old, he can still remember clearly the day on which he got married.
5. Pay attention to the way your partner does the exercise.
6. This is the day on which Lyndon Johnson became president.
7. The resort hotel where we spent our vacation was very luxurious.
8. The little village in France in which we stayed last summer was near Aumont Aubrac.

24g. Punctuation: restrictive and nonrestrictive clauses

Punctuation changes according to different types of adjectival clauses. We'll look at the most common type first.

1. *Restrictive*
   Most of the adjectival clauses we have examined in the reading passage are restrictive; that is, the clause restricts the meaning of the noun phrase preceding it by defining or limiting it. We need the information in the clause to define and limit the referent. For instance, in the sentence

   Students *who sit opposite the teacher* talk more.

   the information in the adjectival clause is crucial to our understanding. If the sentence were just this:

   Students talk more.

   we would ask, "Which students?"
      It is important for you to know the two following points:

   • *Restrictive* adjectival clauses occur more frequently than nonrestrictive.
   • A *restrictive* adjectival clause is not set off from the independent clause by commas.

2. *Nonrestrictive*
   One sentence in the reading passage is this:

> The teacher, who can move about freely while they can't, is important.

Here the adjectival clause describes a familiar and specific teacher (the one in the class) in more detail. It does not define and restrict which teacher the writer means.

The features of nonrestrictive clauses are these:

- They provide additional, not necessary, information about the noun phrase.
- They are set off from the independent clause with commas.
- They are often used with proper nouns, since these are unique and do not need to be further defined and restricted.
- They are never used with *that,* but only with *who, whom, which,* and *whose.*
- No deletions of relative pronouns can occur.

EXAMPLES

> Mrs. McGrath, who lives next door to me, has two children. (nonrestrictive)
>
> The woman who lives next door to me has two children. (restrictive)
>
> Georgia Winston, whom you met recently, goes to school in Manhattan. (nonrestrictive)
>
> The student you met recently goes to school in Manhattan. (restrictive)

If you can delete a relative clause and the sense of the sentence is complete without it, then the clause is nonrestrictive and requires commas.

☆EXERCISE 8

The following sentences are based on the readings. Add commas around adjectival clauses where necessary.

1. Plants that lie on the ground are hard to cultivate.

2. Theo who worked in an art-dealer's shop introduced him to painters.

3. We become aware of the immense strain under which he worked with feverish energy.

4. The paintings on which his fame rests were all painted during three years that were interrupted by crises and despair.

5. He is no different from a lot of us who have fantasies about the things we want.

6. He develops a reality that is infuriating.

7. She lived in a tiny apartment that she shared with "Auntie Tan."

8. I replaced the broken levers with wooden rulers that I connected with nuts and bolts.

9. I handed the drawing to the oldest member of the family who opened his eyes wide with surprise.

10. The experimenters set up three rooms: an "ugly" one which resembled a janitor's closet; an "average" one; and a "beautiful" one.

11. Scarcity is the framework within which economics exists.

12. Children who aren't skilled or interested in these social lies are often a source of embarrassment for their parents.

24h. Quantity words with relative pronouns

Nonrestrictive adjectival clauses are also used with quantity words.

EXAMPLE

She has three sisters.
None of them will help her.
** She has three sisters, none of whom will help her.**

The adjectival clause is set off with commas since it provides additional information rather than information necessary to define and restrict the noun phrase.

☆*EXERCISE 9*

Combine each pair of sentences by making the second sentence into an adjectival clause. Introduce the adjectival clause with expressions like *some of whom* or *which, one of whom* or *which, many of whom* or *which, none of whom* or *which, most of whom* or *which, neither of whom* or *which,* and *both of whom* or *which.*

1. At the lecture there were twenty-two people. Most of them lived in the neighborhood.

2. They waited half an hour for the committee members. Some of them just did not show up.

3. I sang three songs. One of them was "Cheek to Cheek."

4. The cake competition was held last week and she submitted two cakes. Neither of them won a prize.

5. She has four brothers. One of them lives in Australia.

6. She has written over 300 poems. Many of them have been published.

24i. Reduced adjectival clauses

Adjectival clauses can be reduced to phrases.

EXAMPLES

People *who live* in apartments near stairways have more neighbor contacts.

People *living* in apartments near stairways have more neighbor contacts.

The students *who were sitting* next to the teacher avoided talking.
The students *sitting* next to the teacher avoided talking. (See also Chapter 20.)

We perpetuate a seating arrangement *that is reminiscent* of a cemetery.

We perpetuate a seating arrangement *reminiscent* of a cemetery. (See also Chapter 14.)

The students *who were recruited* from the top high schools got good grades.

The students *recruited* from the top high schools got good grades. (See also Chapter 21.)

EXERCISE 10

Rewrite the adjectival clauses in the following sentences as reduced adjectival phrases.

1. She has just bought a house that overlooks the Pacific Ocean.
2. The chairs that are standing in a row over there have to be taken to another room.

3. The people who applaud that comedian must be members of his family.
4. He is the one who is trying to get on TV.
5. The jokes that were told at the party were not at all funny.
6. Any performer who does not offer to go on tour will be dropped from the show.
7. The prize that was awarded at the ceremony went to the youngest performer.

EDIT

What changes would you suggest that the writers of the following passages should make, and why?

A spice container who is badly designed for seasoning is an object that I think is uncomfortable to use it. When I have to season meat, and I have to pour it from this container, it hardly comes out at all because the container has little holes which make the seasoning come out too slowly. It is very annoying. *to season meat with this container because it has little holes—.*

Josephine Asamani, Ghana

One of my school bags is badly designed. It has only a little space *with* which I can put the books I use. On the other hand, it is very deep, so *that where* I have to struggle to find little things in the bottom of the bag. This is one of the less favorite objects that I own. I also dislike the handles of the bag which they are too short. *because they are too short.*

Soonjin Park, Korea

At home I have a desk which *which* chair is so badly designed that every time I sit on it I go crazy. Whenever I sit on the chair, it makes a horrible noise; then, if I try to lean back, it feels as if I am going to fall over. The back of the chair *which* has weak support makes it not steady. Also, when I try to roll it away from my desk, it sticks to the floor and scratches it, I hate that chair. *because*

Ali Rashid, Venezuela

WRITE

Write descriptions of two objects in common use in your daily life that you think are badly designed. (For example, some people search for years to find a well-designed pepper mill and garlic press. Even cups and mugs can suffer from poor design; so can cars, chairs, desks, and typewriters.) Make it clear to your readers exactly how and why the design is so bad. Use some adjectival clauses in your descriptions.

1. Read your piece of writing through carefully. Note where you have used any adjectival clauses. Check the punctuation: use commas only with nonrestrictive clauses—to refer to unique people, places, or objects.

2. Check your use of relative pronouns. Refer to the box in section 24a. Remember that the relative pronoun *that* is not used in nonrestrictive clauses, and it is not used directly after a preposition.

3. If you have used the present tense and *who, which,* or *that* as the subject of its own clause, check the referent to make sure that the verb in the adjectival clause agrees with the referent (The people who are . . . , The person who is . . .).

4. Make sure that you have not added an extra pronoun in the adjectival clause (*She admired the suit that I bought it) or that you have not omitted a preposition (*The house I am living is big).

25 Noun Clauses and Reported Speech

READ

Read the following passage from the reading "The Culture of 'Lead Time,'" which appears with vocabulary glosses on p. 361.

Advance notice is often referred to in America as "lead time," an expression which is significant in a culture where schedules are important. While it is learned informally, most of us are familiar with how it works in our own culture, even though we cannot state the rules
5   technically. The rules for lead time in other cultures, however, have rarely been analyzed. At the most they are known by experience to those who lived abroad for some time. Yet think how important it is to know how much time is required to prepare people, or for them to prepare themselves, for things to come. Sometimes lead time would seem to be
10 very extended. At other times, in the Middle East, any period longer than a week may be too long.

How troublesome differing ways of handling time can be is well illustrated by the case of an American agriculturalist assigned to duty as an attaché of our embassy in a Latin country. After what seemed to him
15 a suitable period he let it be known that he would like to call on the minister who was his counterpart. For various reasons, the suggested time was not suitable; all sorts of cues came back to the effect that the time was not yet ripe to visit the minister. Our friend, however, persisted and forced an appointment, which was reluctantly granted. Arriving a
20 little before the hour (the American respect pattern), he waited. The hour came and passed; five minutes—ten minutes—fifteen minutes. At this point he suggested to the secretary that perhaps the minister did not know he was waiting in the outer office. This gave him the feeling he had done something concrete and also helped to overcome the great anxiety
25 that was stirring inside him.

ANALYZE

1. Some noun clauses have been underlined in the passage. What conclusions can you draw about the types of words that can introduce noun clauses and whether those words can be omitted?

2. In the sentence "Think how important it is to know about lead time," a question is implied within a command. What is the form of the equivalent direct question introduced by the word *how?*

3. Note which tense is used in each of the underlined clauses. Which tense is used in the corresponding independent clause?

STUDY

25a. Form and function of noun clauses

Noun clauses can be used in sentences in the same position as noun phrases or pronouns.

<table>
<tr><td colspan="3" align="center">NOUN CLAUSES</td></tr>
<tr><td>Subject</td><td colspan="2" align="center">Predicate</td></tr>
<tr><td></td><td>VERB</td><td>OBJECT OR COMPLEMENT
OR PREPOSITIONAL PHRASE</td></tr>
<tr><td>His behavior</td><td>was</td><td>wrong.</td></tr>
<tr><td>What he did</td><td>was</td><td>wrong.</td></tr>
<tr><td>We</td><td>noticed</td><td>his behavior.</td></tr>
<tr><td>We</td><td>noticed</td><td>what he did.</td></tr>
<tr><td>We</td><td>heard</td><td>about his behavior</td></tr>
<tr><td>We</td><td>heard</td><td>about what he did.</td></tr>
</table>

Noun clauses are introduced in three ways:

1. By question words: *what, when, where, why, who, whom, whose, which, how, whatever,* etc.
2. By alternative words: *whether, if*
3. By the word *that* or [   ] (omitted *that*)

EXERCISE 1

Write five sentences that tell about cultural differences that surprised you when you were outside your own country. Use a noun clause as the subject of the sentence, according to the following pattern:

How . . . surprised me.
What . . . surprised me.
The fact that . . . surprised me.
The way that . . . surprised me.

EXAMPLE   **How Americans use their knife and fork surprised me.**

Then read your sentences to your classmates.

☆EXERCISE 2

Read the complete selection "The Culture of 'Lead Time'" on p. 361. Write about that same incident as if you were the secretary in the office. What did you see, observe, notice? What did the attaché say, comment, complain? What did the minister tell you to say? Use some of the following expressions in your account:

I was amazed at what . . .
What he did next surprised me because . . .
I couldn't understand why . . .
My boss was puzzled about what . . .
It was obvious to me that . . .

25b. Noun clauses introduced by *that*

There are four important things to remember about noun clauses introduced by *that*:

1. They can fill subject and object positions.
2. They are often used with an introductory *it* as a filler subject.
3. The word *that* can often be omitted in an object clause.
4. No punctuation sets off the *that* clause from the rest of the sentence.

FUNCTIONS OF NOUN CLAUSES WITH *THAT*

Function	*Example*
As subject	That he had made a mistake was clear.
With *it*	It was clear that he had made a mistake.
As object	The minister knew that his visitor was waiting.
As object, with omitted *that*	The minister knew his visitor was waiting.

Noun clauses with *that* also occur frequently in the following contexts:

- In expressions like *the fact that, the reason that, the idea that, the possibility that, the effect that, the way that*

EXAMPLES

> The fact *that he has no money* has changed his lifestyle.
> It is a fact *that he has lost all his money.*

- In expressions like *it is true that, it is clear that, it is obvious that, it is strange that, it is surprising that*

EXAMPLE

> It is obvious that they had different cultural perspectives.

- In expressions like *the fact is that, the advantage is that, the truth is that, the reason is that, the problem is that, the effect is that*

EXAMPLE

> The fact is that he has lost every penny.

- In verb phrases like *be sorry that, be pleased that, be sure that, be disappointed that, be happy that, be surprised that*

EXAMPLE

> I am disappointed that the incident occurred.

☆EXERCISE 3

Write sentences about cultural differences beginning as suggested.

1. When you travel to another country, it is clear that . . .

2. I was astounded by the fact that . . .

3. People don't know the cultural expectations in another country. That is the reason that . . .

4. It is obvious to natives of a country that . . .

5. Visitors to my country are impressed by the idea that . . .

6. They see only too clearly that . . .

7. The main problem with foreign travel is that . . .

8. When I first left my hometown, I was surprised that . . .

25c. Included questions

When a question is included within a statement, it loses question punctuation and question word order.

Whether is used for *if* when a choice is stressed and when *or* follows:

I don't know whether I should apply for this job or the other one.
I don't know whether or not he plans to go.

With a short noun clause, *or not* can occur at the end:

I don't know whether he plans to go or not.

Note: Don't use *that* with a question word in an included clause.

Not   ***He told me that how terrible his boss was.**

DIRECT AND INCLUDED QUESTIONS						
	Introductory Word	*Auxiliary*	*Subject*	*Auxiliary*	*Rest of Sentence*	*Punctuation*
Direct question	What	are	they		doing	?
Included question I don't know	what		they	are	doing	.
Direct question	Where	does	she		live	?
Included question I can't remember	where		she		lives	.
Direct question	Why	did	he		say that	?
Included question I couldn't understand	why		he		said that	.
Direct question		Is	she		working	?
Included question I don't know	if		she	is	working	.
Direct question		Did	he		help	?
Included question I've no idea	if		he		helped	.

280

EXERCISE 4 (oral)

Give full-sentence responses to the following questions, beginning your response with the given phrase.

EXAMPLE

How old is he?
  I don't know how old he is.

1. What is his name? I don't know . . .

2. Why does he stand so close when he talks? I can't understand . . .

3. When will he arrive? He hasn't said . . .

4. When was she born? I don't know . . .

5. What does the ambassador want? I don't care . . .

6. How long has he been waiting? Please tell me . . .

7. Why did he get so angry? I can't understand . . .

8. Whose report is that? I don't know . . .

9. What is the square root of 1,369? I can't work out . . .

10. Why are you staring at me? Please tell me . . .

11. Why did you arrive so early? Please let me know . . .

12. Is it going to be good weather next month? How do I know . . .

13. Does a Scotsman wear anything under his kilt? Nobody knows . . .

14. Did the French win the Battle of Waterloo? I can't remember . . .

EXERCISE 5 (oral)

Write down on a piece of paper a question that you want someone to ask you and that you know you can answer.

EXAMPLE   **What is the capital of Hungary?**

Give the question to a partner. Your partner will turn it into an included question, beginning with *I want to know, Could you tell me, I wonder,* or *I can't remember.*

25d

EXAMPLE   **I want to know what the capital of Hungary is.**

Then tell your partner the answer.

25d. Reported and direct speech

Note the ways in which reported speech can differ from direct speech.

REPORTED AND DIRECT SPEECH	
Direct Speech	*Reported Speech*
"I am happy."	*No quotation marks* He says that he is happy.
"What is she doing?"	*No question mark* He wants to know what she is doing.
"When will they leave?"	*Statement word order* He knows when they will leave.
"I am leaving."	*Past tense cluster after past verb* She said that she was leaving.
"Is she leaving?"	If/whether *when no question word is present* He asked if she was leaving.
She said, "I must leave."	*Third person pronouns* She said that she had to leave.
"I am moving this week."	That *and* those, *not* this *and* these He said he was moving that week.
"Go away!"	*Command introduced by* tell + to He told the caller to go away.
"Please, please, help me."	*No conversational words* She begged them to help her.

☆*EXERCISE 6*

Rewrite the following passage from the first selection in Mark Salzman's "Cultural Exchanges" as reported speech, with no direct quotations. Begin as follows:

When Mark Salzman had finished speaking, Teacher Wu asked him if
. . .

"Your mother is a pianist?"

"Well, she was a pianist. Now she plays the harpsichord."

"Mm. So you know what a piano should sound like, then? You grew up hearing it every day, didn't you?"

"Yes."

☆*EXERCISE 7*

In the second paragraph of section 2 of Mark Salzman's "Cultural Exchanges" on p. 349, there are five instances of included statements. How would the passage change if Salzman had decided to use only reported speech? Rewrite the direct-speech sentences in the form of reported speech.

25e. The conventions of reporting: documentation

When you want to tell a reader about what somebody else has said, you can either quote the words directly if they are particularly apt, or you can paraphrase or summarize their ideas. In either case, you have to let your reader know whose ideas you are relating and where you found them. Read through the selection "The Effects of Our Environment" on p. 351. The authors refer to researchers' studies. Sometimes they use the same words that the researchers used, quoting them directly. Sometimes they just summarize a lengthy article. But each time they include a *reference* in their text to the date of the work, and the section at the end of the article headed "References" gives all the details of the source: for a book, author, title, place of publication, publisher, and date of publication; for an article, title of article, name of journal, volume number, date of publication, and page numbers. There are many formats for such documentation. Some, for instance, ask you to mention in your text, usually in parentheses, the page numbers you are citing. Always find out from an instructor or editor what guidelines you should follow.

25f. Verb form in noun clauses after *insist, suggest,* etc.

In noun clauses introduced by *that* after verbs like *insist, suggest, request, demand, recommend,* and *ask,* use the simple form of the verb, regardless of the subject.

EXAMPLES

The minister insisted that his visitor wait outside.

The attaché demanded that the minister let him in.

The secretary recommended that he not get too excited.

The visitor insisted that he be admitted.

EXERCISE 8

Tell your classmates, in complete sentences, what your parents, family members, or teachers insisted, demanded, recommended, and so on, when you were a young teenager.

EXAMPLE **My older brother demanded that I give him half my allowance.**

EDIT

Some student responses to Exercise 6 follow. They did this exercise before they studied the chapter. What good things has each one done that the other writers should take note of? Where do the writers need to make corrections?

Teacher Wu asked him if his mother was a pianist. He answered that she had been a pianist but that now she played the harpsichord. Then she asked him if he knew what a piano should sound like and that if he had grown up hearing a piano every day and he answered yes.

Ali Rashid, Venezuela

Teacher Wu asked him if her mother was a pianist. He replied positively that her mother was a pianist and then she played the harpsichord. Teacher Wu asked him again that he would know what a piano sound like now and he had grown up hearing it every day. He replied in the affirmative.

Kazi Alam, Bangladesh

Teacher Wu asked him if your mother was a pianist or not. He answered that she had been a pianist. She played the harpsichord at that time. Then she asked whether if he knew what a piano should sound like since he had grown up hearing it every day hadn't he. He said that he knew.

Masayo Ohyama, Japan

WRITE

Listen to a long conversation between two people. You can do this in a public place, such as a college cafeteria or a restaurant, or at your family dinner table. Or you can watch an interview show on television. Make detailed notes about the conversation. Then report that conversation, using no direct quotations but letting your reader know as much as you can about the course of the conversation as accurately as you can. Begin like this:

> **On . . . at . . . (give day and time), I heard a conversation between . . . It went like this: . . .**

EDITING ADVICE

1. Make sure that any noun clauses introduced by *that* are not set off from the rest of the sentence by commas.

2. With reported speech, check to see that you have followed the guidelines in section 25d. Note particularly whether you have used the past time cluster after the introductory past tense verbs, third person pronouns, and statement word order for reported questions.

3. If you find that you have overused the verb *say*, try some alternatives: *reply, respond, comment, observe, mention, add, continue, state, ask, question, wonder, complain, whisper, shout, yell, shriek, insist, demand, request, . . .*

26 Adverbial Clauses: Time, Place, Reason, Result, Purpose, Contrast

READ

Read the following section from Mark Salzman's "Cultural Exchanges," which appears with vocabulary glosses on p. 347.

I asked her not to stay in the apartment <u>while I worked</u>, <u>because it would only make me more nervous</u>, so she prepared a thermos of tea and promised me a good dinner that evening. "And if you need anything, just tell Auntie Tan—she'll be right in the kitchen." Auntie Tan gave me a
5   toothless smile and nodded, and I smiled back.

<u>After Teacher Wu left</u> I began to disassemble the piano. <u>As I was taking off one of the boards concealing the pedal mechanism</u>, I heard a loud squeak and a frantic scratching. I stepped back and watched three large rodents scurry out of the piano, around the room and down a
10 drainpipe.

Using sandpaper and a pair of pliers I managed to get all the hammers loose, and I repaired the pedal system by replacing the broken levers with several wooden rulers that I connected with nuts and bolts. To tune the instrument I damped two of the strings of each note with my
15 thumb and forefinger <u>while I adjusted the third</u>, then tuned each of the others to it. <u>Since I have only semi-perfect pitch</u>, I set middle C according to a Michael Jackson tape played through my Walkman.

ANALYZE

1. Some clauses in the reading are underlined. What relationship (time, place, reason, purpose, result, contrast) exists between each italicized clause and its independent clause?

2. Discuss with other students and with your instructor what other words you could use in place of each one of the introductory words in the dependent clauses underlined in the passage (that is, in place of *while, because, after, as, while,* and *since*).

3. Earlier in that same reading, the following statement occurs:

Though my mother played the piano, I had never learned to tune or repair one.

Underline the independent clause. What is the relationship of the other clause to the independent clause? What could you use to replace *though* in that sentence?

STUDY

26a. Adverbial clauses: position and punctuation

Adverbial clauses, like adverbs, modify either the verb of the independent clause or the whole sentence. Typically, they answer questions like *when? why?* and *where?*

ADVERBIAL CLAUSES	
Before the independent clause	
Dependent Clause	**Independent Clause**
After When Since While etc. } S + V,	S + V.
After the independent clause	
Independent Clause	**Dependent Clause**
S + V	after when since although etc. } S + V.

Adverbial clauses have two important features:

1. They have a S + V structure.
2. That S + V structure is introduced by a *subordinating conjunction,* which serves to link it to the independent clause.

EXAMPLES

Teacher Wu left.
I began to disassemble the piano.
After Teacher Wu left, I began to disassemble the piano.
I began to disassemble the piano after Teacher Wu left.

The subordinating conjunction used here to combine the two sentences is *after.*

The adverbial clause *(after Teacher Wu left)* can come before or after the independent clause. If it comes before, there will usually be a comma separating the two clauses. A comma is not necessary if the adverbial clause comes after the independent clause. Some writers do not follow these conventions exactly (you'll notice variations on this in Salzman's writing). However, your sentences will usually be clear if you follow these rules. The two patterns are shown in the box on the previous page.

26b. Clauses of time and place

Subordinating conjunctions that introduce clauses of time and place are listed in the box on the top of page 289. Note that *while* is used to introduce a subordinate clause *(while* S + V); *during* is a preposition and occurs before a noun phrase:

She slept during the concert.
She slept while he was playing the piano.

___

EXERCISE 1 (oral)

Complete each of the following sentences with an adverbial clause. Pay attention to the verb tenses you use; refer to Chapters 8 through 10 if you need help.

1. I feel afraid when . . .
2. I felt scared when . . .
3. I'll be studying while you . . . (see section 10e in Chapter 10 for verb tense use)
4. I left before . . .
5. We'll leave as soon as . . . (see section 10c in Chapter 10)
6. They will eat dinner when . . . (see section 10c in Chapter 10)
7. She does well whenever . . .
8. We couldn't leave until . . .

288

CONJUNCTIONS OF TIME AND PLACE

Conjunction	Example
Time	
when	When he opened the piano, rodents ran out.
	He had completed the task when she returned.
after	After she left, he took the piano apart.
while	Auntie Tan slept while he was working.
	Auntie Tan slept while he worked.
before	He had completed the task before she woke up.
since	He has played the cello since he was a child.
as soon as	As soon as he arrived, he set to work.
once	Once he started, he worked steadily.
until	He didn't stop until he had finished.
whenever	Whenever he tries something new, he does it well.
by the time (that)	By the time (that) Auntie Tan woke up, the job was finished.
Place	
where	He wants to live where he can practice the cello.

26c. Clauses of reason

Adverbial clauses of reason, answering the question *why?* are introduced by the conjunctions in the box.

CONJUNCTIONS OF REASON

Conjunction	Example
because	I asked her not to stay because it would make me nervous.
since	Since he didn't have perfect pitch, he used his Walkman.
now that	Now that you have a tool, you can tune the piano.
as long as	As long as you are still here, you can help me.

Note that *since* can express time or reason. The meaning is usually clear from the context, as well as from the verb tense used.

EXERCISE 2

Complete each of the following sentences.

1. He feels much more independent now that . . .

2. Because . . . , he has decided to switch jobs.

3. As long as . . . , would you get me a glass of water?

4. Now that the rain has stopped, . . .

5. Since I . . . , I decided to take a taxi.

6. Now that my exams are over, I . . .

26d. *Because* and *because of*

Language learners sometimes have difficulties with the use of *because* and *because of*. The box should help.

BECAUSE AND BECAUSE OF		
	Function	*Example*
because	Introduces a clause (S + V)	He helped her because he had a musical background.
because of	Occurs before a noun phrase	Because of his background, he was able to help her.

EXERCISE 3

Think of six decisions you have made in the past few days and the reasons that you made them. Then write sentences telling the reader the reason for the decisions; use *because* in three sentences and *because of* in the other three.

EXAMPLE

I bought a new school bag.
Reason: It wasn't expensive.
   I bought a new school bag because it wasn't expensive.
   I bought a new school bag because of its low price.

26e. Clauses of result and purpose

Adverbial clauses of result and purpose are formed as described in the box. Note that to express result, *so . . . that* is used with adjectives, adverbs, and the quantity words *much, many, few,* and *little:*

She is so successful that she now has her own business.
She has so many clients that she is busy all the time.

In contrast, *such . . . that* is used before an adjective + noun construction and before *a lot of* + noun:

He has such a successful business that he is making a fortune.
He has such a lot of clients that he works every weekend.

CONJUNCTIONS OF RESULT AND PURPOSE	
Conjunction	*Example*
Result so . . . that	He was so talented that he fixed the piano. He ate so much food that he could hardly move.
such . . . that	He had such a good ear that he was able to tune the piano.
Purpose so that in order that	He worked quickly so (*or* in order) that he would finish on time. Reduced form: He worked quickly (in order) to finish on time. (see section 26g)

EXERCISE 4 (oral)

Use conjunctions of result and purpose to combine the following pairs of sentences into one sentence for each pair.

1. They are rich. They can afford to go skiing in Switzerland twice a year.

2. He had a good time canoeing in Canada. He decided to do it again the following year.

3. She has a lot of free time. She has offered to type my paper for me.

4. He has many books. He doesn't know where to put them all.

5. This book is interesting. I think I'll read it again.

6. This is an interesting book. I think I'll read it again.

7. She ran quickly. I couldn't keep up with her.

8. He traded in his car. He intended to buy a boat.

9. She went to bed early. She wanted to be alert for her exam.

10. The economists made a conservative estimate. They did not want to be accused of being rash.

26f. Clauses of contrast

The subordinating conjunctions in the box occur with adverbial clauses of contrast. Note that *despite* is not used with *of. Despite,* like *in spite of,* is followed by a noun phrase, not by a clause:

Despite his lack of experience, he did the job well.
In spite of his lack of experience, he did the job well.

In some languages, contrast is expressed by a combination of words like *although* and *but.* In English, these do not occur together to express contrast. When you speak or write, you have to choose one or the other.

Although he is young, he is intellectually mature.
He is young, but he is intellectually mature.
He is young; however, he is intellectually mature.

Not *Although he is young, but he is intellectually mature.

CONJUNCTIONS OF CONTRAST	
Conjunction	*Example*
though	Though his mother played the piano, he didn't know how to tune one.
although	Although he plays the cello, he doesn't know how to play the piano.
even though	Even though he was alone, he still felt anxious.
while	While he is musical, he isn't a skilled pianist.
in spite of the fact that	He managed to do the job in spite of the fact that he had had no experience.

☆EXERCISE 5

These passages, adapted from the readings, use *but* or *however* to express contrast. Rewrite each passage using a subordinate adverbial clause.

EXAMPLE

I know what to do in a charcoal gray and pink breakfast nook, but the only thing I can think of to do in a living room is living.

Although I know what to do in a charcoal gray and pink breakfast nook, the only thing I can think of to do in a living room is living.

1. China had been the major supplier of soybeans to the world market. However, the course of postwar politics and the difficulties experienced by the Chinese in recovering from wartime devastation prevented the restoration of prewar trade relations with the West.

2. His baby can't catch him yet, but it's only a matter of time.

3. I haven't had much time to practice it since then, but nowadays I try to play whenever I have free time.

4. My mother played the piano; however, I had never learned to tune or repair one.

5. I had walked along the river many times since meeting the fisherman that day in winter, but I did not see him again until spring.

6. Most people would agree that lying to gain advantage over an unknowing subject is wrong; however, another kind of mistruth—the "white lie"—is both a popular and an often acceptable type of communication.

26g. Reduced adverbial clauses

When an adverbial clause has the same subject as the independent clause, it can be reduced to a phrase with *-ing* or with an infinitive. (See also Chapters 19 and 20.)

EXAMPLES

| After | *I had waited* | an hour, I left. |
| After | *waiting* | an hour, I left. |

| While | *he worked,* | he sang. |
| While | *working,* | he sang. |

Because *he needed a pin,*	he took the key from its hiding place.
Needing a pin,	he took the key from its hiding place.
(omit *because*)	

| He rented a car *so that he could get* | to Boston more quickly. |
| He rented a car *to get* | to Boston more quickly. |

EXERCISE 6

Rewrite each sentence by reducing the adverbial clause to a phrase.

1. He fixed the piano before he ate dinner.

2. She thanked him after she had tried it out.

3. While he was working, he listened to music.

4. He listened to Michael Jackson so that he could set middle C.

5. Because she felt grateful, she made him a wonderful dinner.

6. Before he left, he thanked her for the meal.

26h. Problems with adverbial clauses: fragments

An adverbial clause, even a very long one, must be connected to an independent clause. In formal academic writing, it cannot stand alone. The following adverbial clause is a sentence fragment:

She was happy. *Because he had fixed the piano for her so beautifully.

Sometimes, writers may use a fragment deliberately for stylistic effect, to draw the reader's attention to a particular point. As a general rule, though, avoid fragments. Connect adverbial clauses to independent clauses. (See also Chapter 29.)

EXERCISE 7

The following are sentences from students' compositions. Identify the fragments, and make any necessary corrections.

1. Even though I had a coat, I refused to wear it. Because I thought that

   I looked ridiculous.

2. Sometimes they are very proud that they are from the city. Because they have everything close to them and they can have a good time.

3. Even though the country is healthier, quieter, and has more fresh air. It's still boring, without the fun of entertainment and people.

4. Children who live in the country have more time to study. Because they save time traveling between school and home.

5. Because an only child lives around grown-up people; he doesn't enjoy life as a child.

6. Parents' behavior, education, bad habits, and other negative aspects can be an influence on children; because young children adopt them easily.

EXERCISE 8

Choose one word or phrase that best completes each sentence.

1. He didn't want her to stay in the apartment _____.
   a. during he worked
   b. while he worked
   c. because of he was working hard
   d. until he will finish the work

2. _____, they decided not to cancel the picnic.
   a. In spite of the fact that it was raining
   b. In spite of raining
   c. Despite of the rain
   d. In spite the rain

3. Although he has taken piano lessons, _____.
   a. but he still plays badly
   b. however he plays badly
   c. he plays very well
   d. he still plays badly

4. She decided to leave _____.

   a. after waited an hour
   b. after she has waited an hour
   c. after waiting an hour
   d. after she waiting an hour

5. He waited for the professor _____.

   a. such long time to discuss his grade
   b. so that he could discuss his grade
   c. in order that to discuss his grade
   d. in order to discussed his grade

EDIT

The following are excerpts from pieces of student writing as they were written. What suggestions would you make to the writers for improvement? Would adverbial clauses be of use to make the sentences less choppy? Are there errors that need to be corrected? Where? What details would you like the writers to add? What more would you like to know to get a fuller picture of the event?

My sister Maria when she was sixteen years old helped a lady on the plane get to where she wanted. The lady was traveling alone. She didn't know how to speak English. She began to cry; she didn't know or understand how to fill out the forms. They were both going to Cyprus, so Maria offered to help.

Eleni Mei, Cyprus

The other day I was walking down Riverside Drive. I saw a person changing a tire. He seemed to need help. I offered him my assistance and he accepted. After changing the tire, the man offered me money. I didn't accept his money.

Pablo Arroyo, Puerto Rico

My neighbor Mary, who is a very kind person; asked me to give a hand in her apartment. As I was busy; doing some extra work in my regular job. I told her that I could only help her during the weekend. On Saturday we fixed her floors, painted the walls, fixed the sink, and cleaned the ceilings. Then we went out and she bought me dinner. She was pleased that I had helped her.

Joao Gomes, Brazil

WRITE

Write an account of a time when you helped someone out or someone offered you help when it was needed. Include details about the time, the place, and the people involved. Explain what happened in detail. Let your reader know, too, about the purpose and motives of the people involved (their reasons for acting as they did) and about the results of those actions.

---

1. Read your story through, underlining any subordinating conjunctions you have used (refer to the boxes in this chapter, if necessary).

EDITING ADVICE

2. The clause after the conjunction should have its own subject + verb; in addition, the independent clause of the sentence should also have subject + verb. Underline the verb phrase in the dependent and the independent clause.

3. If you have used a subordinating conjunction as the first word in the sentence, your sentence should follow this pattern:

Conjunction S + V, S + V.

When *because, when, although,* or some other conjunction is the first word in the sentence, there should not be a period at the end of that clause. So check to see if sentences beginning with conjunctions should be attached to the preceding sentence or if they follow the pattern just shown.

---

27 Adverbial Clauses: Conditions

READ

Read the following excerpt from "Economics and Scarcity," which appears with vocabulary glosses on p. 369.

If scarcity exists, then choices must be made by individuals and societies. These choices involve "tradeoffs" and necessitate an awareness of the consequences of those tradeoffs. For example, suppose that you have $25 to spend and have narrowed your alternatives to a textbook or
5 a date. Scarcity prohibits the purchase of both and imposes a tradeoff—a book or a date. Each choice has a consequence. The textbook might enable you to attain a good grade (and increase your knowledge), and the date might mean an evening of merriment.

In arriving at a decision your value judgment plays a key role. A
10 value judgment is what you hold to be important in your estimation of a situation. If you value good grades more than a good time, you may choose the book; if you value a good time more than good grades, you will probably choose the date.

If someone in your family were to win $1,000 in a lottery, the same
15 problem of choice would arise. The $1,000 is a limited sum; it buys only so much. Your family would have to consider alternatives, or tradeoffs, for spending the $1,000. Ultimately, the decision as to how the money would be used would be based on a value judgment of some member of the family.

ANALYZE

1. Underline all the complete verb phrases in the excerpt.

2. Examine the verb tenses used, and determine which verbs belong to the past cluster and which to the present-future cluster. Refer to the box on p. 74 to help you.

3. Note where a switch occurs from one cluster to another. Why do you think it occurred?

4. The passage contains four sentences containing an *if* clause. Three are similar in terms of the verb tenses used; one is different. Which one? Why do you think it is different? How would the meaning of that sentence change if the verb tenses were made to conform with the other three conditional sentences?

STUDY

27a. Features of conditional sentences

Although time reference is usually closely related to verb tense (past tenses indicate past time; present tenses indicate present time; etc.), this is not so with conditional sentences. So everything you have learned about tense-time relationships has to be adjusted with sentences with *if* and *unless*. With conditions, a change in tense does not necessarily signal a change in the time referred to but rather a change in the type of condition expressed. There are four types of conditions you can express in English. Two refer to real or possible situations; the other two refer to hypothetical (imaginary) situations.

REAL OR POSSIBLE	HYPOTHETICAL
fact	speculation
prediction	hindsight (looking back and hypothesizing)

27b. Real conditions of fact

possible fact.

Factual conditions express an idea that is real and true. They express generalizations. In these sentences, *if* is thus the equivalent of *when* or *whenever*. *Unless* indicates that the condition is a necessary one for the situation to occur.

EXAMPLES

If scarcity exists, people make choices.
If water freezes, it turns into ice.
If you hear a quick beep, it's the busy signal.
If she was in class, she definitely took notes.
If I eat breakfast, I feel more energetic.
If she doesn't eat breakfast, she doesn't function well at work.
Unless she eats breakfast, she doesn't function well at work.

Note what happens to the sentence punctuation when the independent clause precedes the conditional clause:

People make choices if scarcity exists.

27c

Water turns into ice if it freezes.
She doesn't function well at work unless she eats breakfast.

The pattern of tenses used for conditions of fact is shown in the box.

REAL CONDITIONS OF FACT		
Meaning	*if or unless Clause*	*Independent Clause*
Fact	Same tense in both	

EXERCISE 1 (oral)

With another student, discuss how you could complete the following sentences, using conditions of fact, with reference to the topic of economics and scarcity.

1. If no scarcity exists, . . .

2. If a person only has $25 to spend, . . .

3. If a society chooses to go to war, . . .

4. There is always less food for the population if . . .

5. If prices go up, demand . . .

6. If demand goes up, . . .

7. Prices of luxury goods fall if . . .

8. Unless people make tradeoffs, . . .

27c. Real conditions of prediction

Often we predict what will happen in the future if a certain condition occurs. We think that that condition is likely or possible.

EXAMPLES

If you value a good time, you will choose to go on a date.
You will choose to go on a date if you value a good time.
If you move to California (and that is possible), you are going to be able to visit us more often.

300

If I have three children (and it is possible that I will), I will send them all to public school.

I will change jobs unless I get promoted.

The pattern of tenses used for conditions of prediction is shown in the box.

REAL CONDITIONS OF PREDICTION		
Meaning	*if or* **unless** *Clause*	*Independent clause*
Prediction	Present tense	*will ('ll)* *be going to* *should* *may* *might* *can* *ought to* + simple form

---

EXERCISE 2

Write six conditional sentences in which you express predictions about the economic situation of yourself or your country.

27d. Hypothetical conditions of speculation and the use of *were*

We can change the meaning and implication of the sample sentences used in section 27c by changing the verb tense, shifting it back from the present-future cluster to the past:

If you *valued* a good time, you *would choose* to go on a date.

The past tense does *not* indicate past time. It shows, rather, that the speaker or writer thinks that you perhaps don't value a good time and makes a hypothesis about the opposite case.

EXAMPLES

If I had some free time, I would help you. (But I don't have any free time, so I can't, and won't, help you!)

We would go to Italy if we knew how to speak Italian. (We don't know how to speak Italian, so we won't go to Italy.)

If you moved to California (but this isn't very likely), you would be able to visit us more often.

In these imaginary conditions, *were* is used as the form of the verb *be*. Note these three points about *were* in hypothetical conditions:

1. *Were* replaces *was:*

   If he were here now, he'd help paint the kitchen.

2. *Were* can be used to make a speculation even more uncertain:

   If the price went down, I'd buy that car.
   If the price were to go down, I'd buy that car. (but the chances are very remote)

3. *Were* is used to speculate about totally imaginary situations:

   If I were you, I'd leave. (But I'm not you.)
   If she were the president, she'd be kind and gentle.

Look at this sentence from the reading:

If someone in your family were to win $1,000 in a lottery, the same problem of choice would arise.

The use of the past tense in this sentence tells us about the attitude of the writers, not about past time. The use of the past tense (and particularly the *were* form) signals the writers' uncertainty that winning the lottery is likely. (Even more uncertainty would be expressed by "If someone in your family should win $1,000 . . .") What the writers imply is that that someone in your family probably will not win $1,000. A more optimistic writer could in fact write:

If someone in your family wins $1,000 . . .

and would then continue with

. . . the same problem of choice will arise.

HYPOTHETICAL CONDITIONS OF SPECULATION

Meaning	if or unless Clause	Independent Clause	
Speculation	Past tense *were (to)* *should*	would ('d) should might could ought to	+ simple form

EXERCISE 3 (oral)

Work with a partner. Change the following statements into the corresponding hypothetical conditions. Remember to shift the tense back.

EXAMPLE

I don't have time, so I can't help you.
 If I had time, I would (*or* I'd) help you.

1. The sun isn't shining today, so we won't play tennis.

2. Lucy isn't in school today, so she can't bring your book home with her.

3. I don't have a car, so you can't borrow it.

4. She isn't a conscientious student, so she doesn't get high grades.
     If she were a conscientious ——
5. The teacher isn't here, so the class can't begin.

6. I don't have any money, so you can't borrow $20 from me.

7. I'm not living in England, so I can't live in a thatched cottage.

8. It's snowing now, so we won't walk to town.
     If it were
9. The price won't go down, so I won't buy that VCR.
     (would) go down
     (were to)
10. My grandfather isn't alive, so he can't enjoy this view.
     were alive

EXERCISE 4

Complete the following sentences with clauses that express appropriate meaning.

1. If I had ten children, . . .

2. If war were declared tomorrow, . . .

3. People would complain bitterly if . . .

4. Students would unite in opposition if . . .

5. If my parents saw that bathing suit, . . .

6. If I weren't a student, . . .

7. Worldwide hunger might result if . . .

8. If the ozone layer were to be even more severely damaged, . . .

Then rewrite each one as two sentences joined with *so*.

EXAMPLE

If I had a lot of money, I'd travel around the world.
   I don't have a lot of money, so I can't travel around the world.

27e. Hypothetical conditions of hindsight

Since the past tense is used to express speculation about present-future time, what do we use to look back to the past and speculate about what might have been? Look at this example:

If my grandmother had seen you in that bathing suit, she would have had a heart attack. (But she didn't see you, so she didn't have a heart attack.)

We shift the tense back from the basic past to the past perfect. The verb forms used to imagine a hypothetical situation in the past and to speculate about its outcomes are given in the box. Note that in conditional sentences, *would* does not occur in the *if* clause, only in the independent clause.

HYPOTHETICAL CONDITIONS OF HINDSIGHT		
Meaning	if *or* **unless** *Clause*	*Independent Clause*
Hindsight	*had* + participle	*would have* *could have* *might have* *should have* *must have* *ought to have* + participle

---

EXERCISE 5

Read the last paragraph of "The Culture of 'Lead Time'" on p. 361. Identify the conditional sentences. Write down the verb forms used in both the conditional clause and the independent clause in a box similar to the one in section 27e.

27f. Wishes

When we express a wish, we shift the tenses back, the same as we do with conditions:

PRESENT-FUTURE	PAST
I don't have a car.	I didn't go to Florida with them.
I wish I had a car.	I wish I had gone to Florida with them.

We also use *were* in present-future wishes:

I wish I were a tap dancer.

EXERCISE 6 (oral)

Make up five sentences of speculation about what you would do and what your life would be like if you were somebody else or if you were in a specific career. Choose people that you admire or a position you would like to have. Then tell your classmates what you would do if you were that person.

EXAMPLE

I wish I were Steffi Graf. If I were Steffi Graf, I'd play tennis every day.

Then make up five more wishes about things you wish you had done in the past.

EXAMPLE

I wish I had learned to drive when I was 17. If I had learned to drive then, I would have bought a car.

27g. Summary of conditional adverbial clauses

For general guidelines to the use of tenses in conditional sentences, consult the box on page 306.

You will also come across mixtures of the categories, as in the second example sentence:

If she had invested her money in a computer company, she would have made a lot of money. (hindsight)

If she had invested her money in a computer company, she would be a rich woman today. (mixed: hindsight and speculation about the present)

CONDITIONAL CLAUSES		
Meaning	*if or unless Clause*	*Independent Clause*
REAL AND POSSIBLE Fact	Same tense in both	
Prediction	present	*will ('ll)* *should* *may* *might* *can* *ought to* } + simple form
HYPOTHETICAL Speculation	past *were (to)* *should*	*would ('d)* *should* *might* *could* *ought to* } + simple form
Hindsight	*had* + participle	*would have* *could have* *might have* *should have* *must have* *ought to have* } + participle

☆EXERCISE 7 (oral)

Look at the following problem.

Assume that a steel pipe is embedded in the concrete floor of a bare room as shown below. The inside diameter is .06″ larger than the diameter of a Ping-Pong ball (1.50″) which is resting gently at the bottom of the pipe. You are one of a group of six people in the room, along with the following objects:

100′ of clothesline
A wooden handled carpenter's hammer

A chisel
A box of Wheaties
A file
A wire coat hanger
A monkey wrench
A light bulb

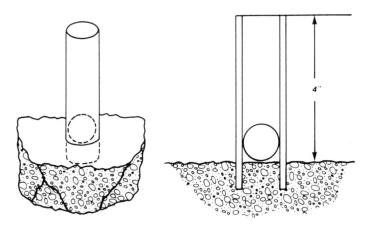

J. L. Adams, *Conceptual Blockbusting: A Guide to Better Ideas*
(New York: Freeman, 1974), p. 32.

Someone says to you, "If your life depended on it, what would you do to get the ball out of the pipe without damaging the ball, the tube, or the floor?" Discuss possible ways with two or three other students. Then together write five sentences explaining the most original ways you find.

EXAMPLE **If we crushed the Wheaties with the hammer, we would be able to pour them into the pipe and . . .**

Use conditions of fact, prediction, or speculation, depending on how certain you are that your solution would work. Read your sentences to the other students in your class.

***

27h. Other conjunctions

The following conjunctions are associated with conditional clauses:

as if   in case
as though   provided that
even if

Do not confuse *as if* and *like: as if* introduces a clause (with S + V), whereas *like* is a preposition and precedes a noun phrase.

307

27i

He acted *as if* he were crazy.
He acted *like* a madman.

In speech, you might hear "He acted like he was crazy," but that is informal. (See also section 16d of Chapter 16.)

EXERCISE 8 (oral)

Discuss with other students ways to complete the following sentences.

1. Even if the meeting is canceled, . . .

2. She bought some more milk in case . . .

3. Provided that the price is low enough, . . .

4. When she arrived after an overnight flight, she looked as if . . .

5. They treated us as though . . .

6. He packed an extra suit in case . . .

27i. Omitted *if*

Occasionally you will see *if* omitted with inversion of the subject and verb.

EXAMPLES

Had I only tried harder, I could have done better.
Were I the president, I'd make a lot of changes.

This is not a frequently used structure.

EDIT

The following passages from students' writing contain some errors. Can you find them and correct them?

1. I once had a lot of money in my savings account. Unfortunately, I spent all of it. If I had kept the money in the account and add more money to it, the amount of money would have grown, and might have even been five or ten times the original amount. If I had kept the money long

enough, I would have bought a house. If I had bought a house, my life would have change because I would have made money from my house by renting it out.

Jin-qiang Luo, China

2. I came to the United States in December 1985. If I had not come here, I would have been a teacher in elementary school in Korea. My life would have been more stable. I would not had an identity crisis and such a feeling of alienation.

Mi-kyung Choi, Korea

3. If I had not been born before 1966, I would have not experienced the Cultural Revolution. I would have not seen my grandmother die because of her suffering. If the Cultural Revolution had not happened, my grandmother even might still be alive now.

Wen-you Zhu, China

WRITE

Write two paragraphs. In one, tell your reader what you would do if you had one thousand dollars to spend in one day. In the other, tell your reader about something you once did that you wish you had not done. How would your life have been different if you had not done it? Pay attention to verb tenses as you write conditional sentences.

---

1. In these paragraphs, you have been asked to speculate about the future and the past. Check the verb forms you have used against sections 27d and 27e.

2. You probably do not need to keep repeating the condition with *if*. But the verb forms in your independent clauses should fit with the pattern for speculation. Don't switch from *would* to *will* for no reason.

3. Check that *would* appears in independent clauses, not in conditional clauses.

EDITING ADVICE

Principles of Written Discourse

28. STYLE
   a. Clarity and directness
   b. Wordiness
   c. Repetition
   d. Old information before new
   e. Sentence variety
   f. Cohesion

29. PUNCTUATION
   a. End-of-sentence punctuation
   b. Semicolon
   c. Comma
   d. Colon
   e. Dashes and parentheses
   f. Apostrophe
   g. Quotation marks

Style

28

Grammatical accuracy isn't enough for writing. Obviously, there will be times when two or more variants would be acceptable in terms of accuracy, but one would fit your context better than the other. Making those decisions as you write means considering stylistic options. This chapter won't go into a lot of detail about rhetorical form and organization of a piece of writing, but it will present briefly a few concepts that are useful for you to bear in mind as you move from one sentence to another in your writing.

STUDY

28a. Clarity and directness

Sometimes writers think that to impress their readers, they have to use a lot of long words and try to sound "intellectual." This is not so. Most readers prefer to read something that is clear, that they don't have to struggle with. They want you, the writer, to do the work. If they have to spend time figuring out what you mean, they'll get impatient. Three principles will help you keep your writing clear for your reader:

1. *Express the action in the verb.* If you use verbs that express action and make their subjects the agents (or performers) of the action, you'll write strong, clear, and direct sentences.

> **My grandfather died when I was 2.**
> *Not* **An event that happened when I was 2 was the death of my grandfather.**

In the second sentence, the subject and verb of the independent clause are as follows:

> s   v
> **an event**   **was**

In the first sentence, the core of the meaning of the sentence is in the subject and verb:

> s   v
> **my grandfather**   **died**

If you use too many nouns formed from verbs, you'll find it hard to be direct:

$$\overset{s}{\text{The death of my grandfather}} \qquad \overset{v}{\text{occurred when I was 2.}}$$

2. *Avoid overusing the verb* be. If you keep using the verb *be*, you won't be able to use many action verbs.

Weak	I am obliged to contribute to the family.
Better	I have to contribute to the family.
Weak	The situation is that there is too much lateness in my school.
Better	The students in my school always come late to class.
Weak	There are a lot of hotels that offer deals.
Better	A lot of hotels offer deals.
Weak	The firm's attempt to hire minorities was not successful until last year.
Better	The firm tried to hire minorities but didn't succeed until last year.

3. *Avoid unnecessary passives.* If you want to tell your reader who performed the action you are writing about, it is usually preferable to use the active rather than the passive voice. It is more direct and less wordy, and it is clearer for the reader.

Not	Success will be achieved by students if they work hard.
But	Students will succeed if they work hard.

Don't use the passive if the active expresses your meaning more directly. (See Chapter 12 for more details on using active and passive forms.)

EXERCISE 1

Rewrite the following sentences to make them more direct.

1. There should be discussion between parents and children about the situation of sex education.

2. In regard to the generation gap, it is a matter that should be recognized by parents.

3. Establishment of the laws in the United States happens at the level of the Senate and the House of Representatives.

4. There are four boys in my family who are always involved in a lot of fighting.

5. There are a few people that I know who refused to continue their studies.

28b. Wordiness

Cut out as many wordy structures as you can. Keep your writing lean; cut out the fat! The following sentence is padded with a lot of unnecessary words and phrases:

> In my opinion, I think that success in school, whether it is elementary, junior high, high school, or college, is a result of the fact that the students are hard-working.

What is it really saying?

> Students succeed in school when they work hard.

The following sentence is padded, too:

> The point I want to make is that the crime rate is increasing in view of the fact that more criminals are inhabitants of the streets.

This can be reduced as follows:

> The crime rate is increasing because more criminals live on the streets.

The following expressions add words but no meaning and should be avoided:

as a matter of fact	what I mean to say is that
because of the fact that	in view of the fact that
last but not least	in my opinion
of a _____ nature /type ("His behavior was of a childish type.")	

28c. Repetition

Note the repetition in these two sentences:

> The doctors used an ultrasound device to test the fetus. This ultrasound device is used frequently in prenatal care.

The sentences could be rewritten like this to avoid repetition:

> To test the fetus, the doctors used an ultrasound device used frequently in prenatal care.

EXERCISE 2

Find a piece of writing (one page or more) you did while using this book. Exchange papers with a partner. Read each other's writing, looking for places where the writing could be cut and made more direct.

28d. Old information before new

We have just noted that it is usually preferable to use action verbs and to make the subject of the sentence the performer of the action. However, at times, a passive is more appropriate.

In English sentences, we tend to present old or given information first, and put new information at the end. In that way, our writing follows a certain linear logic. Look at these sentences:

Researchers have been examining the way people choose where to sit in a library. The choice of seat is often determined by the other people in the room.

The writer of these sentences introduced new information at the end of the first sentence *(where to sit in a library)*. In the second sentence, that old or given information comes first (as *the choice of seat*), and the new information *(the other people in the room)* is left for the end of the sentence.

The following version would be less coherent because it violates the principle of given before new:

Researchers have been examining the way people choose where to sit in a library. The other people in the room often determine the choice of seat.

☆*EXERCISE 3*

How could the second sentence in each sequence be rewritten to preserve the given-before-new principle?

EXAMPLE

A pickup truck is the best vehicle for driving in Texas. People can use it to transport sports equipment.

A pickup truck is the best vehicle for driving in Texas. It can be used to transport sports equipment.

1. The high food value of the soybean made it a natural candidate for livestock feed. They tested the bean and it met the need perfectly.

2. The first public notice of the arrival of soybeans in the West was made by a Swedish biologist. Samuel Bowen introduced them to the New World.

3. While the library was uncrowded, students almost always chose corner seats at one of the empty rectangular tables. After one reader occupied each table, new readers would choose a seat on the opposite side.

4. Research on classroom environments is extensive. Probably Raymond Adams and Bruce Biddle conducted the most detailed study.

28e. Sentence variety

Try to vary your sentence length and structure as you write. You don't want to have all short, simple sentences, or all long, complex sentences. You can get a sense of how varied your sentence length is if you take a colored pen and make a slash mark (/) at the end of each sentence. You'll see then whether these marks occur absolutely regularly or not. A short sentence after a series of longer sentences can be very powerful. Avoid using a lot of sentences with the same structure.

EXAMPLE

When it got dark, we left. Because we were hungry, we drove to a restaurant. Although it was expensive, we ate there.

All three sentences have an adverbial clause before the subject. The effect is monotonous and uninteresting.

When you read your work through, ask yourself if you can combine any sentences; if you can add any short, pointed sentences; or if you could add any questions, for variety.

EXERCISE 4

Revise a piece of your writing specifically for sentence length and variety.

28f. Cohesion

When you write essays, you use devices to link one sentence to another, to make connections between ideas. Some of these devices have been discussed in earlier chapters.

- *Pronouns*

  He saw the bicycle leaning against the wall. It was the one he

  wanted. (See Chapter 18.)

- *Transitions*

  He saw the bicycle. However, he didn't say a word. (See Chapter 23.)

- *Substitution*

  He has a black bicycle, and his sister has a blue one.

- *Ellipsis*

  He got three presents, and she got two. (= two presents)

315

- *Vocabulary*

The words you use provide links from sentence to sentence, too. In Nora Ephron's first paragraph (p. 334), note how many times *living room* is used. Words that are not exactly the same but share the same context also provide cohesion. Note the use of *spend* and *purchase* in the following excerpt from the reading on p. 369:

> **Suppose that you have $25 to *spend* and have narrowed your alternatives to a textbook or a date. Scarcity prohibits the *purchase* of both.**

In the following, note how *money, $25,* and *cost* share the same context and so provide connection:

> **Once time or money is devoted to one thing, the opportunity to use that time or money for other things is lost. If you spend $25 to acquire a textbook, the opportunity cost of that text is what was given up to obtain it.**

In the same way, *textbook* and *text* are connected.

EDIT

The following piece of student writing does not contain grammatical errors, but its style could be improved. Work with other students to rewrite it, editing for elements of style and making it less repetitive and more direct and coherent.

Okushiga is one of the well-known ski resorts in Japan, but in summer, there are not many people who visit Okushiga. It takes about six hours from Tokyo by car or train connecting with the bus. Because of its inconvenient location, and because there is no snow anymore, Okushiga does not attract people in summertime. However, summer in Okushiga is as wonderful as winter. Unlike other resorts in Japan, Okushiga has nothing that distracts people's relaxation, such as souvenir shops, rock music on someone's cassette player, and stands of junk food. In Okushiga, there is only clear, serene nature. People are surrounded by mountains, streams, trees, and flowers. Behind the lodge, there is a small golf course, which is used as a part of a ski slope during the winter. There are also tennis courts and an indoor swimming pool. A narrow river runs in front of the lodge, and people can go fishing if they ignore the coldness of the water. A famous conductor, Seiji Ozawa, who usually conducts the Boston Philharmonic, has his cottage in Okushiga. He really loves the place, and he gives a free concert. On a summer night at the lodge, only lucky people who are there accidentally can listen to his music. He calls the concert "a concert in the forest." The concert is one of the fascinating things in Okushiga, but not many people know about it.

Okushiga is a nice place to spend quiet and gentle days. On the other hand, we can be very active there doing various kinds of sports. We hope Okushiga will never change.

Yuriko Takayama, Japan

WRITE

Write an essay in which you explain which reading passage in this book you enjoyed the most and why. Concentrate not only on editing your work for grammatical accuracy but also on examining it for style and cohesion.

---

1. Make sure that you have varied your sentence length and the types of sentences you have used.

2. Revise any sentences that are wordy and don't have the action expressed in the verb.

3. Read your essay through once to see if you have followed the given-before-new principle.

EDITING ADVICE

---

29 Punctuation

STUDY

29a. End-of-sentence punctuation

The end of a sentence is signaled by a period (.), a question mark (?), or an exclamation point (!). When the meaning connection between two sentences is very close, they may be combined into a single sentence by means of a semicolon.

EXAMPLE

He actually likes babies; he even wants to bring one home.

It is important to signal the end of a sentence (S + V structure) with one of these punctuation marks. Avoid run-on sentences, comma-splices, and fragments. The box on page 319 contains a summary of common problems. See also Chapters 1, 22, 23, and 26 for more examples and exercises.

Note that a period is also used to signal an abbreviation:

Dr.   Ms.   etc.
Mr.   Mich.   Sept.

Usually, no periods are used for abbreviations that use only capital letters:

FBI   NATO   UCLA

No periods are used with abbreviated numbers:

2nd   4th   101st

EXERCISE 1

The following student sentences contain errors. Indicate if a sentence contains a run-on (RO), a comma splice (CS), or a fragment (F).

_F___ 1. For example, when a department store has a bargain sale at the end of the summer. You may buy expensive clothes at a discount price.

_F___ 2. If you have all the time in the world to distract yourself with music, friends, and conversation while studying.

318

PROBLEMS WITH END PUNCTUATION

Problem	Feature	Example
Run-on	No end punctuation	*My brother is funny he likes to get up early.
	Transition: No end punctuation	*My brother works hard however he doesn't make a lot of money.
Comma splice	Comma separates two sentences with no coordinating conjunction	*My brother is funny, he likes to get up early.
	Comma separates two sentences with transition word	*My brother works hard, however he doesn't make a lot of money.
Fragment	No subject	*He is very industrious. Works extremely hard every day.
	No main verb	*Both of them working very hard.
	No independent clause	*Because he wanted to save a lot of money for his vacation.
		*Although he was offered a new job in a new company, which involved a move to California.
		*Wanting to improve his work performance in order to get promoted.

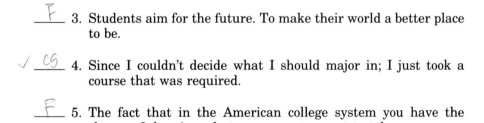

_F_ 3. Students aim for the future. To make their world a better place to be.

✓ _CS_ 4. Since I couldn't decide what I should major in; I just took a course that was required.

_F_ 5. The fact that in the American college system you have the chance of choosing whatever you may want to take.

_CS_ 6. I have a very good friend from Haiti, he has been in college for three years.

_F_ 7. People who are successful in life with money and valuable material possessions.

_Ro_ 8. College prepares you for a career that will make you a lot of money however it costs a lot at the beginning.

319

EXERCISE 2

The following poem by William Carlos Williams relates to the painting by Brueghel that appears on p. 98. The poet wrote it without any sentence punctuation. If you were to write these same words not as a poem but as connected prose, what punctuation would you add?

Landscape with the Fall of Icarus

According to Brueghel
when Icarus fell
it was spring

a farmer was ploughing
his field .
the whole pageantry

of the year was
awake tingling
near

the edge of the sea ,
concerned
with itself ,

sweating in the sun
that melted
the wings' wax

unsignificantly
off the coast ,
there was

a splash quite unnoticed .
this was
Icarus drowning

William Carlos Williams

EXERCISE 3

In the following passage from "Portable Computers," which appears on p. 357, all punctuation, including the end punctuation and capital letters, has been removed. Indicate where sentences should end.

In the early 1960s the first minicomputers were made commercially . they were the size of a two-drawer file cabinet the revolution was on less than a decade later the microcomputer was invented the basic unit of the microcomputer is a tiny silicon chip less than 1 cm on a side each chip is a miniature electronic circuit that serves the different computer functions ‸ amazingly‚ each circuit contains thousands of elements ₒ

29b. Semicolon

A semicolon is used to indicate the end of one sentence when two sentences are so closely related that they are combined into one (see section 29a). A semicolon can also be used in place of a comma to separate items in a list, particularly when the items are long or when they have commas within them.

EXAMPLES

Dying patients especially cannot make decisions about the end of a life: about whether or not to enter a hospital or to have surgery; about where and with whom to spend their remaining time; about how to bring their affairs to a close and take leave.

Transportation in Duluth, Minnesota; Portland, Maine; and Norfolk, Virginia, generates basic jobs.

29c. Comma

Many students overuse commas, sprinkling them over their writing like salt and pepper. There are specific and defined occasions when a comma is appropriate. A useful rule of thumb for you, after you have studied and tried to apply the rules, is this: "When in doubt, leave the comma out."

Commas are usually used in the five instances, each of which is explained and illustrated.

FIVE USES OF COMMAS

1. Before the subject
2. Between items in a list
3. Around inserted material
4. Before a quotation
5. Between clauses joined with a coordinating conjunction.

---

1. A comma is used to set off a phrase or clause that occurs before the subject of the sentence.

   Pattern: ～～～～ ，**S + V**

EXAMPLES

> Last year, I came to believe that the main reason was the lamps.
>
> Arriving a little before the hour, he waited.

2. Commas are used between items in a list.

Pattern: ~~~~~~~~ *x,* ~~~~~~~~ *y,*

and ~~~~~~~~ *z.*

The listed items can be words, phrases, or clauses.

EXAMPLES

> By that time I will be no good at all at eating, sleeping, working, and swimming.
>
> Tofu is simmered with meat, vegetables, and noodles in sukiyaki.
>
> The spotless ashtrays, furniture coverings, and plastic lamp covers sent nonverbal messages telling us not to touch anything, not to put our feet up, and not to be comfortable.
>
> At last Teacher Wu sat down at the piano, took out several books of music, and began to play.
>
> They may prescribe innumerable placebos, sound more encouraging than the facts warrant, and distort grave news.

Note that all the items in the series have to be parallel in structure.

Commas also separate two or more coordinate adjectives, ones that belong to the same category (see Chapter 14) and whose order can be reversed:

> It is a comfortable, inexpensive restaurant.
> It is an inexpensive, comfortable restaurant.
> It is an inexpensive, comfortable French restaurant. (no comma between *comfortable* and *French*)

3. Commas are used to set off words, phrases, and clauses that are inserted into a sentence as supplementary, nonrestrictive, nonessential information.

Patterns:

_____, ~~~~~~~~ , _____.

_____, ~~~~~~~~ .

EXAMPLES

> Doufu, the Chinese name for bean curd, has been made in China for about 2,000 years.

Restaurants use a lot of doufu, the Chinese name for bean curd.

The family, almost hysterical with relief, cheered my decision.

Theo, who worked in an art dealer's shop, introduced his brother to Impressionist painters.

4. A comma is used to set off quoted words from the rest of the sentence.

Patterns: **He said, " 〰〰〰〰〰〰 ."**

" 〰〰〰〰〰〰 ," he said.

EXAMPLES

As she turned to go back, she said, "In your next letter to your mother, tell her you fixed a piano in China for an old lady." "Let's eat first," she said.

A colon can also be used to introduce a direct quotation (see section 29d).

5. A comma is used to separate independent or dependent clauses when they are connected with a coordinating conjunction. The coordinating conjunctions are *and, or, but, nor, so, for,* and *yet.* (See also Chapter 22.)

Pattern: **S + V, conjunction S + V.**

EXAMPLES

I had walked along the river many times since meeting the fisherman that day in winter, but I did not see him again until spring.

They seemed delighted by it, so I tore the sheet out of my block.

I said that it was only a drawing, and [that] I would be happy if he would take it.

Note that the comma comes before—not after—the coordinating conjunction.

Never use a comma in these situations:

• To separate subject and verb:

Not *The course I am taking this semester, takes a lot of my time.

• To set off a clause introduced by *that* from the independent clause:

Not *It was amazing to all of them, that he had done so well.

EXERCISE 4

Examine all the uses of commas in the following passage, taken from the second part of the reading "Cultural Exchanges." Fit each comma into one of the five categories in the box in section 29c.

He exchanged a few words with the family, and they leapt into
_a
action, the women going into the sheltered part of the junk to prepare
_b
food and the men rowing out to meet us in one of two tiny boats lashed to the side. We got in the little boat and returned with them to the junk. We ate a few snacks of different kinds of salted fish, had tea, and
_c _d
then I showed them the drawing. They seemed delighted by it, so I
_e
tore the sheet out of my block. I handed it to the oldest member of the family, a man in his sixties, who opened his eyes wide with surprise
_f _g
and would not take it, saying, "How can I take this? It is a work of art;
_h _i
what do I have to offer you in return?" I laughed, saying that it was
_j
only a drawing, and I would be happy if he would take it just for fun.
_k
But he was serious; when at last he accepted it, putting it down care-
_l
fully on the bed, he began negotiating with Old Ding to choose an
_m
appropriate gift for me.

EXERCISE 5

The commas have been removed from these passages based on the readings. Insert commas where necessary.

1. The 400 people demand services: schools and churches have to be built grocery and clothing stores and livery stables are operated newspapers are published professional personnel are needed and saloons have to cater to visiting cowboys. (p. 367)

2. On the national level if a society chooses to go to war it must give up some consumer goods. (p. 369)

3. In the winter of 1888 while Seurat was attracting attention in Paris and Cézanne was working in his seclusion in Aix a young earnest Dutchman left Paris for southern France in search of the intense light and color of the south. He was Vincent van Gogh. Van Gogh was born in Holland in 1853 the son of a vicar. (p. 343)

4. In the smallest of the portable computers the cathode ray tube has been replaced by a flat electroluminescent display and the disk drives by bubble memory chips. In these computers information is stored on the road in the classroom at conferences at the library or elsewhere. (p. 357)

5. On a hot June afternoon I met the lab's director John McCarthy. . . . McCarthy's appearance when he finally strode into the office struck me as extraordinary. He is about average height five feet nine inches. His build is average with a little age trying to collect itself around his middle. (p. 359)

29d. Colon

A colon introduces explanatory and listed items.

EXAMPLES

Dying patients especially cannot make decisions about the end of life: about whether or not to enter a hospital or to have surgery. . . .

The results teach a lesson that isn't surprising: Workers generally feel better and do a better job when they're in an attractive environment.

Sometimes, when an independent clause is used after a colon, it is introduced with a capital letter, as in the second example. Some teachers and editors prefer a capital, and others do not. Always check to see which form you are expected to use.

A colon often follows the phrase *as follows*. It is not used after *such as*.

Third person pronouns are as follows: *he, she,* and *it*.
Personal pronouns are words such as *you, me, he,* and *they*.

A colon can also be used to introduce a quotation if a complete clause precedes the quotation.

EXAMPLE

It is not until I move closer that I catch the words to the melody: "Get out of here. Get out of here."

29e. Dashes and parentheses

Dashes and parentheses signal an interruption in a sentence. They serve to set off additional information, to present a kind of "aside." Often they present explanations, examples, and comments.

EXAMPLES

Consider a frontier mining town where 100 miners are employed in the town's only basic industry—gold mining.

Another kind of mistruth—the "white lie"—is both a popular and often an acceptable type of communication.

Doufu, called *tofu* in Japan—and now elsewhere—arrived as one of the things associated with the new religion.

White lies are defined (at least by those who tell them) as being unmalicious.

EXERCISE 6

Look through the readings in this book and find three examples each of the use of the colon, dashes, and parentheses. Note how these punctuation marks are used.

29f. Apostrophe

The apostrophe is used in two ways:

1. An apostrophe is used to signal a contracted form in informal writing. It marks the place where letters in a word are omitted:

cannot	can't
did not	didn't
does not	doesn't
would not	wouldn't
he has	he's
he is	he's
I would	I'd
I had	I'd
they are	they're

let us	let's
we will	we'll

IRREGULAR FORM

will not	won't

2. An apostrophe is used to signal possession or ownership. Add *'s* to signal possession. If the noun is a plural form ending in *-s,* add only an apostrophe.

EXAMPLES

> her son's room (one son)
> her daughters' room (two daughters, one room)
> the teachers' books (more than one teacher: plural *-s*)
> the children's books (more than one child, but no *-s* to form plural)

However, *do not* use apostrophes in the following cases:

- With the names of buildings, objects, or pieces of furniture:

Not *the hotel's pool
But the hotel pool *or* the pool in the hotel
Not *the car's door
But the car door *or* the door of the car
Not *the table's leg
But the table leg *or* the leg of the table

- With possessive adjectives and pronouns:

its   yours   hers

Note the use of the possessive adjective in the following sentence:

> The soybean allows the Chinese to feed a quarter of the *world's* population on a tenth of *its* arable land.

EXERCISE 7

Rewrite each of the following pairs of sentences as one sentence, and use an apostrophe. Make the italicized verb the verb of your new sentence.

EXAMPLE

Their daughters took a vacation.
The vacation *was* wonderful
  Their daughters' vacation was wonderful.

1. The child has some toys.
The toys *are* all over the floor.

2. Her children have some dolls.
The dolls *are lying* all over the floor.

3. The director has plans.
Her plans *will be put* into operation.

4. The politicians have plans.
Their plans *might be delayed*.

5. The women have plans.
Their plans *are being attacked*.

EXERCISE 8

In the following sentences based on the readings, identify all the apostrophes, and indicate whether they signal contraction (c) or possession (p). For each contraction, specify what the uncontracted form would be.

_____ 1. It always looks neat and tidy. That's because no one ever uses it.

_____ 2. "How's business?" I would ask.

_____ 3. I salute my friend Lillian's mother.

_____ 4. At times they see important reasons to lie for the patient's own sake.

_____ 5. This has happened to thousands of contemporary cities that have lost industries that represented a portion of the town's basic industry.

_____ 6. I'm not mad at you. It's just been a tough day.

29g. Quotation marks

Quotation marks occur at the beginning and end of directly quoted material, repeating the exact words that were spoken or written. Note the following features of quotations:

- Quotation marks appear at the top of the line:

   He said, "Let's go."

- Quotation marks signal the beginning and end of the exact words quoted.

- Periods and commas go inside the quotation marks:

   The family cheered my decision, saying it had "true spirit."

- For long quotations, do not use quotation marks. Instead, set the passage off by starting it on a new line and indenting every line about ten spaces.

Quotation marks are also used to indicate that one or more words are being used with a special meaning:

The soybean had become "gold from the soil."

EXERCISE 9

In the first part of the reading "Cultural Exchanges" by Mark Salzman on p. 347, you will find some direct quotation and some reported speech. If the author had decided to use all direct quotation, what changes would he have had to make? Change each piece of reported speech to a direct quotation.

EXAMPLE

I asked her how she had managed to get a piano.
I asked her, "How did you manage to get a piano?"

☆EXERCISE 10

In the following passage from the reading "White Lies" on p. 365, a blank has been left at each spot where a punctuation mark originally appeared. Which punctuation marks would you insert in those places?

Although most people would agree that lying to gain advantage over

an unknowing subject is wrong ____ another kind of mistruth ____ the

____ white lie ____ ____ is both a popular and often acceptable type of

communication ____ White lies are defined ____ at least by those who tell

them ____ as being unmalicious ____ or even helpful____

Whether or not they are benign ____ white lies are certainly common ___ In one study ___ . . . 130 subjects were asked to keep track of the truthfulness of their everyday conversational statements ___ Only 38.5 percent of these statements ___ slightly more than a third ___ proved to be totally honest ___ What reasons do people give for being deceitful so often ___ . . .

When subjects in the study . . . were asked to give a lie-by-lie account of their motives for concealing or distorting the truth ___ five major reasons emerged ___ The most frequent motive ___ occurring in 55.2 percent of the lies ___ was *to save face* ___ Lying of this sort is often given the approving label of ___ tact ___ ___ and is used ___ when it would be unkind to be honest but dishonest to be kind ___ (Bavelas, 1983) ___ Sometimes a face-saving lie prevents embarrassment for the recipient ___ as when you pretend to remember someone at a party whom you really don___t recall ever having seen before ___ In other cases a lie protects the teller from embarrassment ___ You might ___ for example ___ cover up your mistakes by blaming them on outside forces ___ ___ You didn___t receive the check ___ It must have been delayed in the mail ___ ___

EDIT

The following passages from student writing contain punctuation errors. What should the writers do to edit these sentences?

1. Basically American restaurants are designed with weak lighting and Chinese restaurants have bright lights. When I go to an American restaurant I have a feeling that I am in a place like a movie theater and I automatically lower my voice.

2. The newspaper report said They were very concerned about the problems".

3. Although vitamins are sold in a lot of stores; their value to health has not been entirely proved.

4. You have to do three things to stay healthy; eat sensibly, exercise, and sleep well.

5. The more successful society is the more developed the country becomes for example, in the United States personal success varies from society to society such as: in the areas of education, science, arts, and business.

6. There are a few people, that go to university and continue studying for many years.

WRITE

Read through one of the following articles:

"The Culture of 'Lead Time' " (p. 361)
"Tau Ceti" (p. 355)
"Artificial Intelligence" (p. 359)
"Economics and Scarcity" (p. 369)

Then close this book and write an informative summary of the ideas contained in the reading passage. Give an account of what the author of the passage says. Refer to the reading again if you want to include any direct quotation.

---

1. Read your summary aloud. Are there any places where you have not put end punctuation where it is necessary?

2. With a different-colored pen—preferably green or red—underline all the punctuation marks in your summary. Examine each one. Consider whether its use is appropriate.

3. Try to fit every comma you have used into one of the five categories explained in section 29c.

4. Review all the uses of punctuation in this chapter. Consider whether you might be able to improve some sentences with, for example, a semicolon, colon, dashes, or parentheses. Aim at variety; it keeps your readers interested.

EDITING ADVICE

PART II

READINGS

Room with View—and No People
Nora Ephron

I have a nice living room. You should come sit in it some day. You will undoubtedly be alone when you do, because no one ever sits in the living room. (Unless we have company. Otherwise, never.) We talk a lot about the fact that no one ever sits in the living room. It makes us all sad. The living room is the prettiest room in the apartment. It has a fireplace and moldings.° It has a slice of a view of the river. It is a cheerful room furnished in light colors. The couches in it were recently cleaned by men with small machines. It always looks neat and tidy. That's because no one ever uses it, I know that, but still. You should see it. I already said that, but I mean it.

Many reasons have been put forward for why we never use the living room. Last year, I came to believe that the main reason was the lamps. So I got new lamps. They are much more attractive than the old lamps. Also, they make the room much brighter. It is now possible to see in the living room. It is even possible to read in the living room. Still, we don't use the living room. Sometimes, in the evening, when we are feeling particularly melancholy° about not using the living room, we wander into it and admire the new lamps and talk about what I have this year come to believe are the reasons why we never use the living room. Perhaps if there were a phone in the living room, but I don't like phones in living rooms. Perhaps if there were a television set, but I feel as strongly about television sets in living rooms as I do about phones. Perhaps new window treatments° would help, but talk of window treatments makes me even more melancholy than the plight° of the living room. Perhaps (this crosses my mind every year at this time) if we put the Christmas tree in the living room, but the living room is so full of furniture waiting for someone to come sit down that there is no room in it for a tree. Anyway, everyone knows the tree belongs in the entrance hall.

Years ago, when I lived in a two-room apartment, I never used the living room either. I used the bedroom. I worked in the bedroom, I ate in the bedroom, I slept in the bedroom. Now I have an apartment with many rooms. I work in the study, I eat in the kitchen, I continue to sleep in the bedroom. Sometimes I think about moving the bed into the living room. This would not solve the problem of why we never use the living room—because the living room would then be the bedroom—but at least we would use the room that is supposed to be the living room for something. The trouble with the idea is that the living room has no closets and is a long way from the bathroom. Also, I am too old to have a bed in the living room.

°moldings decorative borders

°melancholy sad

°window treatments curtains or shades
°plight difficult situation

°**Bloomingdale's**
department store
in New York City

°**Beverly Hills** area
of Los Angeles,
famous for movie
stars' houses
°**color scheme** plan
for use of color in
a room
°**nook** corner

°**salute** praise,
honor

°**marginally**
slightly

°**Victorian** typical
of the reign of
Queen Victoria of
England (1837–
1901)
°**snobbish** arrogant,
feeling superior
°**contemptuous**
scornful

Every time I walk from the bedroom or the study to the kitchen I pass the living room and take a long, fond look at it. It's a lovely room. It might as well be one of those rooms in Bloomingdale's° with a velvet rope in front of it for all the good it does me.

When I was growing up, I had a friend named Lillian who had no living-room furniture. She lived in a large house in Beverly Hills,° and the living room was empty. I always wondered why. I always supposed it was because her mother was having trouble deciding on a color scheme.° Color schemes were important in those days. I had a friend named Arlene whose house was famous for having a color scheme in every room, including the breakfast nook,° which was charcoal gray and pink. Anyway, a few years ago, Lillian was in New York and I finally got up the nerve to ask her why her family had never had any living-room furniture. She told me that her father had given her mother a choice of living-room furniture or a pool, and her mother had chosen the pool. I salute° my friend Lillian's mother. She obviously understood something that I am still having trouble absorbing, which is this: at least you can swim in a pool.

But what can you do in a living room? Tell me. I really want to know. I know what to do in a charcoal gray and pink breakfast nook, but the only thing I can think of to do in a living room is living, and I clearly don't have a clue as to what that consists of, especially if you rule out eating, sleeping, working and swimming. I'm sure that some people are good at it, whatever it is. They probably lie around in a marginally° useful way. They probably contemplate life. They probably have servants and drinks before dinner and linen cocktail napkins that someone irons. They probably think of themselves as civilized. I understand that my living room is part of a long historic tradition—no one sat in the Victorian° parlor either—but that does not in any way make me feel better about its enduring emptiness.

My living room sits in my apartment, a silent snobbish° presence, secretly contemptuous° that I don't know what to do with a room that has no clear function. I'm sure it wishes I were more imaginative; I'm positive it hopes that some day I will grow up and spend a little time in it. And some day I will. Some day when I am very old. By that time I will be no good at all at eating, sleeping, working and swimming, but I won't mind, because I will finally have found a use for the living room. It is obviously the perfect place to die.

WRITE

1. What is Nora Ephron's problem as stated in the article "Room with View—and No People"? How sympathetic are you to that problem? Make sure that you tell your readers your reasons for your point of view.

2. Describe a room in a house that you know. Let your readers know exactly what the room looks like, and show by your explanation what the dominant impression of the room is (for example, is it simple, comfortable, clean, untidy, bare, oppressive, cluttered?).

GRAMMAR REFERENCES

A portion of the reading introduces a chapter marked ‡ .

Subject and predicate: Chapter 1‡

Phrases and clauses: Chapter 2

Questions and negatives: Chapter 3

Proper nouns: Chapter 4

Countable and uncountable nouns: Chapter 5

Articles: Chapter 6

Active and passive: Chapter 12

Verb forms: summary: Chapter 13

Coordinating conjunctions: Chapter 22‡

Style: Chapter 28

The Doctors' Dilemma
Sissela Bok

°**conceal** hide
°**dwarfed** made to look smaller
°**brutal** cruel
°**uphold** keep
°**corruption** dishonesty

Should doctors ever lie to benefit their patients—to speed recovery or to conceal° the approach of death? In medicine as in law, government, and other lines of work, the requirements of honesty often seem dwarfed° by greater needs: the need to shelter from brutal° news or to uphold° a promise of secrecy; to expose corruption° or to promote the public interest.   5

°**gravity** seriousness
°**prognosis** prediction about what will happen

What should doctors say, for example, to a 46-year-old man coming in for a routine physical checkup just before going on vacation with his family who, though he feels in perfect health, is found to have a form of cancer that will cause him to die within six months? Is it best to tell him the truth? If he asks, should the doctors deny that he is ill, or minimize the gravity° of the prognosis°? Should they at least conceal the truth until after the family vacation?   10

Doctors confront such choices often and urgently. At times, they see important reasons to lie for the patient's own sake; in their eyes, such lies differ sharply from self-serving ones.

°**deteriorate** get worse
°**precept** principle, rule
°**transcends** goes beyond

Studies show that most doctors sincerely believe that the seriously ill do   15
not want to know the truth about their condition, and that informing them risks destroying their hope, so that they may recover more slowly, or deteriorate° faster, perhaps even commit suicide. As one physician wrote: "Ours is a profession which traditionally has been guided by a precept° that transcends° the virtue of uttering the truth for truth's sake, and that is 'as   20
far as possible do no harm.'"

°**innumerable** countless, very many
°**placebos** prescribed remedy with no actual medication, sugar pills
°**warrant** demand
°**distort** alter
°**illusory** erroneous, deceptive
°**bestow** give
°**betrayed** deceived
°**advocates** supporters
°**benevolent** well-meaning, well-intentioned
°**autonomy** independence

Armed with such a precept, a number of doctors may slip into deceptive practices that they assume will "do no harm" and may well help their patients. They may prescribe innumerable° placebos,° sound more encouraging than the facts warrant,° and distort° grave news, especially to the incurably ill and   25
the dying.

But the illusory° nature of the benefits such deception is meant to bestow° is now coming to be documented. Studies show that, contrary to the belief of many physicians, an overwhelming majority of patients do want to be told the truth, even about grave illness, and feel betrayed° when they learn that   30
they have been misled. We are also learning that truthful information, humanely conveyed, helps patients cope with illness: helps them tolerate pain better, need less medication, and even recover faster after surgery.

Not only do lies not provide the "help" hoped for by advocates° of benevolent° deception; they invade the autonomy° of patients and render   35
them unable to make informed choices concerning their own health, including the choice of whether to *be* a patient in the first place. We are becoming increasingly aware of all that can befall patients in the course of their illness when information is denied or distorted.

Dying patients especially—who are easiest to mislead and most often   40

337

kept in the dark—can then not make decisions about the end of life: about whether or not to enter a hospital, or to have surgery; about where and with whom to spend their remaining time; about how to bring their affairs to a close and take leave.

°**credibility** reliability

°**scrupulously** totally

°**litigation** lawsuits

Lies also do harm to those who tell them: harm to their integrity and in the long run, to their credibility.° Lies hurt their colleagues as well. The suspicion of deceit undercuts the work of the many doctors who are scrupulously° honest with their patients; it contributes to the spiral of litigation° and of "defensive medicine," and thus it injures, in turn, the entire medical profession. 45

50

°**remonstrating** objecting, criticizing

Sharp conflicts are now arising. Patients are learning to press for answers. Patients' bills of rights require that they be informed about their condition and about alternatives for treatment. Many doctors go to great lengths to provide such information. Yet even in hospitals with the most eloquent bill of rights, believers in benevolent deception continue their age-old practices. Colleagues may disapprove but refrain from remonstrating.° Nurses may bitterly resent having to take part, day after day, in deceiving patients, but feel powerless to take a stand. 55

°**straits** difficult circumstances

°**wary** careful

°**erode** wear away, destroy

°**saw** saying

There is urgent need to debate this issue openly. Not only in medicine, but in other professions as well, practitioners may find themselves repeatedly in straits° where serious consequences seem avoidable only through deception. Yet the public has every reason to be wary° of professional deception, for such practices are peculiarly likely to become ingrained, to spread, and to erode° trust. Neither in medicine, nor in law, government, or the social sciences can there be comfort in the old saw,° "What you don't know can't hurt you." 60

65

WRITE

1. What do you view as the main problems people face in sickness or old age? How are these problems handled in your country?

2. What would you do if you were a doctor facing the dilemma described in the second paragraph of the article—and why? Justify the reasons for your decision. Try to explain them to a reader who holds the opposite point of view.

GRAMMAR REFERENCES

Questions and negatives: Chapter 3‡

Countable and uncountable nouns: Chapter 5‡

Articles: Chapter 6

Active and passive: Chapter 12

-*ing* forms: Chapter 20

The Soybean
Fred Hapgood

Doufu, the Chinese name for bean curd, has been made in China, where it was invented, for about 2,000 years. It is the most important of the foods prepared in the East from the soybean, that remarkable vegetable that not only allows the Chinese to feed a quarter of the world's population on a tenth of its arable° land, but is also a rock on which the Western diet is built and a major hope for averting° world famine.

I had traveled to China in part because the whole story began here, at least 3,000 years ago, when farmers in the eastern half of northern China started planting the black or brown seeds of a wild recumbent° vine.° Why they did this is unclear; plants that lie on the ground are hard to cultivate, and the seeds of the wild soybean are tiny, hard, and, unless properly prepared, indigestible.° Whatever the reason, the farmers persevered,° and evidence suggests that by 1100 B.C. the soybean had been taught to grow straight up and bear larger, more useful seeds. These changes were sufficient to add the bean to the list of domesticated plants.

The new crop° arrived at the right time. The bean is wonderfully abundant° in protein of the highest quality, and, within limits, grows well in soils too depleted° to support other crops. The soybean plant supports colonies° of microorganisms that return rent in the form of soil-enriching nitrogen; this was an important point in a civilization that had been farming many of the same fields for thousands of years. The enthusiasm farmers had for their new crop is suggested by some of the names given different varieties: Great Treasure, Brings Happiness, Yellow Jewel, Heaven's Bird.

Over the next several hundred years the soybean spread from its center of domestication to become a staple° of the Chinese people. As it did, the third virtue° of the bean (together with high food value and ease of production) appeared—a magic versatility.° Dozens of different forms of food were developed from it, of which the most important were soybean sprouts, steamed green beans, roasted soy nuts, soy milk, soy sauce, *miso* (a fermented° soybean paste), soybean oil, *tempeh* (a fermented soybean cake apparently invented in Indonesia), soy flour, and of course doufu, which is the basis for dozens of other soy foods.

I learned all this later, long after I had returned from amusing the people of Chao Lang. At one point during my education, a citizen of Shanghai, an English teacher named Johnny Tong, explained what had happened. "The Chinese consider doufu very common," he said. "Valued, but common. For instance, in our stories a bean curd seller is always a poor man with a good heart. We refer to a girl who is beautiful but poor as *doufu-xishi,* 'a bean curd beauty.' When a man is treating a woman cheaply, taking her for granted,° we say he is just 'eating her doufu.'" What amused the villagers, he suggested,

°**arable** used for cultivation
°**averting** preventing

°**recumbent** lying down
°**vine** climbing plant
°**indigestible** hard to digest, inedible
°**persevered** persisted, did not stop

°**crop** farm produce
°**abundant** plentiful
°**depleted** exhausted
°**colonies** groups

°**staple** major food item
°**virtue** advantage
°**versatility** ability to serve many functions
°**fermented** changed by chemical reaction

°**taking her for granted** not treating her well

339

°**agog** excited
°**high-tech** highly technological
°**breakthrough** new invention

°**slavish** imitative
°**Sinophiles** admirers of the Chinese

°**radically** dramatically
°**shred** cut up into small pieces
°**marinate** soak in spices and herbs
°**subtle** not strong

°**spongy** like a sponge, porous

°**inventory** list

°**diabetic** characterized by an excess of blood sugar

°**lean** not fatty

°**fair** moderate

was that I seemed all agog° over doufu, as if it were some sort of high-tech° breakthrough.°

As we talked, walking through the corridors of plane trees that line the streets of Shanghai, we would pass through the outdoor markets where, under the new economic policies of China, individuals were allowed to sell products 45 of their own manufacture. Sometimes we would see a doufu seller, back on the streets after all these years, and stop to chat. "How's business?" I would ask. "Terrible," I would hear. "I have to stand here all day. Who can compete with the state stores?" (The state stores sold a cheaper, but less tasty, version.) But Tong, after some calculations, advised me that the sellers were doing very well 50 indeed.

In the last half of the first millennium A.D., the Japanese upper classes became slavish° Sinophiles° and imported many aspects of Chinese culture— writing characters, law codes, political institutions, and perhaps most important, Buddhism. Doufu, called *tofu* in Japan—and now elsewhere— 55 arrived as one of the things associated with the new religion. (By this time the soybean itself had been cultivated in Japan for several hundred years.)

Buddhist monks are strict vegetarians, and doufu had become an important food in Chinese monasteries. For several centuries Buddhism was an upper-class religion in Japan; these social associations pushed the 60 development of tofu and its associated soy foods in a different direction than in China.

The Chinese have developed dozens of different ways of reprocessing doufu, most of which change the texture and/or the taste of the food radically.° They press, shred,° slice and marinate,° steam, smoke, deep-fry, ferment, 65 and salt-dry it, often combining more than one process on this list.

In general, Japanese cuisine preserves the simplicity of tofu, its subtle° taste, custardy texture, and "dazzling white robes," in the phrase of a sixth-century monk, in dishes of awe-inspiring elegance. The Japanese do some processing: Dried-frozen tofu, spongy° and highly flavor-absorbent, is a 70 favorite. Tofu is simmered with meat, vegetables, and noodles in *sukiyaki*. Still, the difference in emphasis is unmistakable. . . .

The first public notice of the arrival of soybeans in the West was made by the great Swedish biologist Carolus Linnaeus, who in 1737 included them in an inventory° of plants grown in a garden in Holland. They were introduced to 75 the New World by Samuel Bowen, a merchant who brought seeds back from China in 1765. For the next century the soybean was little more than a botanical curiosity. Then, in the 1880s, French scientists reported that soybeans, unlike other beans, contain virtually no starch, from which the body manufactures sugar, and recommended they be used in diabetic° diets. 80

This was the first of a series of discoveries made by the new profession of nutrition as it examined and analyzed *Glycine max,* the soybean. A second came 20 years later, when the importance of proteins began to be understood: Amazingly, the soybean was found to have an even higher protein content than lean° beef. . . . 85

Forty years ago, I was told, the major crop in Lauderdale County [Tennessee] was cotton, though a lot of corn and other vegetables were grown as well. A fair° amount of livestock° was raised, and there was a good lumber°

340

°**livestock** farm animals
°**lumber** cut wood

°**devastation** ruin
°**restoration** reestablishment
°**affluence** prosperity, riches
°**binge** excess

°**scraps** leftovers

°**Cinderella** fairy tale character: a poor girl who married a prince

industry. Soybeans were attended to only when the cash crops had been taken care of. 90

After the Second World War two things changed. Historically, China had been the major supplier of soybeans to the world market. However, the course of postwar politics and the difficulties experienced by the Chinese in recovering from wartime devastation° prevented the restoration° of prewar trade relations with the West. The world soybean market needed a new source of supply, 95 and the American farmer successfully stepped into the position.

Second, and far more important, postwar affluence° sent the developed world on a binge° of meat eating. By 1973 per capita consumption of chicken had increased by factors of 2, 4, and 15 in the U.S., Europe, and Japan respectively. Supplies of the traditional source of protein in livestock feed— 100 fish meal and scraps° from meat-processing plants—were inadequate to meet these increases in demand. The high food value of the soybean made it a natural candidate. The bean was tested and with a few modifications and supplements met the need perfectly, not only for chickens and hogs, but also for animals as diverse as mink, foxes, shrimp, catfish, eels, trout, bears (in 105 zoos), and even bees and silkworms.

Between 1945 and 1985, as the effects of these changes were felt, the U.S. soybean harvest increased in volume 11 times. The bean became the farmer's most important cash crop and the country's leading agricultural export—in 1985 the United States exported 3.7 billion dollars' worth of soybeans. 110

This was why it was called the Cinderella° crop. A poor relation that had always been given the leftovers in land and time had become "gold from the soil."

WRITE

1. Some people choose to get their protein from soy products, beans, and nuts instead of from meat. What are the reasons for making such a choice? What do you think about the advantages and disadvantages of eating meat?

2. For the next two days, write down all the things you eat. Include food and drink at meals and between meals. Then examine the list, and write about your reactions to it. (Does it seem like a satisfying, tasty, healthy, or nourishing diet? Could it be improved?) What determined what you ate: time, religion, money, circumstances, family preferences? What would be your ideal daily diet?

GRAMMAR
REFERENCES

Proper nouns: Chapter 4‡

Articles: Chapter 6

Verb forms: summary: Chapter 13

Participle forms: Chapter 21

Transitions: Chapter 23‡

The Surprise

Russell Baker

°**stretching a dollar** making a dollar go a long way

°**barged** rushed, intruded

[My mother] was a magician at stretching a dollar.° That December, with Christmas approaching, she was out to work and [my sister] Doris was in the kitchen when I barged° into her bedroom one afternoon in search of a safety pin. Since her bedroom opened onto a community hallway, she kept the door locked, but needing the pin, I took the key from its hiding place, 5 unlocked the door, and stepped in. Standing against the wall was a big, black bicycle with balloon tires. I recognized it instantly. It was the same second-hand bike I'd been admiring in a Baltimore shop window. I'd even asked about the price. It was horrendous. Something like $15. Somehow my

°**scraped together** saved

mother had scraped together° enough for a down payment and meant to sur- 10 prise me with the bicycle on Christmas morning.

°**squandered** wasted

I was overwhelmed by the discovery that she had squandered° such money on me and sickened by the knowledge that, bursting into her room like this, I had robbed her of the pleasure of seeing me astonished and delighted on Christmas day. I hadn't wanted to know her lovely secret; still, 15 stumbling upon it like this made me feel as though I'd struck a blow against her happiness. I backed out, put the key back in its hiding place, and

°**brooded** thought deeply

brooded° privately.

°**intonation** pitch of voice

I resolved that between now and Christmas I must do nothing, absolutely nothing, to reveal the slightest hint of my terrible knowledge. I must avoid the 20 least word, the faintest intonation,° the weakest gesture that might reveal my possession of her secret. Nothing must deny her the happiness of seeing me stunned with amazement on Christmas day.

WRITE

1. Some people think that it is preferable to receive a personal, carefully chosen gift, however small and inexpensive, than a big, expensive gift or simply the gift of money. What do you think, and why?

2. Describe in detail an object that you had always wanted as a child. Explain why you wanted it so badly, whether you eventually got it and how, and what the significance of it is for you now.

GRAMMAR REFERENCES

Countable and uncountable nouns: Chapter 5

Articles: Chapter 6‡

-ing forms: Chapter 20‡

Vincent van Gogh

E. H. Gombrich

°**in seclusion** alone
°**earnest** serious

°**vicar** priest of a
Church of
England parish
°**lay** not part of the
clergy
°**Impressionist**
style of painting
popular in the
1870s in France
°**ungrudgingly**
generously

°**insanity** madness
°**asylum** hospital
°**lucid** sane, rational

°**cypresses** type of
tree

In the winter of 1888, while Seurat was attracting attention in Paris and
Cézanne was working in his seclusion° in Aix, a young earnest° Dutchman left
Paris for southern France in search of the intense light and colour of the
south. He was Vincent van Gogh. Van Gogh was born in Holland in 1853,
the son of a vicar.° He was a deeply religious man who had worked as a lay°   5
preacher in England and among Belgian miners. He had been deeply impressed by the art of Millet and its social message, and decided to become a
painter himself. A younger brother, Theo, who worked in an art-dealer's
shop, introduced him to Impressionist° painters. This brother was a remarkable man. Though he was poor himself, he always gave ungrudgingly° to the   10
older Vincent and even financed his journey to Arles in southern France.
Vincent hoped that if he could work there undisturbed for a number of
years he might be able one day to sell his pictures and repay his generous
brother. In his self-chosen solitude in Arles, Vincent set down all his ideas
and hopes in his letters to Theo, which read like a continuous diary. These   15
letters, by a humble and almost self-taught artist who had no idea of the
fame he was to achieve, are among the most moving and exciting in all literature. In them we can feel the artist's sense of mission, his struggle and triumphs, his desperate loneliness and longing for companionship, and we become aware of the immense strain under which he worked with feverish   20
energy. After less than a year, in December 1888, he broke down and had an
attack of insanity.° In May 1889 he went into a mental asylum,° but he still
had lucid° intervals during which he continued to paint. The agony lasted
for another fourteen months. In July 1890 van Gogh put an end to his life—
he was thirty-seven like Raphael, and his career as a painter had not lasted   25
more than ten years; the paintings on which his fame rests were all painted
during three years which were interrupted by crises and despair. Most people nowadays know some of these paintings; the sunflowers, the empty
chair, the cypresses° and some of the portraits have become popular in col-
oured reproductions and can be seen in many a simple room. That is ex-   30
actly what van Gogh wanted.

WRITE

1. Write about the life of either a famous person in your country or a
person you know personally who should have been successful but hasn't.
Remember that your reader will need details about time, place, and the
person's circumstances.

2. Go to a library and look through a book on van Gogh, or look up van Gogh in an encyclopedia. Choose one that has illustrations. Pick out the painting that you like the best among those illustrated. Write about why you like it and what associations it has for you.

**GRAMMAR
REFERENCES**

Verb phrases: Chapter 7‡

Active and passive: Chapter 12

Verb forms: summary: Chapter 13

Pronouns and pronoun reference: Chapter 18

Punctuation: Chapter 29

Siblings
Anna Quindlen

In the back room the boys are playing, a study in brotherly love. The younger one has the fire engine and the older one has the tow truck, and although entire minutes have passed, neither has made a grab for the other's toy. The younger one is babbling° to himself in pidgin English° and the older one is singing ceaselessly,° tonelessly, as though chanting a mantra.° It is not until I move closer to the two of them, toe to toe on the tile floor, that I catch the lyrics° to the melody: "Get out of here. Get out of here. Get out of here."

Later the older one will explain that he picked up this particular turn of phrase from me, when I was yelling at one of the dogs. (In a similar phenomenon, he always says "Jesus, Mary and Joseph" when I apply the brakes of the car hard in traffic.) When I said it to the dogs, I meant it figuratively°; how Quin means it is less easily classified. I know, because I know where he is coming from. I have vivid° memories of being a small girl reading in a club chair,° and of having my brother, a year younger than I, enter the room and interrupt me. An emotion as big and as bang-bang-banging as a second heart would fill my ribs.° It was, trust me, pure hatred.

This house is full of sibling° rivalry° right now, as colorful and ever-present as my children's Lego blocks.° The preschool class is full of it, too, filled with 3-year-olds in various stages of shell shock° because their moms and dads came home in the car one day with a receiving blanket° full of turf battles,° emotional conflicts and divided love.

Realization has come slowly for some of them; I think it began with Quin one day when the younger one needed me more and I turned to him and said, "You know, Quin, I'm Christopher's mommy, too." The look that passed over his face was the one I imagine usually accompanies the discovery of a dead body in the den°: shock, denial, horror. "And Daddy is Christopher's daddy?" he gasped.° When I confirmed this he began to cry, wet, sad sobbing.°

I cannot remember which of my books described sibling rivalry thus: Imagine that one night your husband comes home and tells you that he has decided to have a second wife. She will be younger than you, cuter than you° and will demand much more of his time and attention. That doesn't mean, however, that he will love you any less. Covers the down side pretty well, doesn't it?

And yet the down side° is not the only one; if it were, "Get out of here" would not have such a sweet little melody. My son loves his brother, who is immensely° lovable; at the same time he dislikes his brother intensely.° He wants him to be around, but only sometimes, and only on his terms. He is no different from a lot of us who have fantasies about the things we want and who are surprised by the realities when we get them.

5

10

15

20

25

30

35

40

°**babbling** chattering
°**pidgin English** simplified English
°**ceaselessly** without stopping
°**mantra** Hindu prayer
°**lyrics** words

°**figuratively** not literally, as an abstraction
°**vivid** very clear
°**club chair** big armchair
°**ribs** bones around the chest
°**sibling** brother or sister
°**rivalry** competition
°**Lego blocks** plastic building blocks
°**shell shock** shock after armed combat
°**receiving blanket** blanket used to hold a newborn baby
°**turf battles** competition over territory
°**den** small, comfortable family room
°**gasped** breathed in sharply
°**sobbing** crying, weeping
°**cuter** more attractive
°**down side** negative side, disadvantage
°**immensely** extremely
°**intensely** deeply

He likes the idea of a brother, but not always the brother himself. When his brother is hurt and helpless, he calls him "my baby." "I don't want my baby to cry, Mommy," he says, which is the kind of line you get into this business to hear.

°**tussle** struggle, fight
°**infuriating** very annoying

But when there is a tussle° over the fire engine, his baby develops a name, an identity, a reality that is infuriating.° "Christopher," he says then, shaking an index finger as short as a pencil stub in the inflated baby face, "you don't touch my truck Christopher. O.K.? O.K. CHRISTOPHER?" 45

°**Maurice Sendak** author of children's books
°**bassinet** baby's bed
°**triumphant** victorious

He actually likes babies; he even wants to bring one home, the 2-month-old brother of his friend Sonia. Eric, he thinks, is perfect: he cannot walk, cannot talk, has no interest in Maurice Sendak° books, Lego blocks, the trucks, the sandbox, or any of the other things that make life worth living, including—especially including—me. One day at Sonia's house he bent over Eric's bassinet° to say hello, but what came out instead was a triumphant° "You can't catch me!" as he sailed away from him. 50 55

°**dovetail** fit exactly
°**insufferable** intolerable, annoying
°**nerd** (slang) person without friends or social life
°**loathed** hated
°**yoked** joined

His baby can't catch him yet, but it's only a matter of time. Then he will have to make a choice: a partner, an accomplice, an opponent, or, perhaps most likely, a mixture of the three. At some point his fantasy of a brother may dovetail° with the reality; mine did when my younger brother, the insufferable° little nerd° with the Coke-bottle glasses whom I loathed,° turned into a good-looking teenage boy who interested my girl friends, had some interesting boy friends of his own, and was a first-rate dancer. But it's not as simple as that, either. In his bones now my elder son probably knows the awful wonderful truth: that he and his brother are yoked° together for life, blood of one another's blood, joined as surely as if they were Siamese twins. Whether the yoke is one of friendship or resentment,° it will inevitably shadow both their lives. That is certainly something to bear, as good a reason as any to look at someone else and wish that he could, impossibly, occasionally, go someplace else. 60 65

°**resentment** anger

WRITE

1. Discuss whether you think that the relationship between siblings is usually characterized by friendship or resentment. Give examples from your own experience or your reading to support the point of view you express.

2. Describe an incident that occurred among siblings or close family members. What did that incident show about the nature of the relationships in that particular family?

GRAMMAR **R**EFERENCES

Verb tenses: overview: Chapter 8‡

Subject-verb agreement: Chapter 17‡

Pronouns and pronoun reference: Chapter 18‡

Coordinating conjunctions: Chapter 22

Cultural Exchanges
Mark Salzman

1

°**cello** stringed
  instrument

After dinner I carried my cello° to [Teacher Wu's] building. It was the first time I had entered a Chinese person's home. She lived in a tiny apartment that she shared with "Auntie Tan," an old woman from the countryside who helped with the shopping, cooking and cleaning. The apartment had cement°

°**cement** concrete
°**sparse** few, scanty

walls, bare except for a calendar and a few photographs, a bare cement floor, a bare light bulb in each room, and sparse° furnishings, with one exception: against one wall stood an upright piano.

I asked her how she had managed to get a piano, and she said that she grew up playing and had continued to study when she was in America. She bought the piano there, and brought it back to China when she returned with her husband. "I haven't had much time to practice it since then, but nowadays I try to play whenever I have free time." She went over, opened it up, and began to play.

°**duet** piece of music
  for two
°**sighed** let out
  breath

The piano was badly damaged—many of the notes did not sound, and those that did were so out of tune I almost wished they hadn't. She invited me to play a duet° with her, but we had to give up. After a pause she sighed° and said quietly, "One night the Red Guards came. They took everything in the house out and burned it. They wanted to take the piano, too, but"—and here she smiled at the floor—"it was too heavy for them to throw out the window! So they just hit it for a while and left. I haven't been able to find anyone to fix it since then." I said I wished that I could help her, but though my mother played the piano, I had never learned to tune or repair one.

"Your mother is a pianist?"

°**harpsichord** key-
  board instrument

"Well, she was a pianist. Now she plays the harpsichord."°

"Mm. So you know what a piano should sound like, then? You grew up hearing it every day, didn't you?"

"Yes."

"Mm." . . .

A week later Teacher Wu appeared at my door early in the morning, breathless with excitement. "I have something here . . ." and she pulled out of her bag something that looked like a bent screwdriver. "I heard that an orchestra was passing through Changsha, so I found them and talked to them.

°**wrench** tool for
  gripping and
  turning

Their pianist had one of these—it is a tuning wrench.° He said I can have it until tonight—can you try?"

"Try what?"

"To tune it—tune the piano!"

"But I don't know how."

"Try!"

347

°**thermos** container that maintains temperature

I asked her not to stay in the apartment while I worked, because it would only make me more nervous, so she prepared a thermos° of tea and promised me a good dinner that evening. "And if you need anything just tell Auntie Tan—she'll be right in the kitchen." Auntie Tan gave me a toothless smile and nodded, and I smiled back. 40

°**pedal** lever for the foot
°**frantic** desperate
°**rodents** rats or mice
°**scurry** hurry
°**pliers** tool for gripping and pulling
°**damped** deadened the sound of

After Teacher Wu left I began to disassemble the piano. As I was taking off one of the boards concealing the pedal° mechanism, I heard a loud squeak and a frantic° scratching. I stepped back and watched three large rodents° scurry° out of the piano, around the room and down a drainpipe. 45

Using sandpaper and a pair of pliers° I managed to get all the hammers loose, and I repaired the pedal system by replacing the broken levers with several wooden rulers that I connected with nuts and bolts. To tune the instrument I damped° two of the strings of each note with my thumb and forefinger while I adjusted the third, then tuned each of the others to it. Since I have only semi-perfect pitch, I set middle C according to a Michael Jackson tape played through my Walkman. 50

I finished just before dinner. I was terribly excited and went into the kitchen to announce my success to Auntie Tan, but saw that she had stuffed her ears with balls of cotton, over which she had tied a thick towel, and seemed to be taking a nap. Teacher Wu arrived shortly thereafter, but did not yet go near the piano. "Let's eat first," she said. 55

°**broth** soup
°**popsicles** ice lollipops

We had a delicious meal of smoked eggs, noodles with pork strips in broth,° and a whole chicken—a real luxury in China, only for special occasions—stewed in a thick yellow sauce. Then we had tea and popsicles° that Auntie Tan had bought for us in the street. At last Teacher Wu sat down at the piano, took out several books of music, and began to play. She played through a few pieces and played them beautifully, but said nothing for a long time. Finally, she stopped playing, looked directly at me, and said in Chinese, "Thank you very much." 60

65

°**rituals** ceremonies
°**pleading** begging

I stood up and said that she was very welcome, but that I had some work to do and should be getting back to the house. She shifted into the rituals° of seeing off a guest, which involve pleading° with the guest to stay, offering him tea and candies, then accompanying him at least part of his way home. This time she walked me all the way to my door. As she turned to go back, she said, "In your next letter to your mother, tell her you fixed a piano in China for an old lady." Then she went home. 70

2

I had walked along the river many times since meeting the fisherman that day in winter, but I did not see him again until spring. It was late afternoon, and I had bicycled to a point along the river about a mile downstream from where we had met, hoping to find a deserted spot to draw a picture. I found a niche° in the sloping floodwall and started drawing a junk° moored° not far from me. Half an hour passed, and just as I finished the 75

°**niche** alcove
°**junk** Chinese ship
°**moored** tied up

80

348

drawing, I heard someone calling my Chinese name. I looked down to see Old Ding scrambling up the floodwall, his boat anchored behind him. I noticed that he limped badly, and when he got up close I could see that one of his legs was shorter than the other and set at an odd angle. Such was his balance and skill in the boats that I only saw his deformity° when he came ashore. He squatted° down beside me and explained that he had just returned from a long fishing trip on Dong Ting, a sprawling° lake in North Hunan. "Big fish up there," he said, gesturing with his arms. Then he asked me what I was doing. I showed him the drawing, and his face lit up. "Just like it! Just like the boat!" He cupped his hands to his mouth and yelled something in the direction of the junk, and right away a family appeared on deck. "Let's show it to them!" he said, and dragged me down to the water. He exchanged a few words with the family, and they leapt° into action, the women going into the sheltered part of the junk to prepare food and the men rowing out to meet us in one of two tiny boats lashed to the side. We got in the little boat and returned with them to the junk. We ate a few snacks of different kinds of salted fish, had tea, and then I showed them the drawing. They seemed delighted by it, so I tore the sheet out of my block. I handed it to the oldest member of the family, a man in his sixties, who opened his eyes wide with surprise and would not take it, saying, "How can I take this? It is a work of art; what do I have to offer you in return?" I laughed, saying that it was only a drawing, and I would be happy if he would take it just for fun. But he was serious; when at last he accepted it, putting it down carefully on the bed, he began negotiating with Old Ding to choose an appropriate gift for me.

Fifteen minutes of vigorous° discussion, all in dialect, produced a decision: they would give me one of the rowboats. I looked at Old Ding and said that that was absolutely ridiculous, that of course I would not take a boat from a poor fisherman's family in return for a charcoal° sketch. "Oh, but it's no problem! They can get a new one!" I realized that the situation was serious, for if I refused and left, they would no doubt carry the rowboat to my house and lay it on the front porch. I looked at the old man. "That is a very fine gift, it is worth thousands of drawings like that one, but we Americans have a custom, and that is we speak directly. If we want something, we say so." Many Chinese people appreciate "talking straight," perhaps because convention almost never allows it, so they applauded this and told me by all means to speak up. "The boat is very fine, but there is something I want more." They all smiled and nodded and said that of course I could have whatever I wanted, but I could see they were deeply nervous. I believe they expected me to ask for the junk. "In my country, we have a superstition. If someone gives you a piece of art, like a painting or a poem, you must give him a piece of art in return, or the feeling will be spoiled. If I take the boat, I will feel sad. I would prefer that a member of your family sing a folk song from your hometown." The family, almost hysterical° with relief, cheered my decision, saying it had "true spirit," and each of them sang something for me.

°deformity physical imperfection
°squatted crouched
°sprawling very large

°leapt jumped

°vigorous lively

°charcoal black carbon pencil

°hysterical excessively emotional

85

90

95

100

105

110

115

120

125

349

WRITE

1. Describe an incident in your life that had to do with dealing with a new culture and with cultural differences. Give details about the time, place, setting, and characters so that your readers get as full a picture of the event as possible.

2. Write about the second story in "Cultural Exchanges," from Old Ding's point of view. Old Ding will be the storyteller (the "I"), telling about the incident with Salzman ("he"). Do this from memory of the story, with the book closed.

GRAMMAR REFERENCES

Verb tenses: past: Chapter 9‡

Verb forms: summary: Chapter 13

Participle forms: Chapter 21

Coordinating conjunctions: Chapter 22

Noun clauses and reported speech: Chapter 25

Adverbial clauses: Chapter 26‡

Punctuation: Chapter 29

The Effects of Our Environment
Ronald B. Adler, Lawrence B. Rosenfeld, and Neil Towne

Physical settings, architecture, and interior design affect our communication. [Recall] for a moment the different homes you've visited lately. Were some of these homes more comfortable to be in than others? Certainly a lot of these kinds of feelings are shaped by the people you were with, but there are some houses where it seems impossible to relax, no matter how friendly the hosts. We've spent what seemed like endless evenings in what Mark Knapp (1978) calls "unliving rooms," where the spotless° ashtrays, furniture coverings, and plastic lamp covers seemed to send nonverbal° messages telling us not to touch anything, not to put our feet up, and not to be comfortable. People who live in houses like this probably wonder why nobody ever seems to relax and enjoy themselves at their parties. One thing is quite certain: They don't understand that the environment they have created can communicate discomfort to their guests.

There's a large amount of research that shows how the design of an environment can shape the kind of communication that takes place in it. In one experiment at Brandeis University, Maslow and Mintz (1956) found that the attractiveness of a room influenced the happiness and energy of people working in it. The experimenters set up three rooms: an "ugly" one, which resembled° a janitor's° closet in the basement of a campus building; an "average" room, which was a professor's office; and a "beautiful" room, which was furnished with carpeting, drapes,° and comfortable furniture. The subjects in the experiment were asked to rate° a series of pictures as a way of measuring their energy and feelings of well-being while at work. Results of the experiment showed that while in the ugly room, the subjects became tired and bored more quickly and took longer to complete their task. Subjects who were in the beautiful room, however, rated the faces they were judging more positively, showed a greater desire to work, and expressed feelings of importance, comfort, and enjoyment. The results teach a lesson that isn't surprising: Workers generally feel better and do a better job when they're in an attractive environment.

Many business people show an understanding of how environment can influence communication. Robert Sommer, a leading environmental psychologist, described several such cases. In *Personal Space: The Behavioral Basis of Design* (1969), he points out that dim° lighting, subdued° noise levels, and comfortable seats encourage people to spend more time in a restaurant or bar. Knowing this fact, the management can control the amount of customer turnover. If the goal is to run a high-volume business that tries to move people in and out quickly, it's necessary to keep the lights shining brightly and not worry too much about soundproofing.° On the other hand, if the goal is to keep customers in a bar or restaurant for a long time, the proper tech-

°**spotless** very clean
°**nonverbal** not spoken

°**resembled** looked like
°**janitor** caretaker
°**drapes** curtains
°**rate** judge the value of

°**dim** not bright
°**subdued** lowered

°**soundproofing** keeping sound out

5

10

15

20

25

30

35

40

351

nique is to lower the lighting and use absorbent building materials that will keep down the noise level.

Furniture design also affects the amount of time a person spends in an environment. From this knowledge came the Larsen chair, which was designed for Copenhagen restaurant owners who felt their customers were occupying their seats too long without spending enough money. The chair is constructed to put an uncomfortable pressure on the sitter's back if occupied for more than a few minutes. (We suspect that many people who are careless in buying furniture for their homes get much the same result without trying. One environmental psychologist we know refuses to buy a chair or couch without sitting in it for at least half an hour to test the comfort.)

Sommer also describes how airports are designed to discourage people from spending too much time in waiting areas. The uncomfortable chairs, bolted° shoulder to shoulder in rows facing outward, make conversation and relaxation next to impossible. Faced with this situation, travelers are forced to move to restaurants and bars in the terminal, where they're not only more comfortable but also more likely to spend money.

Casino owners in places such as Las Vegas also know how to use the environment to control behavior. To keep gamblers from noticing how long they've been shooting craps,° playing roulette° and blackjack,° and feeding slot machines, they build their casinos without windows or clocks. Unless wearing a wristwatch, customers have no way of knowing how long they have been gambling or, for that matter, whether it's day or night.

In a more therapeutic° and less commercial way physicians have also shaped environments to improve communications. One study showed that simply removing a doctor's desk made patients feel almost five times more at ease during office visits. Sommer found that redesigning a convalescent° ward of a hospital greatly increased the interaction between patients. In the old design seats were placed shoulder to shoulder around the edges of the ward. By grouping the chairs around small tables so that patients faced each other at a comfortable distance, the amount of conversations doubled.

Even the design of an entire building can shape communication among its users. Architects have learned that the way housing projects are designed controls to a great extent the contact neighbors have with each other. People who live in apartments near stairways and mailboxes have many more neighbor contacts than do those living in less heavily traveled parts of the building, and tenants generally have more contacts with immediate neighbors than with people even a few doors away. Architects now use this information to design buildings that either encourage communication or increase privacy, and house hunters can use the same knowledge to choose a home that gives them the neighborhood relationships they want.

So far we've talked about how designing an environment can shape communication, but there's another side to consider. Watching how people use an already existing environment can be a way of telling what kind of relationships they want. For example, Sommer watched students in a college library and found that there's a definite pattern for people who want to study alone. While the library was uncrowded, students almost always chose corner

°**bolted** connected

°**craps** gambling
  game with dice
°**roulette** gambling
  game with spin-
  ning wheel and
  numbers
°**blackjack** card
  game, also known
  as 21
°**therapeutic** heal-
  ing
°**convalescent** re-
  covery after
  illness

45

50

55

60

65

70

75

80

85

352

seats at one of the empty rectangular tables. After each table was occupied by one reader, new readers would choose a seat on the opposite side and at the far end, thus keeping the maximum distance between themselves and the other readers. One of Sommer's associates tried violating° these "rules" by sitting next to and across from other female readers when more distant seats were available. She found that the approached women reacted defensively, signaling their discomfort through shifts° in posture, gesturing, or eventually moving away.

°**violating** breaking

°**shifts** changes

Research on classroom environments is extensive. Probably the most detailed study was conducted by Raymond Adams and Bruce Biddle (1970). Observing a variety of classes from grades one, six, and eleven, they found that the main determinant of whether a student was actively and directly engaged in the process of classroom communication was that student's seating position. This finding held even when students were assigned seats, indicating that location,° and not personal preferences, determined interaction.

°**location** position, place

Other studies by Robert Sommer and his colleagues (1978) found that students who sit opposite the teacher talk more, and those next to the teacher avoid talking at all. Also, the middle of the first row contains the students who interact most, and as we move back and to the sides of the classroom, interaction decreases markedly.°

°**markedly** clearly
°**lack** absence
°**perpetuate** make permanent
°**reminiscent of** recalling
°**cemetery** burial ground

With an overwhelming lack° of imagination we perpetuate° a seating arrangement reminiscent of° a military cemetery.° This type of environment communicates to students that the teacher, who can move about freely while they can't, is the one who is important in the room, is the only one to whom anyone should speak, and is the person who has all the information. The most advanced curriculum has little chance of surviving without a physical environment that supports it.

REFERENCES

Adams, Raymond, and Bruce Biddle. *Realities of Teaching: Explorations with Video Tape.* New York: Holt, Rinehart and Winston, 1970.

Knapp, Mark L, *Nonverbal Communication in Human Interaction,* 2nd ed. New York: Holt, Rinehart and Winston, 1978.

Maslow, A., and N. Mintz. "Effects of Aesthetic Surroundings: Initial Effects of Those Aesthetic Surroundings upon Perceiving 'Energy' and 'Well-being' in Faces," *Journal of Psychology* 41 (1956): 247–254.

Sommer, Robert. *Personal Space: The Behavioral Basis of Design.* Englewood Cliffs, N.J.: Prentice-Hall, 1969.

Sommer Robert. *Tight Spaces.* Englewood Cliffs, N.J.: Prentice-Hall, 1978.

WRITE

1. If you could design a classroom or a restaurant, what would it look like? Describe it in detail.

2. Describe the design of the local supermarket or neighborhood store that you use regularly, and comment on the effectiveness of the design.

GRAMMAR REFERENCES	Verb tenses: present and future: Chapter 10[‡]
	Active and passive: Chapter 12
	Verb forms: summary: Chapter 13[‡]
	-ing forms: Chapter 20
	Transitions: Chapter 23
	Adjectival clauses: Chapter 24[‡]
	Noun clauses and reported speech: Chapter 25

Tau Ceti
Lewis Thomas

°**resembles** looks like

°**plausible** acceptable

°**sentient** conscious, with a mind

°**amenities** pleasant remarks

°**party** conversation partner

°**gambling** taking a chance

°**mimeographed** copied

°**durability** ability to last

°**lose the thread** *(idiom)* lose the line of reasoning

°**outset** beginning

°**ambiguity** unclear meaning

°**bragging** boasting

°***Time*** a newsmagazine

°**wincing** embarrassed reaction

°**irrelevant** with no clear connection

Tau Ceti is a relatively nearby star that sufficiently resembles° our sun to make its solar system a plausible° candidate for the existence of life. . . . Let us assume that there is, indeed, sentient° life in one or another part of remote space, and that we will be successful in getting in touch with it. What on earth are we going to talk about? If, as seems likely, it is a hundred or more light years away, there are going to be some very long pauses. The barest amenities,° on which we rely for opening conversations—Hello, are you there?, from us, followed by Yes, hello, from them—will take two hundred years at least. By the time we have our party° we may have forgotten what we had in mind.

We could begin by gambling° on the rightness of our technology and just send out news of ourselves, like a mimeographed° Christmas letter, but we would have to choose our items carefully, with durability° of meaning in mind. Whatever information we provide must still make sense to us two centuries later, and must still seem important, or the conversation will be an embarrassment to all concerned. In two hundred years it is, as we have found, easy to lose the thread.°

Perhaps the safest thing to do at the outset,° if technology permits, is to send music. This language may be the best we have for explaining what we are like to others in space, with least ambiguity.° I would vote for Bach, all of Bach, streamed out into space, over and over again. We would be bragging,° of course, but it is surely excusable for us to put the best possible face on at the beginning of such an acquaintance. We can tell the harder truths later. And, to do ourselves justice, music would give a fairer picture of what we are really like than some of the other things we might be sending, like *Time,*° say, or a history of the U.N. or Presidential speeches. We could send out our science, of course, but just think of the wincing° at this end when the polite comments arrive two hundred years from now. Whatever we offer as today's items of liveliest interest are bound to be out of date and irrelevant,° maybe even ridiculous. I think we should stick to music.

Perhaps, if the technology can be adapted to it, we should send some paintings. Nothing would better describe what this place is like, to an outsider, than the Cézanne demonstrations that an apple is really part fruit, part earth.

What kinds of questions should we ask? The choices will be hard, and everyone will want his special question first. What are your smallest particles? Did you think yourselves unique? Do you have colds? Have you anything quicker than light? Do you always tell the truth? Do you cry? There is no end to the list.

Perhaps we should wait a while, until we are sure we know what we want to know, before we get down to detailed questions. After all, the main question

355

will be the opener: Hello, are you there? If the reply should turn out to be Yes, hello, we might want to stop there and think about that, for quite a long time.

WRITE

1. Tell your readers what you would send to inform inhabitants of another planet about what life on earth is like right now. What objects would give a picture of life in the 1990s?

2. A great deal of money is spent nowadays on space exploration. Do you think that resources should go to space travel, even when there are problems of poverty, food shortage, unemployment, and homelessness to be solved on this planet? Give reasons for your point of view; try to convince readers who might have opposing views.

GRAMMAR REFERENCES

Questions and negatives: Chapter 3

Modal auxiliaries: Chapter 11‡

-ing forms: Chapter 20

Portable Computers
Alexander Taffel

The first digital computer was built in 1946 at the University of Pennsylvania. It weighed 30 tons and filled a large room. It was called ENIAC. In its early days it required 18,500 vacuum tubes to store information. Obviously, a 30-ton computer had its limitations. Scientists and engineers worked to make it better. The use of transistors as small amplifiers° in place of   5
the large vacuum tubes reduced the size and cost of computers. Smaller was better.

In the early 1960's, the first minicomputers were made commercially. They were the size of a two-drawer file cabinet. The revolution was on. Less than a decade later, the microcomputer was invented. The basic unit of the   10
microcomputer is a tiny silicon° chip less than 1 cm on a side. Each chip is a miniature° electronic circuit that serves the different computer functions. Amazingly, each circuit contains thousands of elements.

The great advances in microelectronics have helped achieve the moon landing, satellites, digital watches, computer games, and even computer-   15
controlled automobile engines. Still the computer continues to evolve. One of the latest developments is bubble memory. In bubble memory, the information is stored in tiny magnetic spots or islands that look like bubbles floating on the chip. One great advantage of bubble memory is that it does not lose stored information when the power is turned off.   20

Portable° computers, ranging from briefcase size down to hand-helds, are the latest innovation.° In the smallest of the portables, the cathode ray tube has been replaced by a flat electroluminescent display and the disk drives by bubble memory chips. In these computers, information is stored on the road, in the classroom, at conferences, at the library, or elsewhere, and then   25
transferred to print or conventional disk drive memory later.

Hand-held computers are very light in weight and sit in the palm of one's hand. These miniature computers will prove useful for some situations, but there are drawbacks.° The displays are rarely more than a single short line in length, and the keyboard is so small the user has to peck° rather than type.   30

The computer revolution moves on. In the future, look for tiny chips controlling the functions of stereos, typewriters, telephones, and other appliances, as well as additional advances in the computing industry itself.

°**amplifiers** boosters

°**silicon** a semiconducting element
°**miniature** very small

°**portable** able to be carried
°**innovation** new invention

°**drawbacks** disadvantages
°**peck** typewrite with only one finger

WRITE

1. Most of us have seen advances in technology and have used objects that were not available just a few years earlier. People you know probably remember their family's first television set, their first ball-point pen, their first jet flight, their first video game, and their first use of a computer. Write about where you were and what you were doing when you were first introduced to something new in technology. What difference did it make to you and the people around you?

2. If someone could program a computer robot (like the ones in *Star Wars*) to do five tasks for you on a regular basis, what would you want the robot to do, and why?

GRAMMAR REFERENCES

Verb phrases: Chapter 7

Active and passive: Chapter 12[‡]

Punctuation: Chapter 29

Artificial Intelligence

Philip J. Hilts

°**outpost** building separated from main buildings
°**coiled** in a spiral
°**bristles** short, stiff blades
°**scalp** top of the head
°**recruit** new member
°**contour** outline
°**strode** walked briskly

Eventually I got the chance to go to California and to visit the Stanford Artificial Intelligence Laboratory. On a hot June afternoon I met the lab's director, John McCarthy. I had driven up from the main campus of Stanford University to his outpost° in the hills. He was late, so I waited in his office. It was the head of a long snake of a building which sat coiled° on the hot hill-top. Two walls of the office were glass, and through them I could see the hills outside, which were the color of straw. The short, yellow bristles° of grass made the hills look like the scalp° of a marine recruit.° With the wiry dark hair of bushes and trees shaved off, the bumps and scars of contour° were visible. The few trees out the window were eucalyptus, and they looked dusty and dry as fence posts.

John McCarthy's appearance, when he finally strode° into the office, struck me as extraordinary. He is about average height, five feet nine inches. His build is average, with a little age trying to collect itself around his middle. But his hair encircles his head and his face with a great cloud of silver needles. Amid this prickly gray mist his eyes are two dark rocks.

°**bouts** periods

Our first meeting actually consisted of several conversations, between his bouts° of work. I remember most clearly one moment, a pause between talks. There is a long wooden table in his office, and I recall the form of Professor McCarthy seated before it. His body was hunched° slightly in the shoulders, held motionless, and his eyes were rapt.° A small screen and keyboard were in front of him. The machine was in a little clearing amidst° a jungle of papers and ragged° envelopes. I had come in and sat down, but for a moment my presence was immaterial,° a shade at the rim° of his consciousness. He continued staring into the screen. I recognized this sort of catatonia.° Scientists (as do writers and artists) wander into the paths in the background of their work and cannot find their way back immediately. I didn't interrupt him. . . .

°**hunched** bent forward
°**rapt** attentive
°**amidst** in the middle of
°**ragged** torn
°**immaterial** unimportant
°**rim** edge
°**catatonia** paralysis

There are about three million computers in use in the world now. But not millions or thousands, or even hundreds of them, are dedicated to the sophisticated work of artificial intelligence. Though there has been much celebration of the coming of the computer revolution, it can hardly be said to apply to our current use of these machines: They do little beyond arithmetic and alphabetical sorting. In practice they are no more than automated filing° systems with central controls, and still the chief task they are assigned around the world is to keep track of company payrolls. The promise of computing—"the steam engine applied to the mind" as one professor of computing put it—still remains largely unrealized.

°**filing** record keeping

The one tiny academic discipline in which the limits of computers are being tested is the field of artificial or machine intelligence. Of the hundreds of thousands of computer programmers in the nation, only a few hundred have

359

°**saw** saying

devoted themselves to the question of what computers are finally capable of, asking whether the old science fiction saw° about brains and computers being equivalent is, in fact, actually true. It has been said for fifty years that computers are "giant brains" and that the human mind is merely a "meat computer." In a slightly different form, the same idea has been expressed for 45

°**automatons** robots

more than two thousand years in the construction of automatons° that imitate human and animal behavior. It is only in the past twenty-five years, however, that the questions—what is intelligence and how can it be made mechanical?—have actually been raised to the level of serious academic 50 questions.

°**exotic** unusual and unfamiliar

Within this small, exotic° field, John McCarthy is one of the three or four people who have contributed most. As I sat waiting for McCarthy to finish, I could see him blink a few times and retrieve his thought from the screen before him. I could see he was beginning to recover. He rubbed his eyes be- 55 neath black frame glasses.

°**object** aim, goal

He began by saying that in artificial intelligence the object° is to find out what intellectual activities computers can be made to carry out. He is rather certain that an intelligence smarter than a human being can be built. From time to time, journalists who discover the existence of his laboratory call up 60 McCarthy to ask him about such robots: "Can they be as smart as people?" McCarthy smiles. "No. That is one of the science fiction fantasies, that robots will be *just as smart* as humans, but no smarter. Robots will be smarter, because all you have to do is get the next-generation computer, build it twice as big, run it a hundred times as fast, and then it won't be 65 *just as smart* anymore. . . ." The field of artificial intelligence is a collective

°**souls** people

attempt to create such machines. There are now about three hundred souls° in the United States and perhaps another two hundred in the rest of the world working to make them.

WRITE

1. Hilts describes John McCarthy's appearance and workplace in detail. Obviously, Hilts was very impressed by this man. Describe a teacher you have had whom you admire: describe the teacher's appearance, methods, and the school in which he or she taught.

2. What benefits have computers contributed to society? Describe two things that you think computers do well—probably better than any other means. Give a full explanation for your opinion, and illustrate it with examples.

GRAMMAR
REFERENCES

Verb forms: summary: Chapter 13

Adjectives and noun modifiers: Chapter 14‡

Comparisons: Chapter 16

Punctuation: Chapter 29

The Culture of "Lead Time"
Edward T. Hall

Advance notice is often referred to in America as "lead time," an expression which is significant in a culture where schedules are important. While it is learned informally, most of us are familiar with how it works in our own culture, even though we cannot state the rules technically. The rules for lead time in other cultures, however, have rarely been analyzed. At the most they are known by experience to those who lived abroad for some time. Yet think how important it is to know how much time is required to prepare people, or for them to prepare themselves, for things to come. Sometimes lead time would seem to be very extended. At other times, in the Middle East, any period longer than a week may be too long.

How troublesome differing ways of handling time can be is well illustrated by the case of an American agriculturalist assigned to duty as an attaché° of our embassy in a Latin country. After what seemed to him a suitable period he let it be known that he would like to call on the minister who was his counterpart.° For various reasons, the suggested time was not suitable; all sorts of cues came back to the effect that the time was not yet ripe° to visit the minister. Our friend, however, persisted and forced an appointment, which was reluctantly° granted. Arriving a little before the hour (the American respect pattern), he waited. The hour came and passed; five minutes—ten minutes—fifteen minutes. At this point he suggested to the secretary that perhaps the minister did not know he was waiting in the outer office. This gave him the feeling he had done something concrete° and also helped to overcome the great anxiety that was stirring inside him. Twenty minutes—twenty-five minutes—thirty minutes—forty-five minutes (the insult period)!

He jumped up and told the secretary that he had been "cooling his heels"° in an outer office for forty-five minutes and he was "damned sick and tired" of this type of treatment. This message was relayed to the minister, who said, in effect, "Let him cool his heels." The attaché's stay in the country was not a happy one.

The principal source of misunderstanding lay in the fact that in the country in question the five-minute delay interval was not significant. Forty-five minutes, on the other hand, instead of being at the tail end° of the waiting scale, was just barely at the beginning. To suggest to an American's secretary that perhaps her boss didn't know you were there after waiting sixty seconds would seem absurd, as would raising a storm about "cooling your heels" for five minutes. Yet this is precisely the way the minister registered the protestations° of the American in his outer office! He felt, as usual, that Americans were being totally unreasonable.

Throughout this unfortunate episode the attaché was acting according to the way he had been brought up. At home in the United States his responses

°attaché diplomat

°counterpart person in a similar position
°ripe appropriate
°reluctantly not willingly

°concrete specific

°cooling his heels *(idiom)* waiting

°tail end last part

°protestations complaints

361

°**legitimate** correct would have been normal ones and his behavior legitimate.° Yet even if he had been told before he left home that this sort of thing would happen, he would have had difficulty not *feeling* insulted after he had been kept waiting forty-five minutes. If, on the other hand, he had been taught the details of the lo- 45 cal time system just as he should have been taught the local spoken language, it would have been possible for him to adjust himself accordingly.

WRITE

1. Write about a time when you felt that a person's behavior was "totally unreasonable." Describe exactly what happened.

2. When people travel, they frequently try to learn to least a little bit of the local language. What other things do you think are important for people to know about before they go to foreign countries?

GRAMMAR REFERENCES

Adverbs and frequency adverbs: Chapter 15‡

Transitions: Chapter 23

Noun clauses and reported speech: Chapter 25‡

Adverbial clauses: conditions: Chapter 27

Sizing Up Human Intelligence
Stephen Jay Gould

°**bug** tap
°**minute** tiny
°**irrelevant** unimportant
°**neurons** nerve cells

°**constrained** forced

°**cited** quoted

°**constancy** lack of variation
°**prerequisite** requirement

°**provocative** interesting
°**circumvent** avoid

°**don** put on
°**adhesion** sticking
°**preclude** make impossible
°**boulder** rock
°**homunculus** little man

°**pound** hammer

°**attuned** adapted
°**kinetic energy** energy associated with motion

In this age of the transistor, we can put radios in watchcases and bug° telephones with minute° electronic packages. Such miniaturization might lead us to the false belief that absolute size is irrelevant° to the operation of complex machinery. But nature does not miniaturize neurons° (or other cells for that matter). The range of cell size among organisms is incomparably smaller than the range in body size. Small animals simply have far fewer cells than large animals. The human brain contains several billion neurons; an ant is constrained° by its small size to have many hundreds of times fewer neurons.

There is, to be sure, no established relationship between brain size and intelligence among humans (the tale of Anatole France with a brain of less than 1,000 cubic centimeters vs. Oliver Cromwell with well over 2,000 is often cited°). But this observation cannot be extended to differences between species and certainly not to ranges of sizes separating ants and humans. An efficient computer needs billions of circuits and an ant simply cannot contain enough of them because the relative constancy° of cell size requires that small brains contain few neurons. Thus, our large body size served as a prerequisite° for self-conscious intelligence.

We can make a stronger argument and claim that humans have to be just about the size they are in order to function as they do. In an amusing and provocative° article (*American Scientist*, 1968), F. W. Went explored the impossibility of human life, as we know it, at ant dimensions (assuming for the moment that we could circumvent°—which we cannot—the problem of intelligence and small brain size). Since weight increases so much faster than surface area as an object gets larger, small animals have very high ratios of surface to volume: they live in a world dominated by surface forces that affect us scarcely at all.

An ant-sized man might don° some clothing, but forces of surface adhesion° would preclude° its removal. The lower limit of drop size would make showering impossible; each drop would hit with the force of a large boulder.° If our homunculus° managed to get wet and tried to dry off with a towel, he would be stuck to it for life. He could pour no liquid, light no fire (since a stable flame must be several millimeters in length). He might pound° gold leaf thin enough to construct a book for his size; but surface adhesion would prevent the turning of pages.

Our skills and behavior are finely attuned° to our size. We could not be twice as tall as we are, for the kinetic energy° of a fall would then be 16 to 32 times as great, and our sheer weight (increased eightfold) would be more than our legs could support. Human giants of eight to nine feet have either died young or been crippled early by failure of joints and bones. At half our

5

10

15

20

25

30

35

40

°**wield** handle
°**club** big stick,
   weapon
°**impart** give

size, we could not wield° a club° with sufficient force to hunt large animals (for kinetic energy would decrease 16 to 32-fold); we could not impart° suffi-cient momentum to spears and arrows; we could not cut or split wood with primitive tools or mine minerals with picks and chisels. Since these were es-sential activities in our historical development, we must conclude that the path of our evolution could only have been followed by a creature very close to our size. I do not argue that we inhabit the best of all possible worlds, only that our size has limited our activities and, to a great extent, shaped our evolution.

   45

WRITE

1. Gould tells about an article that explores the possibility of human life at ant dimensions. Think about what kind of perspective an ant would have on human life. That is, if you were an ant, what would you have to say about human beings and their environment?

2. If you were 6 inches shorter or taller than you are now, how would your daily life be affected ?

GRAMMAR REFERENCES

Comparisons: Chapter 16‡

Pronouns and pronoun reference: Chapter 18

Transitions: Chapter 23

White Lies

Ronald B. Adler, Lawrence B. Rosenfeld, and Neil Towne

Although most people would agree that lying to gain advantage over an unknowing subject is wrong, another kind of mistruth—the "white lie"—is both a popular and often acceptable type of communication. White lies are defined (at least by those who tell them) as being unmalicious,° or even helpful.

°**unmalicious** not with bad intention
°**benign** harmless

Whether or not they are benign,°white lies are certainly common. In one study (Turner, Edgely, and Olmstead, 1975), 130 subjects were asked to keep track of the truthfulness of their everyday conversational statements. Only 38.5 percent of these statements—slightly more than a third—proved to be totally honest. What reasons do people give for being deceitful so often? . . .

°**distorting** changing the shape of

When subjects in the study by Turner and his associates were asked to give a lie-by-lie account of their motives for concealing or distorting° the truth, five major reasons emerged. The most frequent motive (occurring in 55.2 percent of the lies) was *to save face*. Lying of this sort is often given the approving label of "tact," and is used "when it would be unkind to be honest but dishonest to be kind" (Bavelas, 1983, p. 132). Sometimes a face-saving lie prevents embarrassment for the recipient,° as when you pretend to remember someone at a party whom you really don't recall ever having seen before. In other cases a lie protects the teller from embarrassment. You might, for example, cover up your mistakes by blaming them on outside forces: "You didn't receive the check? It must have been delayed in the mail."

°**recipient** receiver

The second most frequent motivation for lying was *to avoid tension or conflict* (22.2 percent). Sometimes it seems worthwhile° to tell a little lie to prevent a large conflict. You might, for example, compliment a friend's bad work, not so much for your friend's sake but to prevent the hassle° that would result if you told the truth. Likewise, you might hide feelings of irritation to avoid a fight: "I'm not mad at you; it's just been a tough day." The motive for this sort of lying can be charitably° described as promoting relational stability° (Camden, Motley, and Wilson, 1984).

°**worthwhile** advantageous
°**hassle** *(colloquial)* complications
°**charitably** kindly
°**stability** security, solidity

A third motive for lying (given 9.9 percent of the time) is *to guide social interaction*. You might, for instance, pretend to be glad to see someone you actually dislike or fake° interest in a dinner companion's boring stories to make a social event pass quickly. Children who aren't skilled or interested in these social lies are often a source of embarrassment for their parents.

°**fake** pretend

Affecting interpersonal relationships was a fourth motive for lying, offered as a reason by the experimental subjects 9.6 percent of the time. Some lies in this category are attempts to *expand* the relationship: "I'm headed that way. Can I give you a ride?" "I like science fiction too. What have you read lately?" Lies to make yourself look good also fall into this category, such as calling yourself a "management trainee" when you really are a clerk who might

365

someday be promoted. Other relational lies are attempts to reduce interaction. Sometimes we lie to escape an unpleasant situation: "I really have to go. I should be studying for a test tomorrow." In other cases people lie to end an entire relationship: "You're too good for me. I don't deserve a wonderful person like you." 45

The fifth and last motive revealed by 3.2 percent of the subjects was *to achieve personal power*. Turning down a last-minute request for a date by claiming you're busy can be one way to put yourself in a one-up position, saying in effect, "Don't expect me to sit around waiting for you to call." Lying to get confidential° information—even for a good cause—also falls into the category 50 of achieving power.

°**confidential** secret

REFERENCES

Bavelas, I. "Situations That Lead to Disqualifications." *Human Communication Research* 9 (1983): 130–145.

Camden, C., M. T. Motley, and A. Wilson. "White Lies in Interpersonal Communication: A Taxonomy and Preliminary Investigation of Social Motivations." *Western Journal of Speech Communication* 48 (1984): 309–325.

Turner, R. E., C. Edgely, and G. Olmstead. "Information Control in Conversation: Honesty Is Not Always the Best Policy." *Kansas Journal of Sociology* 11 (1975): 69–89.

WRITE

1. Tell about a time when you or someone you know told a lie. Give all the details of the situation and the people involved. Try to explain the background for the lie and the motive behind it.

2. Which of the five motives for white lies (to save face, to avoid conflict, to guide social interaction, to affect interpersonal relationships, and to achieve personal power) do you find the least acceptable. Why? Which of the five motives would be the most acceptable to you? Why?

GRAMMAR REFERENCES

Active and passive: Chapter 12

Infinitives: Chapter 19‡

Transitions: Chapter 23

Punctuation: Chapter 29

The Basic-Nonbasic Concept
Donald Steila, Douglas Wilms, and Edward P. Leahy

°**imply** suggest
°**consumed** used

°**market** sales
°**component** part
°**sustained**
  supported
°**generated**
  produced

°**taverns** bars

°**integral** essential

°**analogy** parallel
  example

°**livery stables**
  housing for horses
°**saloons** bars

People living in cities are engaged in specialized activities. These activities imply° that cities are centers of trade. In other words, the specialized goods and services produced by a population and not consumed° by that population are exchanged for the specialized goods and services produced by other cities and regions. . . . As we shall see, . . . the labor force of a city can be divided into two parts: (1) [workers] employed in *basic* industries, or "city forming" employment that depends upon areas outside the city for its market,° and (2) the *nonbasic* component,° the "city serving" employment activity that is sustained° from money generated° within the area where it is found.

A city does not serve just those people living within its own municipal boundaries. A city can exist only when it sells its goods and services beyond its borders. When Detroit is recognized as the automobile capital of the United States, we realize that automobiles produced within that city are sold mainly outside its borders. The automobile industry of Detroit, then, is *basic* to that city. *Nonbasic* industries of Detroit produce goods and services that are to be sold within the city. Examples of nonbasic industries are television repair shops, grocery stores, laundries, taverns,° clothing stores, and the like. Similarly, most of the steel produced in Pittsburgh, Pennsylvania, and Gary, Indiana, is sold outside those cities. Each city has its own nonbasic service industries. Whenever an industry of a city produces an item that is intended to be "exported" and consumed mainly outside of the city, then that industry is an integral° component of the city's basic function. As noted earlier, the basic industry of a city may include activities other than manufacturing. Transportation in Duluth, Minnesota; Portland, Maine; and Norfolk, Virginia, generates basic jobs just as those in manufacturing do. A service rather than a product is "exported." Similarly, the authors of this text, who live in a small (population 35,000) "college town," are components of the basic industry of this university community.

Let us draw one further analogy° to demonstrate this important concept of basic and nonbasic industries. Consider a frontier mining town where 100 miners are employed in the town's only basic industry—gold mining. Assume that each of the 100 miners is married and has two children. The basic industry thus supports 400 people. But the 400 people demand services: schools and churches have to be built, grocery and clothing stores and livery stables° are operated, newspapers are published, professional personnel are needed, and saloons° have to cater to visiting cowboys. It has been suggested that there is an average basic/nonbasic ratio of 1:3; that is, for every miner employed in the town's basic industry, three people may be employed in a nonbasic industry. Thus, with 100 miners our community supports 300

367

people employed in the various nonbasic service industries listed above. Let us further assume that . . . the 300 nonbasic personnel are married men with two children. That gives us 1,200 people supported by the nonbasic industries. In other words, the basic mining industry (made up of 100 miners) not only supports its own 300 dependents but also economically supports the 300 nonbasic personnel and their 900 dependents, for a grand total of 1,600 people. (Imagine the size of a modern city that has 50,000 or 100,000 people employed in the basic "export" industries.) But let us return to our miners. Let us assume, for a moment, that the gold vein has run out. What are the consequences? The gold is gone and the 100 miners must seek work elsewhere. The basic industry is gone and nothing is left to support the numerous nonbasic service workers. They too will eventually° leave and our little mining community will become a ghost town. This can and has happened to thousands of contemporary° cities that have lost industries that represented a portion of the town's basic industry.

°**eventually** finally, in the end
°**contemporary** present-day

45

50

55

WRITE

1. Which is the most important industry in your country? Tell your readers as much as you can about it.

2. Imagine that you are one of the gold miners in the frontier town. Write an article for your local newspaper about the decline of the industry from your point of view—how do you feel about it and how will it affect you? Tell your readers about your background, training, family, work, and aspirations.

GRAMMAR REFERENCES

Verb phrases: Chapter 7

Verb tenses: past: Chapter 9

Subject-verb agreement: Chapter 17

Participle forms: Chapter 21‡

Coordinating conjunctions: Chapter 22

Transitions: Chapter 23

Punctuation: Chapter 29

H.w.   1 paragraph. about   goast town.
p199.   Ex 3, Ex 7.
p245~346.

Economics and Scarcity
Patrick J. Welch and Gerry F. Welch

°**scarcity** rarity, short supply

Scarcity° is the framework within which economics exists. Put another way, without scarcity there would be no reason to study economics. This scarcity framework means that there are not enough, nor can there ever be enough, material goods and services to satisfy the wants and needs of all individuals, families, and societies. An examination of your own situation makes this obvious. Do you own the car you would most enjoy? Do you have enough financial resources° for the stereo, tapes, dates, concerts, textbooks, and boots you want? Does your family ever remark that the recent automobile repair bill means hamburgers, beans, and franks this month? Societies face the same scarcity problem on a larger scale. Money spent for roads is money not available for hospitals. Resources devoted to defense are not available for schools or welfare. Gasoline and oil used now for automobiles will not be available in the future. 5

°**financial resources** money

If scarcity exists, then choices must be made by individuals and societies. These choices involve "tradeoffs" and necessitate° an awareness of the consequences° of those tradeoffs. For example, suppose that you have $25 to spend and have narrowed your alternatives to a textbook or a date. Scarcity prohibits° the purchase of both and imposes a tradeoff—a book or a date. Each choice has a consequence. The textbook might enable you to attain a good grade (and increase your knowledge), and the date might mean an evening of merriment.° 15, 20

°**necessitate** make necessary
°**consequences** results
°**prohibits** does not allow

°**merriment** fun
°**key** central
°**estimation** evaluation

In arriving at a decision your value judgment plays a key° role. A value judgment is what you hold to be important in your estimation°of a situation. If you value good grades more than a good time, you may choose the book; if you value a good time more than good grades, you will probably choose the date. 25

°**lottery** gambling game

If someone in your family were to win $1,000 in a lottery,° the same problem of choice would arise. The $1,000 is a limited sum; it buys only so much. Your family would have to consider alternatives, or tradeoffs, for spending the $1,000. Ultimately,° the decision as to how the money would be used would be based on a value judgment of some member of the family. 30

°**ultimately** finally

°**appalling** extremely bad
°**ballot** voting card

Society faces the same scarcity-related tradeoff problem. In some communities, the public school conditions, both physical and intellectual, are appalling.° This may be a reflection of the value judgments of the community. Individuals face on the ballot° the choice of increasing or not increasing tax dollars for their schools. The tradeoff is whether to use household income for schools or for additional shoes, food, furniture, or other preferences of the family. On the national level, if a society chooses to go to war, it must give up some consumer goods° (like jeans and pickup trucks) for defense goods (like uniforms and tanks°). If society chooses to increase its population, there will be less space and fewer resources for each person. Each of these 35, 40

°**consumer goods** household items
°**tanks** armored combat vehicles

369

tradeoffs is necessary because we cannot have everything. And each tradeoff reflects the value judgment of the decision makers.

In making decisions, individuals and societies evaluate both the benefits and the costs of their choices. Because of scarcity, every decision to acquire a 45 particular good or service or to spend time or money in a certain way has a cost attached to it. Economists call these costs opportunity costs. An opportunity cost is the cost of a purchase or a decision measured in terms of a forgone° alternative; that is, what was given up to attain° the purchase or make the decision. Once time or money is devoted to one thing, the opportunity to use 50 that time or money for other things is lost. If you spend $25 to acquire° a textbook, the opportunity cost of that text is what was given up to obtain it—perhaps a date.

°**forgone** given up

°**attain** get

°**acquire** get, obtain

The opportunity cost to parents of choosing to acquire more shoes or food, rather than supporting an increase in a school tax, might be an inferior° 55 education for their children. The opportunity cost of going to war would include the jeans and pickup trucks that were not produced in order to obtain more uniforms and tanks. Because of scarcity, individuals, families, and societies must make tradeoffs—choices based on both the benefits and the opportunity costs of their decisions. 60

°**inferior** worse

WRITE

1. What do you think a government's priorities should be in allocating funds? The following are some areas you might want to consider: education, housing, defense, military, health, social welfare, scientific research, space exploration, manufacturing, farming, transportation, ecology, preservation of natural resources.

2. What decisions do people in your country have to make about the opportunity costs of their purchases? What are the main problems people face when deciding whether to make a purchase?

GRAMMAR REFERENCES

Verb phrases: Chapter 7

Adverbial clauses: conditions: Chapter 27‡

Style: Chapter 28

Punctuation: Chapter 29

Irregular Verbs APPENDIX A

The -s and -ing forms of irregular verbs have been included only in instances where the spelling sometimes causes students trouble.

SIMPLE FORM	-S	-ING	PAST	PARTICIPLE
arise		arising	arose	arisen
be		being	was,were	been
beat		beating	beat	beaten
become		becoming	became	become
begin		beginning	began	begun
bend			bent	bent
bet		betting	bet	bet
bind			bound	bound
bite		biting	bit	bitten
bleed			bled	bled
blow			blew	blown
break			broke	broken
breed			bred	bred
bring			brought	brought
build			built	built
burst			burst	burst
buy			bought	bought
catch			caught	caught
choose		choosing	chose	chosen
cling			clung	clung
come		coming	came	come
cost	costs		cost	cost
creep		creeping	crept	crept
cut		cutting	cut	cut
deal			dealt	dealt
dig		digging	dug	dug
do	does		did	done
draw			drew	drawn
drink			drank	drunk
drive		driving	drove	driven
eat		eating	ate	eaten
fall			fell	fallen
feed			fed	fed
feel		feeling	felt	felt
fight			fought	fought
find			found	found

SIMPLE FORM	-S	-ING	PAST	PARTICIPLE
flee			fled	fled
fly	flies	flying	flew	flown
forbid		forbidding	forbad(e)	forbidden
forget		forgetting	forgot	forgotten
forgive		forgiving	forgave	forgiven
freeze		freezing	froze	frozen
get		getting	got	gotten, got (outside U.S.)
give		giving	gave	given
go			went	gone
grind			ground	ground
grow			grew	grown
hang†			hung	hung
have		having	had	had
hear			heard	heard
hide		hiding	hid	hidden
hit		hitting	hit	hit
hold			held	held
hurt			hurt	hurt
keep			kept	kept
know			knew	known
lay		laying	laid	laid
lead			led	led
leave		leaving	left	left
lend			lent	lent
let		letting	let	let
lie		lying	lay	lain
light			lit, lighted	lit, lighted
lose		losing	lost	lost
make		making	made	made
mean			meant	meant
meet		meeting	met	met
pay	pays		paid	paid
put		putting	put	put
quit		quitting	quit	quit
read		reading	read	read
ride		riding	rode	ridden
ring			rang	rung
rise		rising	rose	risen
run		running	ran	run
say	says		said	said
see			saw	seen
seek			sought	sought
sell			sold	sold
send			sent	sent
set		setting	set	set

†*Hang* in the sense "put to death" is regular: *hang, hanged, hanged.*

SIMPLE FORM	-S	-ING	PAST	PARTICIPLE
shake		shaking	shook	shaken
shine		shining	shone	shone
shoot			shot	shot
show			showed	shown, showed (rare)
shrink			shrank	shrunk
shut		shutting	shut	shut
sing			sang	sung
sink			sank	sunk
sit		sitting	sat	sat
sleep		sleeping	slept	slept
slide		sliding	slid	slid
slit		slitting	slit	slit
speak			spoke	spoken
spend			spent	spent
spin		spinning	spun	spun
spit		spitting	spit	spit
split		splitting	split	split
spread			spread	spread
spring			sprang	sprung
stand			stood	stood
steal		stealing	stole	stolen
stick			stuck	stuck
sting			stung	stung
stink			stank	stunk
strike		striking	struck	struck
swear			swore	sworn
sweep		sweeping	swept	swept
swim		swimming	swam	swum
swing			swung	swung
take		taking	took	taken
teach			taught	taught
tear			tore	torn
tell			told	told
think			thought	thought
throw			threw	thrown
tread			trod	trodden, trod
understand			understood	understood
upset		upsetting	upset	upset
wake		waking	woke	waked, woken
wear			wore	worn
weave		weaving	wove	woven
weep		weeping	wept	wept
win		winning	won	won
wind			wound	wound
withdraw			withdrew	withdrawn
wring			wrung	wrung
write		writing	wrote	written

Spelling

To improve your spelling, it's wise to read a lot and to use a dictionary. In addition, you should learn the following conventions.

1. For a word with *ie* or *ei,* follow the traditional spelling rule:

> *I* before *e*
> Except after *c*
> Or when sounded like "ay"
> As in *neighbor* and *weigh*

For example:

I BEFORE *E*	EXCEPT AFTER *C*	OR WHEN SOUNDED LIKE "AY"
believe	receive	vein
relief	ceiling	reign
niece		

As with most rules, however, there are exceptions to the "*i* before *e*" rule. For example:

conscience	height	science
either	leisure	seize
foreign	neither	

2. For a verb ending in a consonant + *e,* drop the *e* when adding *ing.*

hope	hoping
lose	losing
write	writing
come	coming

BUT NOTE

agree   agreeing (vowel + *e*)

3. For a one-syllable verb ending in one vowel + consonant, double the consonant before *ing* (and before *ed* for regular verbs).

```
step    stepping    stepped
rob     robbing     robbed
chat    chatting    chatted
```

BUT NOTE

    sleep   sleeping (two vowels + consonant)

4. Doubling a consonant signals a short vowel sound.

```
write    writing    BUT    written
hide     hiding     BUT    hidden
```

5. For a two-syllable verb that has the stress on the second syllable and ends in a vowel + consonant, double the consonant before *ing* (and before *ed* for regular verbs).

```
refer      referring     referred
control    controlling   controlled
begin      beginning
```

Do not double the consonant for a verb with the stress on the first syllable:

```
travel    traveling    traveled
```

6. For a verb ending in a consonant + *y*, form the past tense with *ied*.

```
try    trying    tried
cry    crying    cried
```

Verbs ending in vowel + *y* simply add *ed*.

```
play    playing    played
```

EXCEPTIONS

    pay   paid
    say   said

7. For a one-syllable adjective with vowel + consonant, double the consonant in comparative and superlative forms.

```
big    bigger    the biggest
```

8. For a two-syllable adjective ending in *y,* change *y* to *i* before adding *ly* to form the adverb.

happy   happily

9. For an adjective ending in *e,* keep the *e* before adding *ly.*

immediate   immediately

But if the adjective ends in *le,* drop the *e.*

sensible   sensibly

10. With the prefix *anti-* or *ante-,* remember that *anti* = "against," as in *antibiotic,* and *ante* = "before," or "in front of," as in *antecedent.*

11. Add the suffix *-ally* to words ending in *ic.*

basic   basically
tragic   tragically

12. Only four words end in *efy.*

liquefy   rarefy
putrefy   stupefy

Use *ify* in all other words with this ending.

13. When you add *ment* to a word with a final silent *e,* retain the *e.*

require   requirement

EXCEPTIONS

acknowledge   acknowledgment
argue   argument
judge   judgment

14. More words end in the suffix *-able* than the suffix *-ible.* Learn the *ible* words:

forcible   responsible
horrible   terrible
permissible

Add to this list as you come across more *ible* words.

15. There are no useful rules to help with the distinction between the suffix *-ant* and the suffix *-ent*. Keep lists of words in each category:

-ANT	*-ENT*
defiant	independent
reluctant	convenient

16. "Spelling demons" cause confusion. Beware of them!

accept	cloth (plural = cloths)	quite
except	clothes	quiet
affect	custom	real
effect	costume	really
believe (verb)	fell	taught
belief (noun: plural = beliefs)	felt	thought
cite	loose	until
sight	lose	till
site	passed	weather
	past	whether

These spelling demons have unstressed syllables or silent consonants:

comfortable	interesting
government	pneumonia

17. Differences exist between British and American spelling. Adapt your spelling to your audience, and recognize these differences when reading British materials.

AMERICAN		BRITISH	
-or	color	*-our*	colour
-ed	learned	*-t*	learnt
-led	traveled	*-lled*	travelled
-er	theater	*-re*	theatre

18. Use a hyphen to divide a word at the end of a line only if you cannot avoid breaking the word. Remember that you can never hyphenate a one-syllable word (*health* or *watched,* for example).

When you hyphenate words of two syllables or more, divide the word only at the end of a syllable. Check your dictionary for syllable division:

re-spon-si-bil-i-ty
rep-re-sen-ta-tion

Do not separate a word if only one or two letters would remain on a line. That is, do not divide words like *alike* or *added.*

19. Always proofread for spelling errors. Remember that when we read our own work through to check it, our eye often runs ahead, causing us to miss some errors, especially slips like *form* in place of *from* or *to* in place of *too*. So we must devise ways to slow our reading and focus on individual words. The following techniques are useful.

- Put a piece of blank paper under the top line so that your eye cannot move ahead. Touch each word with a pencil point as you say it to yourself
- Read the last sentence first, and work backward through your paper, sentence by sentence. This obviously does not help you check on meaning and logic, but it does slow your reading eye enough for you to concentrate on spelling and internal punctuation.
- Make a copy of your paper and give it to a friend. Ask your friend to read the paper aloud. Follow along on your original. Put a mark by any word that you want to check in the dictionary.

ACKNOWLEDGMENTS

page 7: Van Gogh, Vincent. Three paragraphs from Vincent van Gogh's letter. Adapted from translation quoted in E. H. Gombrich, *The Story of Art,* Oxford: Phaidon, p. 483. From *The Complete Letters of Vincent van Gogh.* By permission of Little, Brown and Company in conjunction with the New York Graphic Society. All rights reserved.

page 144: Definition of the word *put.* Copyright © 1985 by Houghton Mifflin Company. Reprinted by permission of Houghton Mifflin from *The American Heritage Dictionary, Second College Edition.*

page 306: Coles, Jr., William E. From: *Conceptual Blockbusting: A Guide to Better Ideas.* J. L. Adams. W. H. Freeman & Co., 1974.

page 320: Williams, William Carlos. *Collected Poems, Vol. II, 1939–1962.* Copyright © 1960 by William Carlos Williams. Reprinted by permission of New Directions Publishing Corporation.

page 334: Ephron, Nora. "Room with View—and No People." Reprinted by permission of International Creative Management, Inc. First published in *The New York Times Magazine,* December 22, 1985, p. 20. Copyright © 1985 by Nora Ephron.

page 337: Bok, Sissela. "The Doctors' Dilemma" from *The New York Times,* April 18, 1978. Reprinted by permission of *The New York Times* Company.

page 339: Hapgood, Fred. From "The Soybean" as printed in *The National Geographic* 172. July, 1987, pp. 69–76, 80.

page 342: Baker, Russell. Excerpt from *Growing Up* by Russell Baker. Copyright © 1982 by Russell Baker. Reprinted by permission of Congdon & Weed, Inc.

page 343: Gombrich, E. H. Extracts from *The Story of Art* by E. H. Gombrich. © 1972, 1978, 1984. Phaidon Press Ltd., Oxford. Reprinted with permission of Phaidon Press and Prentice Hall, Inc.

page 345: Quindlen, Anna. "Life in the 30's" from *The New York Times,* November 5, 1986, p. C14. Reprinted with permission of *The New York Times.*

page 347: Salzman, Mark. Excerpts from *Iron and Silk* by Mark Salzman. Copyright © 1986 by Mark Salzman. Reprinted by permission of Random House, Inc. and Hamish Hamilton.

pages 351 and 365: Adler, Ronald B., Lawrence B. Rosenfeld and Neil Towne. Excerpts from *Interplay: The Process of Interpersonal Communication,* Third Edition by Ronald B. Adler, Lawrence B. Rosenfeld and Neil Towne, copyright © 1985 by Holt, Rinehart, and Winston, Inc., reprinted by permission of the publisher.

page 355: Thomas, Lewis. Excerpt from "Tau Ceti" in *The Lives of a Cell* by Lewis Thomas. Copyright © 1972 by the Massachusetts Medical Society. Originally published in the New England Journal of Medicine. Reprinted by permission of Viking Penguin, a division of Penguin Books, USA Inc.

page 357: Taffel, Alexander, *Physics: Its Methods and Meanings,* 5th Ed. Newton, Mass: Allyn & Bacon, 1986, p. 477. Reprinted by permission of Prentice Hall.

page 359: Hilts, Philip J., "Artificial Intelligence" from *Scientific Temperaments: Three Lives in Contemporary Science.* New York: Simon & Schuster, Touchstone Books, 1984. Reprinted with permission of Simon & Schuster, Inc.

page 361: Hall, Edward T. "The Culture of 'Lead Time'" from *The Silent Language* by Edward T. Hall. Copyright © 1959 by Edward T. Hall. Reprinted by permission of Doubleday, a division of Bantam, Doubleday, Dell Publishing Group, Inc.

page 363: Gould, Stephen Jay. "Sizing Up Human Intelligence." Reprinted from *Ever Since Darwin: Reflections in Natural History* by Stephen Jay Gould by permission of W. W. Norton and Company, Inc. Copyright © 1977 by Stephen Jay Gould. Copyright © 1973, 1974, 1975, 1976, 1977 by The American Museum of Natural History. Reprinted by permission of W. W. Norton and Company and Andre Deutsch Ltd.

page 367: Steila, Donald, Douglas Wilms, and Edward P. Leahy, Excerpts from *Earth and Man: A Systematic Geography*. Copyright © 1981 John Wiley & Sons, Inc. Reprinted by permission of John Wiley & Sons.

page 369: Welch, Patrick J. and Gerry F. Welch. Excerpts from *Economics: Theory and Practice,* Second edition by Patrick J. Welch and Gerry F. Welch, copyright © 1986 by The Dryden Press, reprinted by permission of the publisher.

Picture Credits

page 6: Van Gogh, Vincent. *The Artist's Room in Arles.* (1889). Musée du Louvre, Paris

page 15: Cartier-Bresson, Henri. (photograph) *Outside a Bistro, France* (1968–69).

page 98: Brueghel, Pieter. *Landscape with the Fall of Icarus.* (1558). Musées Royaux des Beaux-Arts, Brussels.

page 111: Renoir, Pierre-Auguste. *The Luncheon of the Boating Party* (1881). Phillips Collection, Washington, D.C.

page 150: Stevens, M., "Roget's Brontosaurus." Drawing by M. Stevens; copyright © 1985, *The New Yorker Magazine,* Inc.

Index